JOSEPH PRIESTLEY

"A COMET IN THE SYSTEM"

by
John Ruskin Clark

Introduction by
William N. Richardson, Ph.D.
Site Administrator, The Joseph Priestley House
The Pennsylvania Historical and Museum Commission

The Friends of Joseph Priestley House, Inc.
Northumberland, Pennsylvania
1994

ISBN 0-9642064-0-4

Published by the Friends of Joseph Priestley House, Inc.
472 Priestley Avenue
Northumberland, PA 17857

Printed by Chernay Printing Inc.
Coopersburg, PA 18036

Table of Contents

PREFACE

We live in a time when the forces of religious and political conservatism are again on the rise. Also present in England and continental Europe two hundred years ago, such forces were then attacking the civic and religious ideals of freedom in the British unwritten constitution, American Declaration of Independence and Constitution, and the French Revolution's Declaration of the Rights of Man, which were ardently defended by Dr. Joseph Priestley.

It was in Philadelphia and ultimately Northumberland, Pennsylvania, that Joseph Priestley, the subject of John Ruskin Clark's biography, found refuge from the persecution he suffered, as a courageous liberal and Unitarian minister, in the Birmingham Riot of 1791. Since the British Establishment could not openly attack him for his religious heresies, he was charged with being a seditious revolutionary.

Not only a pioneer in science, best known as the discoverer of oxygen, Joseph Priestley was also an apologist for a Christianity purged of the corruptions that made it unacceptable to thoughtful and scientifically-oriented people, while seeking also to provide rational men and women grounds for understanding and appreciating the essential teachings of historic Christianity that he claimed was unitarian.

The non-scientific writings of Joseph Priestley, as collected and published by John Towill Rutt, fill 26 volumes. To master this immense and diverse body of writings by a man who was intimate with Benjamin Franklin and Thomas Jefferson on the one hand, and Theophilus Lindsey and Thomas Belsham, also leaders of English Unitarianism, on the other, has been the task Dr. Clark has undertaken for many years. It has been a privilege for me to hear chapters of his biography presented at annual meetings of Collegium, a liberal religious scholars association.

Dr. Clark will in 1990 have served in the Unitarian Universalist ministry fifty years. A distinguished graduate of Meadville/Lombard Theological School in Chicago, he successfully served, for more than two decades, the growing congregation that built a splendid new meeting-house in San Diego, California, where he is now Minister Emeritus. His first book, *The Great Living System,* is nearly sold out of its second publication by Skinner House Books.

It is a distinct privilege for me to write the preface commending this book to both religious liberals and the general public about one who fought for complete freedom of religion and of the written and spoken word. For, in this age, our religious freedom, and responsible independence and interdependence, is again threatened by the religious and political right, against which Priestley so courageously fought two centuries ago.

Spencer Lavan, PhD
Dean/CEO, Meadville/Lombard Theological School
Chicago, Illinois

Introduction To The
1994 Edition

Joseph Priestley counted Thomas Jefferson and Benjamin Franklin among his closest American friends. Franklin, whom Priestley met in London in the 1760's, encouraged the young, dissenter minister to take his natural philosophy inquires seriously as befitted his apparent talents. Franklin's encouragement resulted in Priestley's publication of *The History and the Present State of Electricity With Original Experiments* (London, 1767) in which Franklin's well known kite experiment is chronicled. Thomas Jefferson both admired and revered Priestley immensely and, with his help, crafted the curriculum for the University of Virginia. This new, liberal arts curriculum subsequently determined the content of nineteenth-century, American, progressive education. While Priestley lay on his death bed in 1804, he finished correcting the proofs for a pamphlet comparing the lives of Jesus and Socrates. Jefferson was so impressed by this writing that he began his "Jefferson Bible."

Priestley's nineteenth-century admirers included American scientists who met at his Northumberland home in 1874 to celebrate the one-hundredth anniversary of Priestley's discovery of oxygen and to discuss the possibility of forming a scientific society. Those discussions led to the formation of the American Chemical Society some two years later at Brooklyn College in New York. On August 1, 1994, representatives of the American Chemical Society will again meet at Priestley House to designate his American home and laboratory as a national historic chemical landmark.

As the preeminent intellect of the Anglo-American enlightenment, priestley sought to create a holistic philosophy. He saw no distinction between "science" – then called natural philosophy – and religion. Likewise, he made no distinction between matter and spirit. William Blake, a contemporary of Priestley who knew him through their mutual publisher Samuel Johnston, saw Priestley as a materialist who exhalted reason. For Blake, faith was more important. English

i

Joseph Priestley

Unitarians largely forsook priestley for the materialism that William Blake disliked in Priestley.

Like Blake, Ralph Waldo Emerson, who was a Unitarian minister and later the father of the transcendentalists, also saw Priestly as a materialist lacking in spirituality. In early nineteenth-century New England, American Unitarians transformed the religion that Priestley first brought to Philadelphia from England and rejected the whole of science and religion that Priestley sought to unite. This legacy is reflected in some Unitarian congregations today.

John Ruskin Clark, author of Joseph Priestley, *A Comet in the System,* certainly numbers among Priestley's most valued friends of this generation. Clark has made Priestley's message accessible to contemporary audiences. Priestley's theological writings often seem irrelevant to the twentieth century mind concerned with a more material reality. His science was often more narrative than empirical, though none the less brilliant. Clark sees Priestley as Priestley saw himself. Priestley saw no difference between matter and spirit, the pivotal point of disagreement between not only him and Blake but the British theological establishment of the time. Clark presents the whole as Priestley saw it: matter and spirit united by seeking one truth.

John Ruskin Clark was born in 1911 in the Philippines where his father was an officer in the constabulary. He was graduated from Beloit College in 1937 and from Meadville Theological School – then associated with the University of Chicago – in 1940. During the Second World War, Clark served as a Unitarian chaplain in the Marine Corps in China and the Pacific. On his discharge from the military, he completed two years of graduate study at the University of Chicago. Clark served as Unitarian minister for New Hampshire and California congregations. He is the author of *The Great Living System – The Religion Emerging From the Sciences* (1977) and *Joseph Priestley – A Comet in the System* (1990).

Clark became interested in Priestley in the late sixties and began to read and research Priestley's life. When he retired from active ministry in 1977, Clark began his Priestley biography. My own introduction to Joseph Priestley, about whom I knew equally little when I began working for the Pennsylvania Historical and Museum Commission as Site Administrator of the Joseph Priestley House, a Commonwealth of Pennsylvania property, was through Clark's book. From 1991 to 1993, Joseph Priestley House sold out the remaining stock of Clark's 1990 publication, and in the Fall of 1993, I asked Clark if he intended to republish the volume that has been so valuable to our many visitors to Joseph Priestley House. At that time John Ruskin

Introduction

Clark, in a spirit that I can only describe as emulatory of the Priestley I have come to know in my research, agreed to make a deed of gift of the rights and royalties to his work to benefit the newly formed Friends of Joseph Priestley House, a 501-C-3 not-for-profit organization whose mission statement is to educate the public about the life and times of Joseph Priestley. All proceeds from this publication go to the furtherance of that mission statement. The Friends of Joseph Priestley House are profoundly grateful to John Ruskin Clark and delight in sharing his message of the whole Priestley – minister, educator, historian, linguist, natural philosopher – and his search for a singular truth to unify all knowledge.

William Richardson, Ph.D.
Site Administrator, The Joseph Priestley House
The Pennsylvania Historical and Museum Commission

April 20, 1994
Northumberland, Pennsylvania

iii

INTRODUCTION

Joseph Priestley (1733-1804)inspired my interest when in 1966 I was desperate for a sermon topic and decided to do a biographical sermon on him. I knew little about him, except that he was a distinguished English Unitarian minister and scientist. My library provided me with information for a sketch of his life and achievements, highlighting his minor but popular scientific invention of a way to less expensively manufacture sodawater, though he is best known for his discovery of oxygen. Then I searched my library for a Priestley quotation to use as a reading.

On a bottom shelf, I found two books with broken spines and brown with age that I was amazed to find were a first edition in two volumes of the *Memoirs of Dr. Joseph Priestley to the Year 1795, Written by Himself: With a Continuation, to the Time of his Decease, by his son, Joseph Priestley....* published in Northumberland, Pennsylvania, in 1806. I had bought them while a student at Meadville Theological School in 1942 when the library sold them as duplicates.

I spent the rest of the day and most of the night reading Priestley's Memoirs, and found a suitable reading from his 1768 *An Essay on the First Principles of Government* that was influential in the political theory for the American and French Revolutions, and the reform of the British government, as I later learned. He ardently defended civil and religious liberty: complete freedom of thought and expression were essential to ascertaining truth in all fields of endeavor. He was a liberal in politics as well as in religion--except for his expectation of the early establishment of the Kingdom of God on earth. He associated with leading political, philosophical, and scientific leaders of his time in Europe and America--three of the authors of the Declaration of Independence were his friends and admirers.

With this introduction to Priestley, I wondered why such an outstanding man was not better known and widely appreciated outside of scientific circles. I wanted to redeem his reputation and decided to write his biography after I retired from active ministry in the San Diego Unitarian Church in 1977. That year, I published *The Great Living System--Religion Emerging from the Sciences*, so I was intrigued that Priestley, a scientist and theologian, had in the 18th century, on grounds of a unified empirical-epistemology, integrated science and theology--still a problem for theologians.

His biography, I thought, would contribute to the history and development of important ideas.

I learned that Priestley was a paragon of the Enlightenment--an 18th century philosophical movement that rationally and critically examined previously accepted doctrines and institutions. He made enduring and progressive contributions to physical sciences, political science, cosmology, psychology, education, the study of history, and historical criticism of the Bible. His zeal for historical "pure Christianity," that he claimed was unitarian in theology, was prompted by his mission to convert skeptics and unbelievers to Christianity, which he thought had been corrupted by Platonic philosophy.

In consequence of his theological controversies, he suffered the destruction of his home, library and laboratory in the 1791 Birmingham Riot, and continued persecution forced him and his family in 1794 to flee England for asylum in Pennsylvania.

It is still assumed that Priestley was the first victim of the Riot because he was a "seditious revolutionary." He supported the American Revolution, and then the French Revolution, with many other Englishmen, when it was an effort to reform the French government as a constitutional monarchy on the English model. He condemned the French Revolution when it turned into a Reign of Terror. His real offense was his heresy. He had a bad press. Hence, his innovative contributions to the history of ideas in England and America are shamefully ignored, except by scientists. Now, as then, he is maligned by those who do not know him very well.

For instance, James Burke slandered Priestley: "Mary's husband was a preacher who failed in the pulpit because of his stammer. He was, in common with the times, a scientific dabbler--and to judge by his letters, he was also permanently afflicted by a concern for money. He had evidently married Mary for her money, and when he found she had little, had turned to her brothers. By the late 1760's he and Mary, supported by John, were living in Leeds, where Joseph divided his time between preaching badly enough to be fired, and investigating the behavior of gases in the brewery next door." [Burke 1978, 176]

> # References in this form are to secondary sources: the author's name, date of publication, and page number, which can be identified by name and date in the list of references at the end of the book.

*References in the above author-date style are used in
natural and social sciences works. This style is simple and
efficient for the nature of the references in this biography,
especially the many references to Priestley's collected works,
identified by the volume number.*

In Leeds (where he did begin his experiments with gasses), as in
Birmingham, Priestley was a very successful minister, he was not
fired, and his salary exceeded that of most Dissenter ministers.
Scientists do not consider him a "dabbler." However, his wealthy
brothers-in-law and other benefactors did often subsidize his extra-
curricular activities in science, Biblical criticism, and philosophy.

Jacob Bronowski claimed that the ascent of man "is made by
people who have two qualities: an immense integrity, and at least a
little genius. Priestley had both." [Bronowski 1973, 144]

Priestley was not a systematic thinker, but he transformed
chemistry, physics, and theology by his seminal insights. He was,
concludes Robert Schofield, engaged in "a too sophisticated endeavor to answer questions that his contemporaries were not asking, with concepts so antique they would not again be modern for
nearly one hundred years." [Schofield 1980, 38] His creative concepts are now modern. Priestley so candidly revealed himself that
he does not need to be psychoanalyzed to understand his motives,
which he exposed in his writings. He was open and honest, except
for his few theological prejudices. August Montague Toplady, an
Anglican cleric, friend and critic, wrote: "Transparency is, in my
opinion, the most valuable of all social virtues. ... Give me the person
whom I can hold up as I can a piece of crystal, and see through him.
For this, among many other excellencies, I regard and admire Dr.
Priestley." [I-i, 310]

*References in this form are to The Theological and Miscel-
laneous Works of Joseph Priestley, edited with notes in 26
volumes by John T. Rutt, published in London 1817-1832:
volume number followed by page number.*

Priestley had many interests that he developed and modified
throughout his life. To help comprehend his dynamic thought, I
have gathered his major themes in chapters, not in chronological
order.

I have adopted Priestley's policy about what material to focus on.
He wrote: "All the disputes which have in no way contributed to the
discovery of truth, I would gladly consign to oblivion." I have

chosen to emphasize what is still relevant and significant in his thought. Though he pioneered in the historical-method of Biblical criticism, I do not dwell on his eschatalogical faith or volumes of Bible commentaries.

Also, I have adopted his justification for quotations: "That I might not misrepresent any writer, I have generally given the reader his own words...." Priestley wrote well, and I have selected his most concise and mature statements on the various subjects. I suspect that one reason his writings are not widely known is that he published so much, and repeated himself. I have used the most easily understood expressions of his thought. I do not tell you how much I know about Priestley, but let him speak for himself as much as is pertinent to my purpose, while providing background information.

With my apology to readers in Great Britain, I have changed Priestley's English spelling to the alternate American spelling, "connexion" to "connection," for instance. I thought Americans would be as distracted as I was by English spelling. I have not copied Priestley's frequent use of italics for emphasis and I have not altered Priestley's now-confusing punctuation.

Priestley is widely known as a creative experimental scientist in chemistry and physics, but I am not competent to elucidate such achievements; this has been done in books and monographs about him by scientists or philosophers of science, to which I refer. But I have noted his scientific achievements and theory of science as counterpoint to the development of his thought in other fields.

I am indebted to Priestley's chapel-member, friend and devoted admirer, John Towill Rutt (to whom this book is dedicated), who gathered and edited, with extensive footnotes, Priestley's non-scientific writings, including letters by Priestley and a few from his friends, in *The Theological and Miscellaneous Works of Joseph Priestley* in 25 volumes published in London 1817 to 1832, by subscription of his many admirers. I own a photocopy of the first edition by Kraus Reprint Co.

Priestley scholars warn that Rutt's editing of Priestley's letters is unreliable because passages in the manuscript letters are omitted without indication, and other letters are combined. In my reading of the manuscript letters, where the omissions are underlined by Rutt or a subsequent scholar, in Dr. Williams Library in London, I concluded that the omissions were made out of respect for the Priestleys' expressed desire for family privacy. Priestley left instructions to burn his correspondence that remained after the riot. Mary Priestley destroyed her correspondence. So Rutt's omissions are primarily to respect the Priestleys' wishes. Deletions were references to private family matters (unfortunately removing evidence of how much he was concerned with the welfare of his family), or were unkind remarks about contemporaries, or were illegible. No claim that Rutt made substantial changes in Priestley's published works is alleged by Priestley scholars.

Rutt noted Priestley's mistakes and misapprehensions, and I have written no hagiography, acknowledging his prejudices with their sources. But I have focused on his significant and enduring contributions to the history of ideas.

I am grateful for the resources of libraries and the help of librarians at the University of California San Diego; Meadville Theological School, Chicago (Neil Gerdes); Harvard University; American Philosophical Society, Philadelphia; Library of Congress; Huntington Library, San Marino, California; Birmingham Central Library, England; Manchester College, Oxford (Barbara Smith); and Dr. Williams Library, London.

I am obliged to Alan Ruston of London, a Unitarian historian, for his helpful advice and guidance.

My appointment by the Minns Committee of Boston to give four endowed lectures on Priestley in 1982, sponsored in the San Francisco Bay area by the Starr King School for the Ministry, Berkeley, was a supportive challenge to preparing early drafts of material for this book.

My daughters, Harriet C. Shaftel and Susan C. Silk, have been helpful, critical readers of the entire manuscript, and I am grateful to my wife Alma for proofreading and for her patience with my Priestley obsession. Members of Collegium, a liberal scholars group that meets annually, have critically read and discussed four drafts of this work, and a member has provided the Preface. The San Diego Independent Scholars have responded to my presentation of the first chapter, and Ariss Treat Sedgwick, President, has been a very helpful copy editor, as has Ruth Valleau. In the San Diego Unitarian Church, helpful and encouraging readers have been Reverend Tom Owen-Towle, Dr. Hugh Frank, Burton Johnson, Willis Perry, and Dr. Christopher Stowell, who has guided me through the mysteries of computers and prepared the camera-ready copy for electronic printing.

John Ruskin Clark, D.D.
San Diego, California

Carbon dust portrait of Joseph Priestley by Ruth Valleau, commissioned by John Ruskin Clark, 1987.

I

"CHURCH AND KING!"
"The great odium that I have incurred"

Joseph and Mary Priestley were preparing to play a game of backgammon by candlelight after supper, as they usually did, when there was a violent rapping at the door. Some young men from his congregation, "breathless with running," reported that a great mob had assembled at about eight o'clock outside the hotel in Birmingham where the Constitution Society had earlier dined, demanding Priestley. After stoning the hotel windows, they went to burn two Dissenter chapels, Priestley's New Meeting and the Old Meeting. The mob threatened Priestley's home and person, shouting "Church and King!" and "To Dr. Priestley's." His home was two miles out of the city.

Thinking such violence improbable, Joseph and Mary Priestley only hid some valuables. When Samuel Ryland's carriage came for them (they had none of their own), they were prevailed upon to get in and flee with only the clothes they had on. Dr. Joseph Priestley, one of England and America's great Eighteenth Century scientists, political scientists and heretical Unitarian theologians, was the first victim of the Birmingham "Church and King Riot" in 1791. He was later harassed into seeking asylum with his family in the United States. He was caricatured and denounced as a seditious revolutionary; he was controversial, but was he guilty as charged?

The alleged cause of the riot was a July 14th public dinner sponsored by the Constitutional Society of Birmingham to celebrate the second anniversary of the Fall of the Bastille that began the French Revolution. Priestley had been advised by friends not to attend the three o'clock dinner in a hotel. An anonymous handbill had been widely distributed several days earlier implying that the dinner had a seditious purpose. Scurrilous rumors focused animosity on notorious Priestley.

Though he was a founding member of the Constitutional Society, he had little to do with planning the dinner celebration, explaining, "I am well known to all my friends to be averse to public entertainments." He did not attend. [XIX 373]

> *References in this form are to The Theological and Miscellaneous Works of Joseph Priestley edited with notes in 26 volumes by John T. Rutt, published in London 1817-1832. Volume number and page number.*

Instead, he and his wife Mary entertained dinner guests, a lecturer on natural philosophy and his family from London. After the guests had left, at a little after five three intimate friends who had attended the Celebration came by to report to Priestley that the dinner had been a success with eighty gentlemen in attendance. They had departed without incident, since the crowd that had hissed them as they gathered at the hotel had dispersed by the five o'clock adjournment. The mob did not reassemble at the hotel until about eight. [XIX 374]

Priestley refused the offer of the young men of his congregation to defend his home from the mob. In a 1787 sermon on "Taking the Cross and Following Christ" he had said, "My brethren, ... if we be not ready and determined, when called upon, to bear persecution, and even death, in the cause of Christ, we are no true Christians." [XV 174] Any resort to violence by others should be born patiently, said Priestley: "It is generally a proof that our adversaries have nothing better to offer, and therefore is a presumption that we have truth on our side; and surely the sense of this may well enable us to bear up under any insult to which we may be exposed." [XV 189]

The fleeing Priestleys stopped a mile away at the home of his intimate friend and staunch supporter William Russell. By midnight, word came that the mob was demolishing the Priestley home.

Their third child, twenty-year-old William, had remained at their home to extinguish all flames while friends got the neighbors to do the same before the mob came. When the vandals came, they tried in vain to get a spark to light a fire from Priestley's electrical machine (when cranked, it generated only static electricity that could not ignite a flame), but they plundered the house. Not until the next morning did the vandals secure live coals from a tavern across the fields to burn the Priestley home, laboratory, library and manuscripts, and the curtains Mary had stitched by hand.

Priestley walked across fields toward the riot and on that calm, clear moonlight night he could hear the shouts of the mob and the blows of the instruments destroying his home, and see the flames consuming the two Dissenter chapels--his own and another whose minister never voiced his political opinions and had not attended the Dinner.

Martha Russell, daughter of William whose home was later burned by the rioters, wrote her recollection of Priestley's reaction to the pillaging of his home: "Undaunted he heard the blows which were destroying his house and laboratory that contained all his valuable and rare apparatus and their effects, which it had been the business of his life to collect and use. Not one hasty or impatient expression, not one look expressive of murmur or complaint, not one tear or sigh escaped him...." [Holt 1970, 163]

> *References in this form are to secondary sources: the author's name and date of publication followed by the page number, which can be identified by name and date in the list of references at the end of the book.*

His Christian faith sustained his composure, as he wrote to William Russell fifteen days after the riot: "It is, indeed, an alarming crisis that things have come to. But we cannot doubt that a wise and good Providence superintends and directs the whole." [I-ii, 125]

The Priestleys were preparing to go to bed at four in the morning when word came that the mob had been reinforced by hundreds and was advancing toward the Russell home. They fled five miles further to the home of their daughter Sarah and son-in-law, William Finch, at Heath Forge where they thought they would be safe. Arriving before breakfast, they brought the first news of the disaster in Birmingham.

Priestley paid no attention to reports that the Birmingham mob was pursuing him until he was awakened at eleven that night and warned that the mob would soon be there. His family urged him to escape. Mary remained with her daughter who was about to give birth to a child. "My wife behaves with wonderful courage," wrote Priestley at the time. However, her spirits later became "distressed" by continuing persecution of her family.

Priestley and a servant mounted horses and started for London, riding most of the night. The next day, learning that all was quiet in Heath, they turned back to the Finch's and arrived that evening. Priestley was received with "great consternation" by his family as

William Finch had just returned from a neighboring town with the report that a riot was expected there too; a mob threatened the meeting-house, minister's home and homes of the Dissenters.

Priestley and his servant, "though much fatigued, and greatly wanting sleep," again headed for London but in the dark lost their way and rode nineteen miles in a circle. The next day he drove a light carriage to Worcester where he caught the mail- coach for London. Traveling all night, he arrived in London the next morning. He had been on the road with little sleep for four nights and three days. He went to the home of his closest friend and colleague, Theophilus Lindsey, minister of the first named Unitarian chapel in England.

The fears of Priestley's friends for his safety were justified. A party from the mob was sent to capture Priestley, wrote a member of the Established Church on Sunday during the riot: "Should the Doctor not be able to elude their vigilance, it is much to be apprehended that they will murder him, as he is considered the mischievous author of the treasonable hand-bills that have been circulated about the town, and which first produced the riot." [XIX 545]

The Birmingham Gazette reported: "On Friday morning, as they recovered from the fatigue and intoxication of the preceding night, different parties of the rioters entered the town to the great consternation of all the inhabitants. The doors of every ... [prison] were thrown open, and ... [the inmates] paraded through the streets, armed with bludgeons, loudly vociferating 'Church and King!', words which all the inhabitants now chalked upon their window-shutters and doors for the security of their dwellings." [Holt 1970, 169]

The magistrates (civil officers charged with the administration of the law) then tried "by the most conciliating language, to induce them to separate and desist from further violence," warning "Friends and Fellow Churchmen" that the reparations would increase their property taxes. The magistrates had lost control of the mob, but nonetheless refused permission for citizens to form an armed posse to disperse the rioters.

The *Gazette* reported that by Saturday, the rioters had been joined by thieves and drunken prostitutes, and small bands wandered throughout the town levying contributions on the inhabitants: "There was scarcely a house-keeper that dared refuse them meat, drink, money, or whatever they demanded." [Holt 1970, 170]

The riot continued from Thursday night to Sunday evening, when government troops finally galloped into town to establish order. The mob had burned eleven homes. They pillaged one that was so close to its neighbor that to torch it might set the house next door afire, which was not on their list to destroy. In addition to the two chapels in Birmingham, the mob burned a Dissenter chapel and minister's home in a neighboring town. (Meeting-houses of only the Church of England were called "churches." Dissenters met in "chapels.") Eight rioters, including seven women, were so intoxicated that they could not flee the flames and were burned to death.

Priestley wrote of the class of people whose homes were listed for destruction by the mob: "No member of the Establishment (Established Church), though present at the dinner, suffered at all; and the only sufferers were that very description of men against whom the popular resentment had been excited several years before, viz. the Unitarian Dissenters in general, and myself in particular, whether we were present at the dinner, or concerned in promoting it, or not. ... Of the principal sufferers, who were ten in all [two of whom lost two houses], only three were at the dinner, and their houses were the last that were destroyed." [XIX 468] (In Birmingham at the time, "Unitarian" was used interchangeably with "Presbyterian," since it was mainly Presbyterians who, following Priestley, were evolving into Unitarians.) At the beginning of the riot, reported the *London Chronicle*, the Methodists, still nominally affiliated with the Church of England, on their declaring for Church and King, "were assured that they should remain unmolested. The Church people walk about as usual, without the smallest apprehension of danger." [I-ii 117]

At the celebration dinner, Captain James Keir had presided, but was unmolested. He was a member of the Church of England and a prominent chemist and industrialist who was concerned that lucrative trade with France not be interrupted. After the dinner adjourned, he returned to his home in the country about eight miles from Birmingham and did not learn of the riot until the next day. Rioters went out of town to burn Dissenter's homes; two miles to Priestley's, three miles to Russell's, to the "country" for Hutton's second home, and to Kingwood for the Dissenter minister's home and chapel. But as a "churchman," Keir's home was not on the list of homes to be destroyed by the rioters.

Captain Keir wrote a letter to the editor of *The Birmingham and Stafford Chronicle* protesting that "many gross falsehoods have been circulated through the country, in order to inflame the minds of the people concerning the meeting held last Thursday, to commemorate the French Revolution." He had accepted the invitation of the Birmingham organizers of the dinner to preside, "never conceiving that a peaceable meeting, for the purpose of rejoicing that twenty-six millions of our fellow creatures were rescued from despotism, and made as free and happy as we Britons, could be misinterpreted as being offensive to a government whose greatest boast is liberty, or to any who profess the Christian religion, which orders us to love our neighbors as ourselves." [XIX. 548]

The "gross falsehoods" he rebutted were: "it is reported that we drank disloyal and seditious toasts"--he printed a list of the toasts as evidence that they were loyal, peaceable and charitable; "that Justice Carles was insulted and turned out of the room"--he was never in the room; "that a seditious hand-bill" had been distributed by the organizers of the meeting several days prior to the dinner-- the organizers had immediately published and widely distributed a disavowal of the anonymous, inflammatory hand-bill and declared their loyal attachment to the King, Lords and Commons; and that at the dinner, Priestley had drunk a toast to "The King's head on a platter." Priestley was not even present.

Keir concluded: "Nevertheless, these false reports are all the pretenses for the late horrible Riots; but the event shows that they were only pretenses, and that the Dissenters were the true object of the fury of the mob, as many of those gentlemen who suffered from the Riots were not present." [XIX 548-550]

"Dissenters" dissented from the authority and liturgy of the government-established Church of England. King Henry VIII had rejected the authority of the Pope and established a national church with himself at the head. His daughter, Queen Elizabeth, had as- serted her authority as supreme head of the Church and by edict required uniformity in religion: "Subscription" by all subjects to the Thirty-Nine Articles defining the doctrines of the Church of England, and use of the Book of Common Prayer in public worship.

All "nonconformist" clergy were required to be reordained by the Episcopal rite. Some 2000 nonconformist clergy refused and were "ejected" from their pulpits and "livings." People who thought Henry VIII's reformation of the Established Church had not gone far enough were persecuted; the Pilgrims and Puritans fled to New England to secure freedom in religion for themselves.

Though Dissenters were elected to Parliament, they were by law denied royal appointment to public offices by the requirement that they annually receive Anglican communion. However, the penalties for "occasional conformity" in order to qualify for office, and for other derelictions in religion, were not strictly enforced. Many Dissenters did so qualify, including William Russell--the zealous member of Priestley's congregation who was magistrate of a neighboring town.

Nonconformists were permitted by the 1689 Act of Toleration to have their own places of worship and to appoint and dismiss their own preachers, who had to take an oath of loyalty to the crown and subscribe to most of the Thirty-Nine Articles, but who were not permitted to officiate at marriages. By the late 18th century, they flourished in a number of denominations, generally known as Dissenters, including Congregationalists, Presbyterians, Independents, Baptists, Quakers and Unitarians.

While voluntarily supporting their own churches, Dissenters were still taxed the "church rate" to support the Established Church. They organized and financed their own colleges--they were denied degrees from the tax-supported universities of Oxford and Cambridge unless they subscribed to the Thirty-Nine Articles.

Priestley wrote of the Dissenters: "They acknowledge no authority in any man, or any body of men, to settle articles of faith or rules of discipline for them. In all these things they judge and act for themselves, holding themselves answerable to God and their own consciences only." [XIX 198] Their authority in religion was not a government-prescribed creed but the Bible, rationally interpreted. They were free to follow their reason through theological changes without government interference. They cherished a de facto separation of church and state.

The dinner in Birmingham that celebrated the second anniversary of the beginning of the French Revolution was organized by members of the Constitutional Society, which had been formed the previous month to promote a more equal representation in the British Parliament. [XIX 373] They proposed to have annual dinners on the 4th of November and the 14th of July to celebrate the liberation of the English and of the French people from despotic rule.

The "4th of November" was the anniversary of the English Revolution of 1688: that year the Dutch Prince of Orange, fourth in the line of English royal succession, at the invitation of powerful Englishmen antagonized by the pro-Catholic policies and the despotic rule of King James II, invaded England with an army. In the almost bloodless revolution, King James II fled to France. Parliament declared that the king had abdicated and offered the vacant throne to William and Mary. King William III was hailed as a liberator and Protestant hero.

The English Revolution established the right of citizens to resist abused authority and change the government; established a constitutional monarchy, a separation of powers with Parliament exercising restraints on the king; and granted, by Parliament's 1689 Act of Toleration, limited religious freedom (except to Jews, Catholics and Unitarians). These rights became precedents for the civil and religious liberties of citizens in the unwritten British constitution.

For nearly a century in London, the Society for Commemorating The Revolution had annually celebrated the historic event on November 4th. In 1788, the Society of 300 gentlemen, including Anglicans and Dissenters, had celebrated the centennial of the British Revolution, as did a similar society in Birmingham--though in that Dissenter's stronghold, the clergy of the Established Church did not attend because the Society refused to include a toast to the Church of England. [I-ii 14]

The French and the English revolutions were celebrated because both gave citizens more liberty and influence in government. The celebrants anticipated that the French Revolution would establish a constitutional monarchy on the English model, as the French were then attempting to do. But members of the Establishment, who had recently lost the American Colonies by revolution, were frightened by perceived threats from the revolutionary fervor to the siamese twins of English Church-and- State.

The Dissenter William Russell (to whose home the Priestleys first fled) was the principal organizer of the Birmingham dinner. He was a wealthy magistrate of a neighboring town, and he mounted his horse in a vain attempt to get the Birmingham magistrates to quell the mob. Neighbors were removing and hiding his home furnishings. His wife had recently died. His two mature daughters and a son were urged to flee the approaching mob. They fearfully set out on foot until their father caught up with them in a carriage and told them that their home had been burned. After four harrowing nights on the road, they arrived in London. They also later fled to America.

Russell recorded his experience after leaving the celebration dinner: "Neither myself, nor the company in general, who went out together at the front door, met with any Rioters, or the least annoyance in leaving the hotel; and in repeatedly walking the streets some hours afterwards I did not perceive any disturbance.... My opinion is, that no disturbance would have happened, had not uncommon measures been used to promote it." [XIX 563]

Some of the "uncommon measures" that Russell cited were: prior to the riot, a meeting of Church and King partisans had considered "how to punish these damned Presbyterians"; the rioters were heard to frequently declare that they had the magistrates' protection as they were doing the magistrates' bidding; and the rioters had a list of houses to pillage and burn. Though the magistrates were present while the rioters were destroying the homes of Priestley and others, the magistrates never read the "Riot Act"--an English law providing that if twelve or more persons unlawfully assemble and disturb the peace, they must disperse when the Act is read to them or be guilty of a felony. [XIX 558-567] The wife of the lord lieutenant of Birmingham County, "speaking of the rioters" to an attending physician, said that "they went farther than we intended."

One of the men who had not attended the dinner but whose town house was sacked and country house burned by the mob was William Hutton. "He was a victim of revenge," wrote his daughter Catherine: as a commissioner of the Court of Requests, "he had compelled ten thousand blackguards to pay their just debts, and at this time of general license they were let loose upon him." [Hutton 1875, 24]

William Hutton, a Dissenter but not a member of Priestley's congregation, recorded his explanation of the riot, complaining: "However just might have been Dr. Priestley's sentiments, yet had he not promulgated them on one side, and party violence opposed them on the other, perhaps the peace of my life had never been wrecked in the terrible tempest of ninety-one.... If the doctor chooses to furnish the world with candles, it reflects lustre upon himself, but there is no necessity to carry one. It is the privilege of an Englishman to walk in darkness if he chooses." [I-ii 188]

Hutton added that he was surprised that men of a liberal education should quarrel over religion, declaring that "every religion upon earth is right." Priestley responded that "whatever any man deems to be important truths, he must wish others would embrace. Hence, you should not condemn the spirit of proselytism. You cannot, indeed, do it without condemning the conduct of the apostles and reformers in all ages." [I-ii 187]

Hutton's daughter Catherine and her brother were members of Priestley's congregation. She had written to a friend: "The celebrated Dr. Priestley has taken up his residence among us for the sake of facilitating his philosophical experiments, and Mr. Hawkes, one of the preachers at the New Meeting, having resigned his place, it has been offered to the Dr., and it is generally believed he will accept it. If he do, you may expect to hear of my becoming a convert to his religion, for I am weary of Calvinistical monotony and nonsense."

However, she reflected the opinion of her father that Priestley's religious zeal "rendered Birmingham a likely theater for mischief." She wrote a friend: "I look upon Dr. Priestley as a good man, attached to his King and country, and meaning well to every creature; but, though unintentionally, and himself the first sufferer, he was, I think, one of the primary causes of the Riots in Birmingham, by rousing the spirit of bigotry and all uncharitableness in others. He was himself so unconscious of having done wrong, nay, he was so certain of having done only right, that his friends took him almost by force from his house, and saved him from the vengeance of the mob who would have torn him to pieces." [Hutton 1875, 24]

When Priestley moved to Birmingham in 1780 he was renowned for his *The History and Present State of Electricity, with Original Experiments* and discoveries in chemistry. He intended to devote full time to his experiments in science; instead, he became involved in bitter theological controversy. In spite of his earlier successful ministry at Leeds, his theological studies had led him to adopt opinions so different from those of most Dissenters that he did not expect a large chapel to invite him to their pulpit and thought he would only occasionally be employed as a guest preacher.

Mary Priestley's brother John Wilkinson, a wealthy ironmonger, invited the Priestleys to settle near him and rented a house for them at Fair Hill in the country two miles from the city of Birmingham. A visiting French geologist described it as "a charming house, with a fine meadow on the one side and a delightful garden on the other. There was an air of perfect neatness in every thing connected with this house, both without and within it." He added: "Dr. Priestley received with greatest kindness. He presented me to his wife and daughter, who were distinguished by vivacity, intelligence and gentleness of manner." [*Transactions* 1931, 48]

Benefactors built a two-story laboratory in the yard to house Priestley's expanding scientific equipment, which kept the stench and occasional explosions of his experiments out of his home. Mary took care of the house, but the neatness of the laboratory was Priestley's responsibility: he said that it was "no more than my duty" when a friend thought it was "condescension" for Priestley to be sweeping the floor.

Other wealthy benefactors, "lovers of experimental philosophy and disinterested promoters of it," subsidized the cost of his laboratory supplies--a source of research grants in his day, since he would not accept royal patronage. He was ready to pursue his avocation as an experimental scientist.

However, on the resignation of the senior minister at New Meeting Presbyterian Chapel, Priestley was surprised and pleased to receive an almost unanimous invitation to be minister of the chapel, in spite of his radical heterodoxy and stammer. He accepted, three months after settling in Birmingham, "on the express condition of the congregation having no claim upon me except on Sundays; the rest of the week being devoted to my philosophical and other pursuits. The other duties of the place were discharged by my worthy colleague Mr. Blythe." [XIX 360] As it turned out, "other pursuits" in Biblical studies absorbed more of Priestley's time than his scientific work, and embroiled him in religious controversies--to the dismay of his philosophical friends.

The New Meeting, established in 1692, "had attained a degree of liberality of sentiment hardly equalled in any other place," wrote Priestley, due to his immediate predecessors in the pulpit. The congregation concurred with every proposal that Priestley made: the establishment of a library in the Meeting House, the annual election of twelve "elders" to superintend the affairs of the congregation,and especially the organization of three Sunday school classes for children and young people ages five to thirty, whom he personally taught each Sunday. He was beloved for the work he so enjoyed with young people. When grateful parents raised a generous donation for Priestley, he accepted on condition that he give half to his associate minister who cared for the rest of the pastoral office. [I-i 340]

A young member of the Church of England, who later "was an indignant witness of the destruction of Dr. Priestley's library, manuscripts, and apparatus" by the Church and King rioters, wrote his impression of Priestley as a teacher:

"Though differing in religious opinions, I was in the habit of associating with those who regularly attended the instruction of Dr. Priestley; and had I formed my notions of him ... from the representations which I often heard from the pulpit in the church, I must indeed have deemed him 'the deamon of heresy;' but happily I had been accustomed to exercise my own faculties in the pursuit of truth. Much as I had heard and read about Dr. Priestley, I did not know his person till the year 1788, when curiosity induced me to accompany a friend to hear a lecture which he delivered on a Sunday afternoon. Amongst various other designations, we had been told that he was 'a deluded visionary,' and 'a proud and haughty scorner;' but we discovered such a delineation to be unjust, having no resemblance to reality."

The young convert continued, "When we entered the place, we found a man of about middle stature, slenderly made, remarkably placid, modest, and courteous, pouring out, with the simplicity of a child, the great stores of his most capacious mind to a considerable number of young persons of both sexes, whom, with the familiarity and kindness of a friend, he encouraged to ask him questions, either during the lecture or after it, if he advanced any thing which wanted explanation, or struck them in a light different from his own. The impression made upon us was so strong, that we never failed afterwards to attend on such occasions in order to profit by his lessons, and we frequently went to hear him preach, until he was driven from this town in 1791."

The young man concluded with a characterization of Priestley: "His lectures were peculiarly instructive, and the general tenor of his sermons was practical, urging the cultivation of universal benevolence, the earnest pursuit of knowledge, and the most un-restrained free inquiry upon all important subjects. He was the most unassuming, candid man I ever knew; and never did I hear from his lips, either in lecture or sermon, one illiberal sentiment, or one harsh expression concerning any persons who differed from him, not even of the individuals who were so much in the practice of abusing and traducing his character." [I-ii 162]

"Traducing his character" continued after the Riot. Besides attacks on his patriotism in Parliament and in caricatures, and on his religion in the press, the government suspected the young men who were his disciples. A report to the Government on the situation in Birmingham eighteen months after the Riot said that "the only people there from whom any thing is to be apprehended, are some young men brought up under Priestley." [XV 498]

Some 38 years later, young men were still meeting once a month as the Priestley Society: one of their members would give a "retrospect of the advance or retrogression of civil and religious liberty since their last meeting. Once every year (the anniversary of Dr. Priestley's birthday), the members and friends of the society dine together." [I-ii 366] The memory and principles of Priestley were long celebrated in Birmingham, if not in the rest of England.

Priestley began writing his memoirs at the peak of his career in 1787 while spending a month at the home of his brother-in-law John Wilkinson. At the time, he wrote:"I esteem it a singular happiness to have lived in an age and country, in which I have been at full liberty both to investigate, and by preaching and writing to propagate, religious truth; that though the freedom I have used for this purpose was for some time disadvantageous to me, it was not long so, and my present situation is such that I can with greatest openness urge whatever appears to me to be the truth of the gospel, not only without giving the least offense, but with the entire approbation of those with whom I am particularly connected [his congregation]." [I-i 349]

A few months later in Birmingham, he added: "As to the dislike which I have drawn upon myself by my writings, whether the Calvinistic party, in or out of the Church of England, those who rank with rational Dissenters, (but who have been exceedingly offended at my carrying my inquiries farther than they wished any person to do,) or whether they be unbelievers, I am thankful that it gives less disturbance to me than it does to themselves; and that their dislike is much more than compensated by the cordial esteem and approbation of my conduct by a few, whose minds are congenial to my own, and especially that the number of such persons increases." [I-i 349] He claimed that the number of Unitarians increased ten-fold. [XIX 367]

Four years later in *An Appeal to the Public, on the Subject of the Riots in Birmingham*, Priestley (who knew English constitutional law from teaching it at Warrington) wrote in the opening paragraph: "It has hitherto been your great boast, that you were possessed of the best form of government in the world; that in England all men are subject to the laws, from the king upon the throne to the meanest person in the realm; that no man can long be confined, much less punished, without the sentence of law; that whenever any man is accused of a crime, opportunity is given him to make his defense, in the presence of his accusers and of the witnesses against him; and that in all cases he must be tried by his peers, by persons in a situation in all respects similar to his own, so that they themselves may expect the same treatment in the same circumstances. Without this you are sensible there can be no equal law, or equal liberty. It has also been the great pride of an Englishman, that with us the press is free; so that any opinion whatever, civil or religious, may be openly proposed and discussed without any apprehension of danger. ... I was born an Englishman ... and supposed I had the protection of ... [the] constitution and laws for my inheritance. But I have found myself greatly deceived; and so may many of you, if, like me, you should, with or without cause, be so unfortunate as to incur popular odium." [XIX 347-48]

Priestley denied the official justification for persecuting him and in 1794 gave his reason for leaving England in the preface to a sermon to his last congregation in England: "As to the great odium that I have incurred; the charge of sedition, or of my being an enemy of the constitution or peace of my country, is a mere pretence for it, though it has been so much urged, that it is now generally believed, and all attempts to undeceive the public with respect to it, avail nothing at all." [XV 524]

He concluded: "If, then, my real crime has not been sedition or treason, what has it been? For every effect must have some adequate cause, and, therefore, the odium that I have incurred must have been owing to something in my declared sentiments or conduct that has exposed me to it. In my opinion, it cannot have been any thing but my open hostility to the doctrines of the Established Church, and more especially to all civil establishments of religion whatever. This has brought upon me the implacable resentment of the great body of clergy; and they have found other methods of opposing me, besides argument, and the use of the press which is equally open to us all." [XV 526]

The popular justification for victimizing Priestley--his sympathy with the French Revolution--still is repeated so often that he is ignored as controversial, except by physical scientists who recognize his notable achievements in their fields. His progressive and enduring contributions to cosmology, political science, psychology, education, historical method in Biblical criticism, and theology are not generally recognized.

During the degeneration of the French Revolution into a Reign of Terror, the king and queen plus thousands of citizens (including Priestley's friend and father of modern chemistry, Antoine Lavoisier, who had served in the King's administration) were guillotined. Fear that the revolutionary fervor might spread caused mounting hysteria in England.

Birmingham had been riven by the "party spirit" of churchmen before Priestley settled there. He was a zealous exponent of free thought and expression and of religious and civil liberty, and was a critic of the corruptions of Christianity and of the Established Church. The odium of his religious reforms made him a primary target of the reactionary violence in England.

II

"MIXING ACTION WITH SPECULATION"
"Party spirit in Birmingham"

The intent of the instigators of the Birmingham Riot was realized. Priestley was opposed by "other methods" than argument; his career was blasted at its peak, and he was finally driven from the country. Until 1791 he had been positive and creative, but for the rest of his life he was persecuted and defensive, even in America. At age 58 he was so stigmatized that many former friends withdrew from him. However, his loyal friends defended and helped him, and he was called to be the successor of his colleague Price in a wealthy suburban-London pulpit.

He never returned to Birmingham. Immediately after the Riot, his congregation addressed him, sympathizing with his "unmerited and painful suffering": "Accept, dear Sir, our unfeigned testimony to your exemplary diligence, your eminent abilities, your unremitted zeal, your distinguished humility, your unquestioned sincerity, and your uniform love of peace, Christian forbearance, and moderation; and permit us to assure you how affectionately and tenderly we sympathize with you under your present sufferings, and how sincerely we wish their removal. And although you are not immediately returning to us, yet we look forward with pleasure to those happier times when you may resume your pastoral labors here, with safety and satisfaction." [I-11, 134]

Two months later, his congregation--worshiping with the Old Meeting in temporary quarters until a new meeting house could be built, with Sunday school classes led by young members--earnestly urged him to return to their "happy connection, as pastor and people." [I-ii, 159] Priestley responded that he had expected to return, "but every account that I have received having represented the party spirit as more inveterate than I had imagined it to be, so that in all probability my return would only inflame it, and, in consequence of this, my situation, if safe, would be uncomfortable, and perhaps hurtful, it is my deliberate opinion that it will be better for some other person less obnoxious to popular prejudice to take my place, and that I may be more usefully fixed in London, or its neighborhood." [I-ii, 164] After the Riot, he received many letters of sympathy and appreciation: from the young people of the Birmingham New Meeting ("We have seen the great apostle of civil and religious liberty driven from among us."); from his former Leeds chapel; from the Committee of the London Society for Commemorating the English Revolution ("as friends to the general rights of human nature ... to ascribe to the commemoration of the French Revolution the late devastation at Birmingham, would be to insult the understandings of mankind." Priestley responded, "Violence is temporary, but truth is eternal."); from the Committee of Protestant Dissenters at York; from the Philosophical Society at Derby; from an Assembly of Dissenting Ministers ("... we heartily congratulate you on being able, in so trying circumstances, to display to the view of the public the exercise of the most difficult and magnanimous virtues."); from the Dissenters of Bristol and Bath; and from the students at the Dissenters New College, plus many friends, including a few Anglican clergy. The Royal Society, to which he had contributed so much, was dominated by the Establishment and did not condole him, though individual members helped resupply his laboratory.

In his memoirs, Priestley wrote: "I consider my settlement at Birmingham as the happiest event in my life, being highly favorable to every object I had in view, philosophical or theological. In the former respect I had the convenience of good workmen of every kind [to make his laboratory instruments], and the society of persons eminent for their knowledge of chemistry." In his theological pursuits, he had the society of friendly Biblical scholars and theologians. [I-i, 338]

At the time of the Riot, the Priestley children were scattered. Sarah, 28 and married to William Finch, was pregnant and living in the nearby town of Heath. Joseph, Jr., 23, was married to Eliza Ryland (daughter of Samuel Ryland who brought the carriage to carry the Priestleys to safety from the mob) and was just beginning a mercantile partnership in Manchester--which was cancelled when his father was made notorious by the Riot. William, 20, had recently returned from Paris and was distressed by his experience with the rioters. Henry, 14, whom Priestley wished to make a scholar to carry on his work in science and theology, was safely living and studying with Priestley's friend and fellow theologian in Bristol, about 80 miles from Birmingham.

Priestley was concerned for the welfare of his children, especially after the Riot when his sons found it impossible to secure employment and finally ventured to America. He had always doted on his children. "Nothing gave the Doctor more pleasure than to please us," wrote John Ryland of his earliest recollections of accompanying his mother when he was eight to play with the Priestley children. "To please his young friends," Priestley gave them slight shocks of static electricity from his generating machine and exhibited his "magic lantern." When his sons begged him for the air gun he had designed, Priestley took them to the coal cellar and set up the block, on which his wig was dressed, for the boys to shoot at. [Ryland 1844, ms]

"Mrs. Priestley ... was a woman of great energy and strength of character," recalled John Ryland. She was an excellent homemaker, managing the servants, keeping the accounts, and relieving her husband of every domestic care so he could devote his time to his scientific and theological pursuits. She wrote beautiful letters and maintained life-long friendships.

When Priestley's younger brother Timothy, a Calvinistic Dissenter minister, deplored his brother's heterodoxy to Mary, he soon learned that she was "no dox." [Gordon 1970, 124] She was even less orthodox than her husband: she did not share the Christian piety Priestley considered a necessary motive for virtue. "She did not believe in an afterlife and had 'the most rooted aversion' to his preaching and other ministerial activities. His wife's skepticism was disturbing to Priestley, but he acknowledged that she 'had attained the end, the most benevolent and disinterested disposition I ever knew, with but little of the means.'" [Lesser 1970, 93] Nor was she concerned with his scientific activities. [Holt 1970, 93] She created the environment for him to pursue his interests without domestic distractions, in spite of her frequent bouts with tuberculosis in which she spat up blood.

Though Priestley's health had been good since he was 18, just before moving to Birmingham he suffered from gall stones, which sometimes gave him "exquisite pain." The first summer he was in Birmingham, he spent several weeks in August at the summer home of William Russell at Brighton, a seaside and health resort on the south coast of England. Priestley later reported that "by confining myself to a vegetable diet I perfectly recovered, and have now so long been free from the disorder, that I am under no apprehension of its return." [I-i, 343] He continued his vegetarian diet the rest of his life, with a single glass of wine with his dinner.

Priestley's preoccupation with chemistry disturbed Mary. When his laboratory was in their home, the noise and stench from his experiments pervaded the house--until Shelburne provided him with a separate laboratory at Bowood. When the family moved from Leeds to Calne, Mary packed everything and Priestley offered to help by fastening and roping the boxes. "On their arrival, Mrs. Priestley opened them and found, under the cover of each box, a medley of minerals and mixtures of chemicals. Priestley begged her not to worry if the clothes 'were a little injured,' for the other things stood up to the journey perfectly well." [Gibbs 1965, 87]

In the *Life of Joseph Priestley*, his contemporary John Corry described Priestley as "about middle stature, or five feet eight inches high. He was slender and well proportioned; his complexion was fair, his eyes grey and sparkling with intelligence, and his whole countenance was expressive of the benignity of his heart. He often smiled, but seldom laughed. He was extremely active and agile in his motions. He walked fast and very erect, and his deportment was dignified. His common dress was a black coat without a cape, a fine linen or cambric stock, a cocked hat, a powdered wig, shoes and buckles. The whole of his dress was remarkably clean.... During his residence at Far Hill, Dr. Priestley rose about 6 o'clock, and commonly retired to his study, where he continued till eight, when he met his family at breakfast. He breakfasted on tea, and after breakfast again went to his study, accompanied by his amanuensis [who could transcribe Priestley's short-hand, though no one now can]. In the afternoon he usually took a walk to Birmingham, and spent some time at the printing office where several of his controversial publications were printed, and he afterwards visited some respectable friends. Being an excellent economist of time, he returned home at an early hour, and generally sat down to supper at eight o'clock. ... After supper the Doctor called all his family together to prayers, and retired to rest about ten o'clock." [Cory 1804, 43]

Joseph, Jr., wrote that his father thought his chemical experiments were a relaxation from his theological studies, enabling him to be so productive. He read widely, including novels and plays. For many years of his life he spent two or three hours a day playing games such as cards, backgammon, and especially chess, with Mary after supper. When the children were old enough to play, they turned to whist or "some round game at cards," which Priestley enjoyed as much as any of the family, but never played for money. He got plenty of exercise: in his laboratory he did all his own work "as he never employed an operator, and never allowed any one even to light a fire." Since he never owned a horse, he walked a great deal with a regular pace of four miles an hour. At Calne and Northumberland, he enjoyed working in his garden. [Priestley 1806, Vol. I, 185]

By his self-discipline, Priestley made time for his multifarious enterprises and recreation. He rose before the rest of his family or servants, made his own fire, and shaved himself--which he did every morning until a few days before his death. [Priestley 1806, Vol. 2, 162] He budgeted his time for reading, writing and experimenting, laying his watch on the table before him so he would keep to his schedule. He wrote the first draft of his compositions in shorthand and transcribed it himself, until in Birmingham he could afford to hire a transcriber. His writings benefited by at least two drafts, plus criticism by his friends, before publication. He deliberately scheduled time each day to enjoy the company of his friends and family.

He was not fussy about being disturbed while writing: "It has been a great advantage to me that I have never been under the necessity of retiring from company in order to compose anything. Being fond of domestic life, I got a habit of writing on any subject by the parlor fire, with my wife and children about me, and occasionally talking to them without experiencing any inconvenience from such interruptions....many persons greatly distress themselves, and others, by the idea that they can do nothing except in perfect solitude or silence." [I-i, 347]

His international reputation as a scientist was already established by the time he moved to Birmingham. He had published his classic *History and Present State of Electricity, with Original Experiments.* Benjamin Franklin evaluated his friend's experiments, concluding: "Upon the whole Dr. Priestley appears to be a very intelligent, ingenious, and indefatigably diligent Experimenter; and to have contributed considerable Materials for the Improvement of the Electrical Branch of Natural Philosophy." [Schofield 1966,67]

In the developing field of chemistry, he discovered eight chemical elements: oxygen, nitrogen, nitrous oxide, nitric acid, nitrogen dioxide, ammonia, hydrogen chloride, and sulfur dioxide. For his experiments in chemistry, especially devising a more efficient method of manufacturing artificially carbonated water (then thought to be a cure for scurvey and other diseases), he had been awarded the highest honor of the Royal Society, the gold Copley Medal, on Franklin's recommendation. He discovered the function of the blood in respiration, and photosynthesis as the process by which common air was purified--he had wondered how the Creator refreshed air polluted by respiration, oxidation, and combustion, a theological question in his mind. Priestley published some 150 scientific books and articles between 1757 and 1804. [McEvoy, March 1978, 39]

In recognition of his many scientific achievements, Priestley was elected a member of the Royal Society, London; the French Academy of Sciences; the Imperial Academy of Sciences at St. Petersburg, Russia; the Philosophical Society at Orleans, France; the Society at Haarlem, Netherlands; the Lisbon Royal Academy of Sciences, Portugal; The American Philosophical Society at Philadelphia, and the American Academy of Arts and Sciences at Boston. [Schofield 1966, 412]

"I am far from pretending a complete knowledge of chemistry," wrote Priestley. Though he had been exposed to chemical experiments when teaching at Warrington Academy, he was 34 years of age and living in Leeds before he was led to begin his own research in chemistry. But his skill as an experimenter and observer produced such significant findings that he influenced the leading chemists of his day; John Dalton in England and Antoine Lavoisier in France, among others. Lavoisier in 1777 invited Franklin to be present for a repeat of "a few of the principal experiments of M. Priestley on different kinds of air." [Schofield 1966, 160]

Priestley devised his own laboratory techniques and improvised inexpensive apparatus. He used an ordinary ceramic wash-tub, with his own additions, as a "pneumatic trough" to collect gases over water, or over mercury if they were water- soluble. He discovered a more efficient and accurate way to measure the fitness of air for breathing than by seeing how long a mouse or candle flame could survive in a sealed bottle of air: he mixed nitric oxide with the air to be tested and then measured how much oxygen was absorbed--the amount the air was diminished.

He considered his discoveries in science as contributions to knowledge for the benefit of humanity and, like his friend Franklin, patented and profited by none of them. His laboratory expenses burdened his family budget. Wishing to preserve himself "independent of every thing connected with the court," he twice declined overtures to secure him a government pension: one by his influential friend from Leeds, John Lee while Solicitor General, and the other by a Bishop "in whose power it was to have procured it." Instead, he preferred "the assistance of generous and opulent individuals, lovers of science, and also lovers of liberty." [I-i, 216] After he left the employ of Lord Shelburne, who had subsidized his experiments during his most prolific period,his financial backers in Birmingham included many of his intimate philosophical friends; moreover, Josiah Wedgwood freely supplied him with everything he needed made of ceramics, and a London glass-worker with every instrument made of glass. [I-i, 216]

Priestley was a model of the emerging empirical scientist who rolled up his sleeves and, as he said, mixed "action with speculation" by "giving some employment to hands and arms, as well as to the head," testing his hypotheses by experiments. [XXV, 346]

He was not only a skilled experimenter; he had an explicit philosophy of science that integrated it with and supported his theology. In the preface to his *History of Electricity* he expressed his conviction that science reinforced religious sentiments: "A life spent in the contemplation of the productions of Divine powers, wisdom, and goodness, would be a life of devotion. The more we see of the wonderful structure of the world, and of the laws of nature, the more clearly do we comprehend their admirable uses to make all the percipient creation happy." [XXV, 351]

He wrote that in science "we see the human understanding to its greatest advantage, grasping at the noblest objects, and increasing its own powers, by acquiring to itself the powers of nature, and directing them to the accomplishment of its own views, whereby the security and happiness of mankind are daily improved." [XXV, 343] But, said Priestley, "Before we can improve upon nature, by an artificial combination of its powers, the laws of nature must be understood; and they are only to be understood by a careful observation of what does in fact take place in consequence of them." [XXIII, 197]

Science tends to make us humble, he said, "as it shows in the strongest light, the immensity of nature, the unsearchable wisdom of the Author of nature, and the narrowness of our comprehension. Other persons hear of these truths, but experimental philosophers feel them." [XVIII, 357]

Science keeps us humble because it teaches us that no discovery of truth is final: "Such is the necessary connection of all things in the system of nature, that every discovery brings to our view many things of which we had no intimation before....The greater is the circle of light, the greater is the boundary of the darkness by which it is confined.... In time, the bounds of light will be still farther extended; and from the infinity of the Divine nature and the Divine works, we may promise ourselves an endless progress in our investigations of them, a prospect truly sublime and glorious." [XXV, 372]

In the history of electricity, he wrote, "we see a gradual rise and progress in things." When we see "a perpetual progress and improvement" and "an actual increase in a long period of time past, we cannot help forming an idea of an unlimited increase in futurity, which is a prospect really boundless and sublime." [XXV, 341] This principle of gradual progress substantiated his confidence in the inevitable but gradual improvements of government and religion, as well as of science. Franklin shared Priestley's optimism about science. Soon after Priestley was settled in Birmingham, Franklin wrote to him from France: "I always rejoice to hear of your being still employed in experimental researches into nature, and of the success you meet with. The rapid progress true science now makes, occasions my regretting sometimes that I was born too soon. It is impossible to imagine the height to which may be carried, in a thousand years, the power of man over matter. We may, perhaps, learn to deprive large masses of their gravity, and give them absolute levity, for the sake of easy transport. Agriculture may diminish its labor and double its produce: all diseases may by sure means be prevented or cured, (not excepting even that of old age,) and our lives lengthened at pleasure, even beyond the antediluvian standard. Oh that moral science were in as fair a way of improvement, that men would cease to be wolves to one another, and that human beings would at length learn what they now improperly call humanity!" [I-i, 329]

The advancement of science required a history of its development so scientists could benefit from the achievements and mistakes of the past, and an easy channel of communication about all new discoveries, said Priestley, who reported his experimental mistakes and failures as well as his successes. The popularity of his *History of Electricity* encouraged him to attempt the history of all branches of science. However, his hastily written *History of the Present State of Discoveries Relating to Vision, Light, and Colors* was so poorly received that he lost money and abandoned the project. However, the book is still in demand--it was reprinted in 1978.

Priestley believed that science would engender religious reforms: the rapid increase of knowledge, "which like the progress of a wave of the sea, of sound, or of light from the sun, extends itself, not this way or that way only, but in all directions, will, I doubt not, be the means under God of extirpating all error and prejudice, and of putting an end to all undue and usurped authority in the business of religion as well as of science.... and the English hierarchy (if there be anything unsound in its constitution) has equal reason to tremble even at an air-pump or an electrical machine." [XXV, 375] The spread of knowledge, not violence, was the agency Priestley believed would inevitably reform the political as well as the religious order.

Priestley always worked in a community of intimate friends with whom he interchanged ideas and criticisms in science and religion, in person or by mail. In Birmingham, "the society of persons eminent for their knowledge of chemistry" that Priestley enjoyed was chiefly in the Lunar Society, so named because its monthly meetings were near the full moon. They met for dinner and conversation in various homes from two to eight--hence the full moon to drive home by. Over the years, there were fourteen members called "Lunatics," seven of whom were members of the Royal Society.

Priestley's special friends in the Lunar Society-- with many of whom he had corresponded before moving to Birmingham and joining the Society-- included Erasmus Darwin, Matthew Boulton, James Watt, James Keir, William Withering, and William Small, plus Josiah Wedgwood--an occasional guest.

They were an influential group in the Industrial Revolution, "for the Lunar Society was a brilliant microcosm of that scattered community of provincial manufacturers and professional men who found England a rural society with an agricultural economy and left it urban and industrial." [Schofield 1963, 3] The Society was a forum for ideas in the sciences, pure and applied, to which Priestley had already made so many contributions.

Conversation was spontaneous at meetings of the Lunar Society as there was no agenda or scheduled papers. Dr. Erasmus Darwin wrote to Matthew Boulton, both original members since 1765: "I am sorry the infernal divinities who visit mankind with diseases, and therefore are at perpetual war with Doctors, should have prevented my seeing all you great men at Soho today. Lord! what inventions, what wit, what rhetoric, metaphysical, mechanical and pyrotechnical, will be on the wing, bandied like a shuttlecock from one to another of your troop of philosophers!" The Lunatics did not take themselves too seriously. When James Watt was host, he wrote to Darwin: "I beg that you would impress on your memory the idea that you promised to dine with sundry men of learning at my house on Monday next, and that you will realize the idea. For your encouragement there is a new book to be cut up, and it is to be determined whether or not heat is a compound of phlogiston and empyreal air, and whether a mirror can reflect the heat of a fire. I give you friendly warning that you may be found wanting whichever opinion you may adopt in the later question; therefore, be cautious. If you are meek and humble, perhaps you may be told what light is made of, and also how to make it, and the theory proved by synthesis and analysis." [Holt 1970, 128]

Priestley recorded that at meetings of the Lunar Society, "neither politics nor religion ever were the subjects of our conversations. Philosophy engrossed us wholly." [I-i, 211] So he could not respond with religious arguments when Erasmus Darwin proposed his theory of evolution, foreshadowing his grandson Charles. Erasmus was impressed by fossil shells and bones he found in caves he visited in 1770 and speculated that all animals evolved from shelly sea creatures. [King-Hele 1977, 75] However, one of Priestley's last publications in America was a refutation of Erasmus's published theory of evolution; Darwin's assumption of "spontaneous generation" as the origin of species countered Priestley's assumption of the Creator as the "first cause."

Erasmus Darwin was a prosperous physician who had studied medicine at the Universities of Cambridge and Edinburgh, a poet, an inventor, corpulent and lame from an accident in a carriage he had designed, and an engaging conversationalist in spite of a stammer (like Priestley's) which he claimed was a convenience: "It gives me time for reflection and saves me from asking impertinent questions." [Ritchied-Calder 1982, 136]

Matthew Boulton, a Lunatic with whom Priestley had corresponded before moving to Birmingham, had built a large iron works at Soho outside of Birmingham that was a popular tourist attraction. The die pressing machine, for stamping out buttons and popular steel buckles, was powered by a water-wheel that lacked sufficient water in the summer. Darwin suggested to Boulton that James Watt might help him solve his power problem.

Watt was a scientific-instrument maker at the University of Glasgow who, in repairing a model of a Newcomen steam engine, had hit upon a way to improve it by condensing the steam that powered the piston in a separate boiler, which kept the cylinder at a more efficient constant heat. When Watt was in England surveying for the canal developers, he visited Birmingham where William Small, a Lunatic, showed him around the Soho works and introduced him to Boulton.

Boulton bought Watt's patent on the improved steam engine and made him a partner in the Soho factory for the manufacture of the Boulton & Watt engine. A further improvement of the engine was provided when John Wilkinson, Mary Priestley's brother and an occasional guest of the Lunar Society, designed and built a lathe for more accurately boring cannon barrels, which provided the precision necessary for boring the eighteen inch cylinder of Watt's steam engine. [Ritchie-Calder 1982, 144] Most of the Lunatics, except Boulton, had supported both the American and French revolutions and feared the Church and King mob. Watt's son had been denounced as a French agent by Edmund Burke in the House of Commons. At the Soho factory, Boulton and Watt had armed their workers to withstand an attack. [Ritchie-Calder 1982, 144] Soho was unmolested. But after Priestley was falsely accused of sedition, Boulton broke off his friendship with Priestley.

Before settling in Birmingham, Priestley had also corresponded about chemistry with Captain James Keir, who did not share Priestley's phlogiston theory about the nature of oxygen. Keir was the Lunatic who presided at the Birmingham dinner celebrating the French Revolution. He had been a medical student with Erasmus Darwin at the University of Edinburgh and, after a period in the British army, settled near Birmingham. He directed manufacturing operations for Boulton at Soho for a time, and later operated a large chemical works at neighboring Tipton, where he innovated a process for producing industrial alkalis. He wrote articles on chemistry, geology, politics and military strategy. [Ritchie-Calder 1982, 140, and Schofield 1966, 361]

William Withering, whose improved glass apparatus with valves Priestley had recommended (rather than his own device) for manufacturing carbonated water, was another long-time friend and correspondent of Priestley. Withering had earned a medical doctorate at the University of Edinburgh and was a prominent physician in Birmingham. From his studies in botany, he introduced a derivative of the foxglove plant, digitalis, as a cardiac stimulant. He wrote articles on gases and minerals--the "witherite" he discovered is used in many manufacturing processes. On Sunday evening of the Riot, the mob gathered around his home but it was saved by the arrival of the troops. It is now a Birmingham golf-club house.

One of the original members of the Lunar Society, with Boulton and Darwin, was William Small, who was educated in medicine and science at Marischal College in Aberdeen. At age 24 he went to Williamsburg, Virginia, to be professor of natural philosophy at the

College of William and Mary. His pupil Thomas Jefferson later wrote of him: "From his conversation I got my first views of the expansion of science and the system of things in which we are placed," and added, "Small probably fixed the destinies of my life." On Small's return to England in 1764, he attended a Royal Society meeting as the guest of Franklin, who gave him a letter of introduction to Matthew Boulton recommending Small as a physician who wished to settle in Birmingham. [Ritchie-Calder 1982, 136, and King-Hele 1977, 60]

Josiah Wedgwood did not regularly attend Lunar Society meetings as he lived 40 miles from Birmingham at Hanley, near his pottery. He and Priestley had become friends and correspondents years before, sharing a passionate interest in chemistry. Wedgwood sought technical advice from Priestley, including the possibility of gilding by electricity. Priestley sent him new materials and minerals to experiment with, and he supplied Priestley with ceramic vessels for his laboratory. Wedgwood's application of the findings of science to his pottery manufacture enabled him to produce chinaware of high quality--the firing he controlled by his invention of a ceramic pyrometer for measuring high temperatures in kilns. To solve his problem of pottery broken in transit by carts over rough roads he, with his later partner Thomas Bentley and Erasmus Darwin, promoted building the Trent-and-Mersey canal, part of a network of canals financed by the growth of country banking fostered by provincial industrialists. The canal enabled Wedgwood to ship his wares safely and inexpensively to Liverpool and Hull for export.

Besides the circle of scientists he regularly met and corresponded with in England, Priestley's letters show him "as a member of an international community of scientists who visited or wrote to one another, communicating news of their researches even during war time." [Schofield 1966, 188] Priestley believed in the importance of such information exchange, but he found his extensive correspondence burdensome in foreign languages. He had met many foreign scientists during a three-month tour on the Continent with Lord Shelburne in 1774.

The ministry was Priestley's vocation, while science was an avocation, a means of finding answers to theological questions about the processes of Creation and, as he acknowledged, lending weight to his "attempts to defend Christianity, and to free it from those corruptions which prevent its reception with philosophical and thinking persons." [I-i, 200]

Priestley alienated many people by his research and publications in religion. He felt he had a call to convert unbelievers to "pure

Christianity" by challenging the orthodox corruptions of its pristine form. In Birmingham he had a congenial society of theologians and Biblical scholars to support his enterprise: "We met and drank tea together every fortnight. At this meeting we read all the papers that were sent for the *Theological Repository*, which I had revived some time after coming hither." [I-i, 339] "For want of sufficient sale" and because of personal financial loss, he had to discontinue the project after publishing six volumes in all between 1769 and 1788. He thought the *Repository* "one of the most useful works I ever undertook." [XX, 509]

The purpose of the *Repository* was to "promote Religious Knowledge" by free inquiry, said Priestley. On the model of his *History of Electricity* that consolidated in one source reports of experiments, Priestley sought in religion to "promote the early communication of new thoughts, concentrate...valuable knowledge, and prevent useless and tedious publications. ... It is meant to be a common channel of communication, which shall be open for all new observations that relate to theology....open, not only to all denominations of Christians, but to persons who disbelieve Christianity and revelation in general," including Deists whose criticisms, he said, had led to improvements in Christian knowledge. [VII 514]

However, only Dissenters contributed, most of them Socinian (or Unitarian) friends--no orthodox Christians, Deists or even Arians. More than a third of the articles were by Priestley. He was denounced, but not responded to in the *Repository* , by Methodists and Calvinist Dissenters.

He first published his radical ideas in theology in the *Repository* to get feedback so he could benefit by reactions to his new or doubtful opinions. In it, Priestley published his articles on "the miraculous conception of Jesus" and on "the intricate business of Platonism," despite advice not to advance such controversial ideas.

As usual with his theological writings, Priestley had sent his best friend Theophilus Lindsey, founder of the first Unitarian Chapel in London, a copy of his essay on the proper humanity of Jesus for corrections and comments. Lindsey was alarmed that publication would "be attended with ill consequences to his friend, by creating enemies, injuring his character, or impeding his usefulness" and warned him not to publish it, hoping "to save him from the odium which ... would accrue from pursuing the principle to its just consequences." [Belsham 1873, 142]

Priestley did not heed the warning and did incur "odium." If evidence convinced him that he was mistaken, he would modify his position, but not out of fear. "I have written with as much impartiality as I am capable of; following such lights as my reading and observation have been able to supply. I pretend not, however, to have written under the influence of all the virtues, that of discretion, in subjects of this nature, being almost out of my system." [XXII, 336] In Birmingham, he expanded his controversial ideas in *An History of the Corruptions of Christianity* in two volumes (1782) and *An History of Early Opinions Concerning Jesus Christ* in four volumes (1786), both trenchant criticisms which further enraged the orthodox, particularly in the Established Church, and alarmed most of the non-Unitarian Dissenters. For eight years in Birmingham he was engaged with Anglican clergy in an acrimonious public theological controversy.

Without access to a university library, the expense of acquiring works of the early Christian writers to consult for his histories was considerable but, said Priestley, "I have found my theological friends even more liberal than my philosophical ones." They included Mrs. Rayner, a life-long benefactress and member of Lindsey's Unitarian Chapel; William Tayleur, a zealous Unitarian who also generously contributed to the founding of the London Chapel; and leading members of Priestley's Birmingham congregation, at the instigation of William Russell. [I-i, 215] Although his salary in Birmingham exceeded his earlier expectations from the ministry, it could not have supported his scientific and theological researches without such encouragements from his many benefactors who thought he was contributing to knowledge in both fields. Priestley contributed to two great advances of his century, the Industrial Revolution and the Enlightenment (new light by reason and experiment)--for both of which Birmingham was a center.

The city of Birmingham was in the Midlands about 108 miles northwest of London, a three-day journey by horse and carriage. With a population of about 100,000, Birmingham had long been a manufacturing center of labor-intensive "cottage industries," principally smiths who made buckles and buttons, bridle-bits and nails, knives and swords. They manifested their independence during Cromwell's Civil War when the iron workers manufactured sword blades for the Parliamentary forces but declined orders for weapons from the Royalist forces.

The Industrial Revolution was engendered by the invention of the spinning jenny, flying shuttle, power loom and the improved steam engine, which moved weaving, as well as the industries that manufactured the machines, into large factories and concentrated labor in cities such as Birmingham.

A new class of influential citizens emerged. Wealth could be accumulated not only by the ownership of estates but of industries, and wealthy entrepreneurs resented their lack of power and prestige. The industrialists were rankled by outmoded government regulations and by rule of the Establishment--the exclusive class of nobility, land owners, Churchmen and clergy, court pensioners, and graduates with school-ties from the "public" Universities.

During most of Priestley's adult life, an inept king reigned, King George III whose stubborn insistence on taxing the American Colonies led to their independence by revolution. The Royal prerogative of appointing government officials, and dispensing offices and perquisites, surrounded the king with sycophants who administered the government. King George, a devoted family man who patronized the arts, was intellectually incapable of seeing a problem dispassionately, felt his own inadequacy, had bouts of madness, and ended his life violently insane.

During his reign, political parties emerged--though yet unorganized: the Tories were conservative supporters of the king in the wars against the American Colonies and revolutionary France, while the Whigs were liberal opponents of both wars and sought government reforms. Priestley, most of his friends, and most of the Dissenters, were Whigs.

Birmingham was not a self-governing city until after the Reform Act of 1832 (for which Priestley was an early exponent), and did not receive a charter of incorporation until 1838. Prior to that, Birmingham was administered by the Lord of the Manor.

Manorial authority gave Birmingham some immunity from royal interference; when the nonconformist clergy were ejected from their livings by the Act of Uniformity in the 17th century, they found refuge and employment in Birmingham. The city became a strong center of Dissenters whose numbers were increasing, as Priestley asserted in a post-riot letter to the Anglican clergy of Birmingham: "In the last eleven years, in which you have shown a disposition peculiarly hostile to the Dissenters, they have increased in an unprecedented proportion. Not less than ten new congregations of Dissenters, or [of] Methodists, have been formed in that time. ... In the meantime, though your places of worship are but five, those who attend public worship in them are little, if at all, increased." [XIX, 592]

By Priestley's time in Birmingham, Dissenters were a majority of the middle class commercial and manufacturing people. Priestley recorded a cause of the Riot: "It is the opinion of many, that envy of the prosperity of Dissenters was one considerable stimulus to the mischief done to them in Birmingham." [XIX, 419] In no other city where the second anniversary of the French Revolution was celebrated was there even a disturbance, let alone a riot.

The increasing influence of Dissenters aggravated unusual "party spirit" in Birmingham. The clergy, said Priestley, "long before I went thither, as well as during the whole time of my residing there,...refused to go in the same coach with Dissenting Ministers at funerals, or to walk with them in the procession. When I gave the late Bishop of St. Asaph an account of this behavior of the clergy of Birmingham, he expressed much concern at it, and said that he thought such bigotry had now existed no where." [XIX, 361]

An exception to the estrangement was that in 1788 Priestley happily found himself concurring with all other Birmingham Christians, Anglican and Dissenter alike, in preaching a sermon on the same Sunday in opposition to the slave trade. It was satisfying "to go with the multitude," for a change, on the Biblical theme "He hath made of one blood all nations of men to dwell on all the face of the earth." [Acts 17:26]

Priestley based his anti-slavery exposition not only on Scripture, but also on the dignity of human nature and the common rights of humanity, including Negroes. All mankind, he said, are brethren and neighbors, with no subordination according to race. In Jesus' parable of the Good Samaritan, Priestley argued that "he who showed mercy" was neighbor, not only to relations and friends, but to the outsider who fell among thieves, which was the case with "the great and growing enormity of slavery," the traffic in the human species on the sugar plantations of the West Indies by English owners (including one of his friends who was at least kind to his slaves).

Priestley asked his hearers to identify with the slaves: "What these poor wretches are made to suffer while they are conducted to such a distance, for such a purpose, before they reach the ships; what they suffer on the ships, and in their cruel bondage afterwards, may, in some measure, be imagined by us, when we consider that these men have the same feelings with ourselves, and conceive themselves to be as unjustly treated as we should do, if we were violently seized, conveyed away from all our friends, and confined to hard labor all our lives in Africa. [XV, 371]

He recited the suffering of the slaves: "In general, it is said, that in our plantations slaves are employed so many hours every day, excepting Sundays, in the service of their masters, that they have only one for themselves, and but little for sleep. For remissions in labor they are severly beaten, and for rebellion (as any attempt to recover liberty is called), they are generally gibbetted alive. The shocking indecencies to which the females are subjected during the voyage, and afterwards, and the cruel separation of the nearest relations and friends, husbands and wives, parents and children, both when they are put on board the ships, and at the place of sale, would be heard with horror by all but those who are habituated to this traffic." [XV, 371]

He claimed that "both natural and revealed religion inculcate a humane and equitable treatment of all that come under our power. We are still under obligation to do to others what we would that they should do unto us." [XV, 376]

He denounced a rationalization of slavery: "Some Europeans, finding Negro slaves in this wretched, degraded condition, to which they themselves have reduced them, have had the assurance and the folly to pronounce them to be a species of men greatly inferior to themselves." [XV, 379]

Priestley concluded: "We should be all means, then, if we have any idea of the dignity of human nature, and if we have at heart the real interest of the master, as well as that of the slave, put an end to this unnatural and improper distinction among those who are partakers of the same common nature." [XV, 380] Nineteen years later, in 1807, the slave trade was abolished by Great Britain, long before the Americans became sensitized to the enormity of the slave trade.

Two incidents worsened relations between Anglicans and Dissenters. Priestley wrote to a friend in 1787 about the "affair which has made a great noise around here," the controversy about the Birmingham library (Priestley had originally proposed it on the model of the one he had organized in Leeds). A motion was made to exclude from the library "all books of controversial divinity," especially Priestley's, who responded in a letter of protest to all subscribers. The Anglican clergy did its utmost to gain support for the motion. At the annual meeting of the subscribers (a majority were Dissenters), Priestley wrote: "The chief speakers were the rector of the principal church on one side, and Mr. Russell on the other; and though no measures were concerted by us, the motion was rejected by about two thirds of the company present, so that the high-church party is thoroughly humbled." [I-ii, 6] John Ryland later claimed that the library controversy "began the feelings that were finally vented in the riots." [Ryland 1844 ms]

"Party spirit" also emerged when "Sunday Schools," for the secular education of children who worked the rest of the week, were started by subscription of "persons of all religious persuasions" acting in concert, said Priestley. "It was agreed that the children should go to whatever places of public worship their parents should choose." Since no children of Dissenters attended the school, all of the students attended the Established Church. "But the high-church party, not being content with this, at a meeting of the subscribers, the business of which was not advertised, the former rule was rescinded, and the children were then absolutely ordered to do what they had ever done, and always might have done, that is, attend the worship of the Established Church, and no other." After continuing their subscriptions for a year in the vain hope that the high-church party would revert to its former liberal policy, the Dissenters subscribed to the opening of their own Sunday School, and provided that parents could send their children to public worship wherever they chose. [XIX, 362]

"Wishing to discover the cause of this excessive party- spirit," wrote Priestley, "and to apply, if I should be able, some remedy to it, I found the Dissenters were in possession of all the civil power in the place, by having the nomination of all the offices; and though they constantly gave the principal office, viz. that of High Bailiff, to a member of the Church of England, they choose to retain the power of nominating of which they had long been in possession. This power ... I took pains, from the beginning of my residence in Birmingham, to persuade the Dissenters to relinquish; and I gradually brought over to my opinion some of the principal of them." [XIX, 364] At the time of the Riot, both magistrates in Birmingham were members of the Established Church. [XIX, 398]

Though it was Priestley's theological writings that enraged people, the English tradition of formal religious freedom precluded direct attack on his religion. During the hysteria over the French Revolution, the unfounded charge against Priestley was that he was a seditious revolutionary. Quotations used against him were not from his political publications but were taken out of context from his theological ones. He wrote: "I never preached a political sermon in my life, unless such as, I believe, all Dissenters usually preach on the Fifth of November, in favor of civil and religious liberty, may be said to be political." [XV, 525] His political opinions were expressed in his publications, not in the pulpit.

The odium Priestley incurred resulted from his early development of "more rational notions of religion." It was adolescent anxiety about salvation and rejection of his application for chapel membership as a "not quite orthodox" young man that set him on a course of theological development to Unitarianism, and to his radical psychological and cosmological theories. However, he continued in the Christian piety of his childhood, including belief in the revealed truths which he thought were necessary to virtuous living and a future life ("that fine place" to which Priestley was consoled his mother went after her death); the moral teachings of Jesus, the resurrection of the body on the Day of Judgment and the providence of God in making this the best of all *possible* worlds.

III

"MORE RATIONAL NOTIONS OF RELIGION"
"A Deep Reverence for Divine Things"

Priestley's "odium" began when he was young and acquired "more rational notions of religion." He spent the rest of his life vindicating, freely expanding, and modifying his evolving affirmation of liberal Christianity, from Calvinism to Unitarianism. He became so heretical for his time that he frightened Dissenters and enraged Anglicans.

He was the eldest child, born March 13, 1733, at Fieldhead, in Yorkshire, about six miles southwest of Leeds and two miles from the village of Birstal, where today there is a Priestley statue. His father Jonas, a "cloth dresser," dyed and finished cloth. Yorkshire was the center of woolen cloth manufacture, a major "cottage industry" done in homes on a piece-work basis. His mother was a farmer's daughter.

In his memoirs, Priestley recalls, "It is but little that I can recollect of my mother. I remember, however, that she was careful to teach me the Assembly's Catechism, and to give me the best instructions the little time that I was at home [until he was about four]." He explained, "My mother having children so fast, I was very soon committed to the care of her father, and with him I continued with little interruption till my mother's death." [I-i, 3-4] In six years, she had born four sons and two daughters. "She died in the hard winter of 1739, not long after being delivered of my youngest brother, and having dreamed a little before her death that she was in a delightful place, which she particularly described, and imagined to be heaven, the last words which she spake, as my aunt informed me, were 'Let me go to that fine place.'" [I-i, 6]

Through all his rational purifications of orthodox Christianity, Priestley never abandoned faith in "that fine place" where the sufferings of this life would be compensated, though not immediately in heaven. Retribution would come on the biblical Judgment Day, when the Kingdom of God would be established on earth, and all the dead resurrected and rewarded for their virtue or punished for their sins. Such was the sanction for virtue, and he thought that instilling virtue was the purpose of Christianity. Priestley's childhood conviction of an afterlife makes understandable his incongruous faith in the coming Judgment Day, unaffected by his other rational reforms of Christianity.

After his mother's death, Priestley was taken to live with his father for three years. "But being without a mother, and my father being encumbered with a large family, a sister of my father's, in the year 1742, relieved him of all care of me, by taking me entirely to herself, and considering me as her child, having none of her own. From this time she was truly a parent to me, till her death in 1764." [I-i, 6-7] His Aunt Sarah Keighley also adopted a "deformed" niece who was raised with Priestley. His Uncle John Keighley, a Dissenter who led his family in prayer twice daily and taught them, including servants, the Assembly's catechism, was a farmer with substantial property who lived in Heckmondwike, three miles from Priestley's family home.

Keighley's home, where Priestley lived for ten years, was "Old Hall," originally built in the 15th Century of stone with a half-timbered hall and stone-slate roof. A door from the attached barn could admit sick or birthing animals into a stall in the hall where they could be cared for in the warmth of the stone fireplace. Old Hall was restored in 1981 as an attractive pub. Both the Priestleys and Keighleys were members of the orthodox Calvinist Congregational Chapel in Heckmondwike. Joseph saw a good deal of his own family; he lived in what we would now call a supportive "extended family."

Soon after Priestley went to live at the Old Hall, Mr. Keighley died, leaving most of his estate to his wife: "By this truly pious and excellent woman, who knew no other use of wealth, or talents, than to do good, and who never spared herself for this purpose, I was sent to several schools in the neighborhood." [I-i, 7] As well as reading and writing English, he learned Latin, Greek and, with a tutor, Hebrew. On his own, he learned "Annet's shorthand" and, thinking he could make some improvements (as he did with most every thing that interested him) he wrote Annet. Though Priestley was not yet 16, his letter began a correspondence that lasted several years; they argued over Annet's "necessarianism" and Priestley so ably defended "free will" that Annet asked permission to print the correspondence, which Priestley refused. [I-i, 19] Twenty-eight years later Priestley was an ardent advocate of the "necessity" of decisions by the will, instead of a "free" will.

"From the time I discovered a fondness for books, my aunt entertained hopes of my being a minister, and I readily entered into her views: but my ill health obliged me to turn my thoughts another way; and with a view to trade, I learned the modern languages, French, Italian and ... [German], without a master; and....I translated and wrote letters for an uncle of mine who intended to put me in a counting-house in Lisbon....but getting better health, my destination for the ministry was resumed, and I was sent to Daventry [academy]." [I-i, 8] His "ill health" was a "complaint in his lungs" that afflicted him during his adolescence. He completely recovered.

Priestley's inquiring mind was given free reign by the tolerance of his extended family. His father was a pious Calvinist, "... but without giving much attention to matters of speculation, and entertaining no bigoted aversion to those who differed from him on the subject." [I-i, 10] His Aunt Sarah "was truly Calvinistic in principle, but was far from confining salvation to those who thought as she did on religious subjects. Being left in good circumstances, her home was the resort of all the Dissenting ministers in the neighborhood, without distinction; and those who were most obnoxious on account of their heresy, were almost as welcome to her, if she thought them honest and good men, ... as any others." [I-i, 10]

Priestley was exposed to liberal influences as a youth. His tutor in mathematics before entering college "was a little more liberal than the members of the congregation in which I was brought up, ... and his general conversation had a liberal turn, and such as tended to undermine my prejudices. But what contributed to open my eyes still more, was the conversation of a Mr. Walker....who preached as a candidate....[for the pulpit in the Priestley's chapel]. He was an avowed Baxterian, and being rejected on that account, his opinions were much canvassed, and he being a guest at the house of my aunt, we soon became very intimate, and I thought I saw much of reason in his sentiments." [I-i, 14] A "Baxterian" was influenced by the theology of the popular 17th century Puritan minister Richard Baxter who developed a position midway between the "predestination" of Calvin and the free-will acceptance of salvation of James

Arminius, a Dutch theologian who rejected Calvin's unconditioned election to salvation.

Priestley was later to become Walker's successor in the Leeds pulpit. When they met again just before Priestley departed for America, Priestley said, "Ah, Walker, it was you that first led me astray from the paths of orthodoxy." [Gordon 1896, 106]

Mr. Graham, one of "the most heretical ministers in the neighborhood," was frequently a guest at his Aunt's. Priestley later wrote of him: "We kept up a correspondence [frequently in Latin] to the last, thinking alike on most subjects." [I-ii, 11]

In his memoirs, Priestley reflected on his Calvinist rearing: "Though, after I saw reason to change my opinions, I found myself incommoded by the rigor of the congregation with which I was connected, I shall always acknowledge with gratitude that I owe much to it. The business of religion was effectually attended to in it. We were all catechised in public till we were grown up, servants as well as others: the minister always expounded the Scriptures with as much regularity as he preached; and there was hardly a day in the week in which there was not some meeting of one or other part of the congregation. On one evening there was a meeting of the young men for conversation and prayer. This I constantly attended, praying extempore with others, when called upon."

"At my Aunt's there was a monthly meeting of women, who acquitted themselves in prayer as well as any of the men belonging to the congregation. Being a first child in the family, I was permitted to attend their meetings...." "The Lord's-day was kept with peculiar strictness. No victuals were dressed on that day in any family. No member of it was permitted to walk out for recreation, but the whole of the day was spent at the public meeting, or at home in reading, meditation, and prayer...." [I-i, 17] Priestley used Sunday afternoon to outline the sermon he had heard that morning, which he said helped develop his composition style. Years later, after studying Jewish Sabbath customs, Priestley concluded that "social and cheerful entertainments, such as were not improper on other days, are by no means inconsistent" ... with the requirements of the Lord's-day. [XX, 351]

About his Calvinist training, Priestley continued: "By these means, not being disgusted with these strict forms of religion, as many persons of better health and spirits might have been.... I acquired in early life a serious turn of mind. Among other things, I had at this time a great aversion to plays and romances, so that I never read any works of this kind, except Robinson Crusoe, until I went to the academy. I well remember seeing my brother Timothy reading a book of knight-errantry, and with great indignation I snatched it out of his hands, and threw it away. This brother, afterwards, when he had for some time followed my father's business, ... became, if possible, more serious than I had been; and, after an imperfect education, took up the profession of a minister among the Independents [orthodox Calvinist] in which he now continues." [I-i, 17] Priestley thought Timothy's diversion of "shooting" was cruel, urged him to join the church, and successfully did everything possible to press him into the service of religion.

Priestley continued: "Thus I was brought up with sentiments of piety, but without bigotry; and having, from my earliest years, given much attention to the subject of religion, I was as much confirmed as I well could be in the principles of Calvinism, all the books that came in my way having that tendency." [I-i, 11]

Priestley recalled a distressing delusion: "It was my misfortune to have the idea of darkness, and the ideas of invisible malignant spirits and apparitions, very closely connected in my infancy." [I-i, 5] The existence of "spirits" of any kind, good or evil, became one of the orthodox assumptions later challenged by Priestley.

His identification with Calvinism induced an adolescent religious crisis: "The weakness of my constitution, which often led me to think that I should not be long-lived, contributed to give my mind a still more serious turn; and having read many books of experiences, and, in consequence, believing that a new birth, produced by the immediate agency of the spirit of God, was necessary to salvation, and not being able to satisfy myself that I had experienced any thing of the kind, I felt occasionally such distress of mind as it is not in my power to describe, and which I still look back upon with horror. Notwithstanding I had nothing very material to reproach myself with, I often concluded that God had forsaken me, and that mine was like the case of Francis Spira, to whom, as he imagined, repentance and salvation were denied. In that state of mind I remember reading the account of 'the man in an iron cage,' in the 'Pilgrim's Progress,' with the greatest perturbation."

However, he concluded by expressing his confidence that Divine Providence made everything work for good: "I imagine that even these conflicts of mind were not without their use, as they led me to think habitually of God and a future state. And though my feelings were, then, no doubt, too full of terror, what remained of them was a deep reverence for divine things, and in time a pleasing satisfaction which can never be effaced, and, I hope, was strengthened as I have advanced in life, and acquired more rational notions of religion. The remembrance, however, of what I sometimes felt in a state of ignorance and darkness, gives me a peculiar sense of the value of rational principles of religion." [I-i, 12]

His next-younger brother Timothy wrote: "At four years of age Joseph could repeat the Assembly's Catechism, without missing a word. When about six and a half, he would now and then ask me to kneel down with him while he prayed." [Priestley, T. 1805]

When news of Priestley's death reached Calvinist minister Timothy in England, in a memorial service Timothy censored his brother's theology: "None so entirely overthrow the grand design of Jehovah, in making manifest that love which is his peculiar glory, as those who deny the divinity of Christ" and the atonement." [Priestley,Timothy,1805,V]

In a biographical supplement to his sermon, Timothy recalled Priestley's early interest in science: "Joseph began to discover a taste for experiments when about eleven years old. The first he made was on spiders; and by putting them into bottles, he found how long they could live without fresh air." ... "When he began to learn astronomy, he used to be frequently in the fields with his pen and papers: this spread his fame, as it was a science at that time very little known." ... "Whenever he discovered any new experiment, his pleasure cannot be well described. Once, in an attempt to melt metal, when he saw it fuse, he exclaimed, 'Oh, had Sir Isaac seen such an experiment!'" [I-i, 34-35] Delight in the beauty of his scientific discoveries remained a source of satisfaction to Priestley.

Another determinative event in Priestley's religious development, besides his adolescent terror at feeling that, by orthodox definition, God had forsaken him, was his exclusion from membership in the Calvinist church in which he had been raised. Before he left home at age 19 to study for the ministry, Priestley was "very desirous of being admitted as a communicant in the congregation which I had always attended, and the old minister, as well as my aunt, were as desirous of it as myself; but the elders of the church, who had the government of it, refused me, because, when they interrogated me on the subject of the sin of Adam, I appeared to be not quite orthodox, not thinking that all the human race (supposing them not to have any sin of their own) were liable to the wrath of God, and 'the pains of hell for ever,' on account of that sin only; for such was the question put to me. Some time before, having then no doubt of the truth of the doctrine, I well remember being much distressed, that I could not feel a proper repentance for the sin of Adam; taking for granted, that, without this, it could not be forgiven me." [I-i, 14] Like Robert Frost's "Road Not Taken," by rejecting "original sin" Priestley "took the one less traveled by" and that "made all the difference." He spent the rest of his life reforming Christianity to conform to his rational interpretation of Christian history.

Consequently, Priestley nearly did not become a minister. By the time he was ready to leave home to study for the ministry, he was an "Arminian," rejecting the Calvinist scheme of predestination and election in favor of belief in human freedom to voluntarily accept salvation through Christ, a belief popularized by the then new but burgeoning Methodist movement in England. Hence, he "resolutely opposed" the intention of his aunt to send him, at her expense, to an academy in London where he would be required to testify to his "experience of salvation" and every six months reaffirm his belief in "ten printed articles of the strictest Calvinist faith." He might not have studied religion--he had thought of medicine as an alternative-- had not a former schoolmaster persuaded his aunt that he would receive a better education at Daventry Academy. [I-i, 21]

The Academy was a four-year Dissenter's college founded in 1729 in Northampton by Philip Doddridge, a distinguished educator who refused to apply for a bishop's license for his school and was able to keep the school open in 1733 only through the personal intervention of King George II, who declared that in his reign there should be no persecution for conscience sake. [Holt, A. 1970, 10] Just before Priestley enrolled, Doddridge died and the Academy was moved to Daventry, a small town on a main thoroughfare in central England.

Dissenter academies had been opened as private enterprises by some of the "ejected clergy" in the 17th century to train the ministry for their dissenting religious movements, as well as educate Dissenters for medicine, commerce and the bar, without benefit of the government support received by the two established universities, which the Dissenters could not attend unless they subscribed to the Established Church.

The Dissenter academies provided a better education than was then available in the tax-supported universities: "During a period when the grammar schools slept and the Universities were sterile,'... [Dissenter academies] were 'thoroughly alive and active.' At a time when, according to Gibbon, the Oxford dons had absolved their consciences from the toil of reading, thinking, writing, and teaching, 'while their dull and deep potations increased the intemperance of youth,' and when unreformed Cambridge, according to Chester-field, was 'sunk in the lowest obscurity,' these Academies were the real centers of higher education in England." [Willey 1977, 185]

English universities, as well as others on the continent of Europe, said Priestley in a 1791 address to the supporters of New College in Hackney, "were sufficiently adapted to the times in which they were instituted. They formed such men, and such writers, as the age required. But if the times change, those old establishments do not, as they ought to do, change with them; and, in consequence of this, institutions which were at first highly useful, as indeed most institutions have been, (having been suggested by real and pressing occasions,) may not only cease to be useful, but grow into a real nuisance. ... It is therefore from Dissenters alone, not shackled by the fetters of our universities, that free inquiry into matters of religion can be expected." [XV, 430-31]

Fortunately, Priestley attended an academy where sectarian policies did not prevail and free inquiry was encouraged or his experience at Daventry would not have been so rewarding. Priestley was a mature 19 years old when he entered Daventry as an advanced student. During the years that he had been withdrawn from formal schooling because of his ill-health, he had studied on his own or with tutors and had learned "geometry, algebra, and various branches of mathematics, theoretical and practical. And at the same time I read 'Gravesande's Elements of Natural Philosophy' [an introduction to Newton's philosophy], 'Watt's Logic,' 'Locke's Essay on the Human Understanding,' etc., and made such a proficiency in other branches of learning, that when I was admitted at the academy [on a scholarship] ... I was excused all the studies of the first year, and a great part of those of the second." [I-i, 13] Priestley spent three years at Daventry, he wrote, "with that peculiar satisfaction with which young persons of generous minds usually go through a course of liberal study, in the society of others engaged in the same pursuits, and free from the cares and anxieties which seldom fail to lay hold of them when they come out into the world." [I-i, 22] "In my time," he wrote, "the academy was in a state peculiarly favorable to the serious pursuit of truth, as the students were about equally divided upon every question of much importance, such as liberty and necessity, the sleep of the soul [no consciousness between death and the resurrection], and all the articles of theological orthodoxy and heresy; in consequence of which, all these topics were the subject of continual discussion. Our tutors also were of different opinions; Dr. Ashworth taking the orthodox side of every question, and Mr. Clark, the sub-tutor, that of heresy, though always with the greatest modesty."

"Both of our tutors being young, at least as tutors, and some of the senior students excelling more than they could pretend to do in several branches of study, they indulged us in the greatest freedoms, so that our lectures had often the air of friendly conversations on the subjects to which they related. We were permitted to ask whatever questions, and make whatever remarks we pleased; and we did it with the greatest, but without any offensive, freedom. The general plan of our studies ... was exceedingly favorable to free inquiry, as we were referred to authors on both sides of every question, and were even required to give an account of them. ... In this situation, I saw reason to embrace what is generally called the heterodox side of almost every question. Notwithstanding the great freedom of our speculations and debates, the extreme heresy among us was Arianism and all of us, I believe, left the academy with a belief, more or less qualified, of the doctrine of the atonement." [I-i, 23]

"Arianism" was a doctrine advanced in the 4th century that the Son was created by and essentially different from the Father, which was declared a heresy by the Council of Nicene --making the doctrine of the Trinity orthodox. Nevertheless, in the 18th century many Anglican divines flirted with Arianism until they were called to heel by the Church.

At Daventry, all the lectures were in English, not in Latin as was the custom in the universities at that time. The students paid tuition and for board and room, and brought their own sheets, sent out their washing to be done, supplied their own candles, and provided their own tea and sugar if they drank tea in the morning.

The daily schedule began with a roll call at 6:10, followed by prayers and private reading. At eight was "Family Prayer" and breakfast. Lectures were from 10:00 to 2:00, followed by dinner. Afternoons were free for reading, conversation or recreation-- rambling in the countryside. Evening prayer was at 7:00, followed by individual sessions with tutors. Supper was at 9:00, the gates of the Academy were locked at 10:00 and by 10:30 the students had to be in their rooms. For missing Family Prayer or for being late to a lecture, fines were exacted or the student was publicly reproved. [Holt 1931, 11]

Since at Daventry there was no provision for teaching the "learned languages," Priestley and his roommate agreed to rise early enough before roll-call at 6:10 "to read every day ten folio pages in some Greek author, and generally a Greek play in the course of the week besides." [I-i 25]

Priestley's "attention was always more drawn to mathematical and philosophical studies" than to Greek. "Dissenting academies regularly offered the most complete formal instruction in contemporary science available in the eighteenth century." [Schofield 1966, 4] At Daventry in Priestley's time the curriculum included lectures in geometry, algebra, trigonometry, the laws of motion of the planets based chiefly on the propositions of Isaac Newton, applied mathematics, the study of weight and its mechanical effects, optics or the study of light and sight, the study of gases, astronomy, and the anatomy of the human body. Scientific equipment was available to illustrate these studies.

Priestley's activities and reading are recorded in the few of his diaries that escaped the Birmingham Riots, including two from his years at Daventry. His son, Joseph Jr., in the "Continuation" of Priestley's memoirs records that, in addition to assigned readings, Priestley read mostly in the sciences: algebra, anatomy, geometry, and the theory of chemistry. Thus Priestley had as good a formal education in the sciences as was then available in England.

Priestley's diary reveals that at Daventry he generally spent afternoons visiting or walking with friends. He was fond of walking--his regular pace was four miles an hour. A club met evenings twice a week to debate questions, deliver orations, or read essays of their own composition. Other evenings Priestley spent in company with some of the students in their rooms. [Boyer 1964, 141]

Delivering sermons and orations disturbed Priestley: "I was much discouraged even then with the impediment in my speech, which I inherited from my family, and which still attends me. Sometimes I absolutely stammered, and my anxiety about it was the cause of much distress to me." However, he hoped the speech impediment would make him less disputatious in company, prevent his being "seduced by the love of popular applause as a preacher," and make him more attentive to what he said than how well he said it. [I-i, 27] He was, however, popular as an interesting conversationalist, then and for the rest of his life.

"All the time I was at the academy," wrote Priestley, "I never lost sight of the great object of my studies, which was the duties of a Christian minister, and there it was that I laid the general plan which I have executed since." In preparation for the ministry, he composed the first draft of a series of essays on "Institutes of Natural and Revealed Religion," which he later used in his churches as lectures to adults, or to older youth in his Sunday schools, with great success. In writing the lectures, he had the benefit of discussing the subjects with his favorite tutor, the liberal Clark who perused every section. He published the revised and expanded "Institutes" in three volumes over three years while a minister in Leeds. A second edition came out while he was in Birmingham, and after his death a number of editions were printed and circulated by the Unitarian Societies.

The "general plan" that Priestley projected as a student for his studies as a minister was a disciplined schedule that enabled him to regularly accomplish so much. Priestley later said that his daily study schedule took only five hours; "All of which may be conveniently dispatched before dinner, which leaves the afternoon for visiting and company, and the evening for exceeding in any article if there be occasion." [Boyer 1964, 141] Whatever modifications of his plan were occasioned by his various employments, his discipline produced a steady stream of publications in many fields.

Priestley's ministry in his first parish was unsuccessful. He had accepted the first proposal by his tutor, Clark, that he become a candidate for the Presbyterian pulpit in Needham Market near the east coast of England. He accepted, "though it was very remote from my friends in Yorkshire, and a very inconsiderable place." [I-i 28] The congregation of about 100 had been without an assistant to their semi-retired minister for a year because the salary was so small.

Everything, he wrote, "for the first half year appeared very promising, and I was happy in the success of my schemes for promoting the interest of religion in this place." He catechised children of all ages and gave lectures to people regardless of age or sex on the theory of religion from his "Institutes of Natural and Revealed Religion." "But in this I soon found that I had acted imprudently. ... when I came to treat of the 'Unity of God,'... several of my audience were attentive to nothing but the soundness of my faith in the doctrine of the Trinity." [I-i, 30]

"So extremely unpopular was I for some years after my first settlement as a minister, though I had never preached a controversial sermon, or done any thing that I thought would irritate ... that, besides losing the greatest part of my hearers, when I printed and circulated Proposals for opening a school [to augment his income], for which I was not thought to be unqualified, I never got a single scholar." [XV, 29]

He had thought that the congregation had accepted his anti-trinitarian Arianism when, to avoid compromising himself, he refused the salary subsidy from funds of the Calvinistic Independents, and the congregation agreed to make up the difference. It didn't; he lost a fourth of his income and church attendance declined, "especially as the old minister took a decided part against me." [I-i 31]

At the same time, his Aunt Sarah, who had assured him that if he chose to be a minister, she would keep him financially independent, stopped sending him remittances,[owing in part to the ill offices of his orthodox relations, plus the care of and future provision for her deformed niece]. Though he already suffered hardship, he graciously accepted the additional cut in income: "I was satisfied she was not able to perform her promise....She had spared no expense in my eduction, and that was doing more for me than giving me an estate." [I-i, 32]

However, before leaving Needham, he did seek her help in overcoming his handicap. He had been distressed that preaching was so painful that it would preclude invitations to a better church, as well as to pulpit exchanges. [I-i 33] At his request she paid for his first trip to London for a month's treatment for his stammer, from which he received some temporary benefit but soon relapsed.

In London, Priestley was introduced to Dr. Benson, who now and then procured him "an extraordinary five pounds from different charities", and to Dr. Kippis, Dissenting minister of a chapel in London, later a supporter and contributor to the *Theological Repository*, fellow tutor at New College, and life- long intimate friend. Thus began the growing network of friends Priestley enjoyed in London.

Notwithstanding the unfavorable circumstances, he was far from being unhappy at Needham: "I was boarded in a family from which I received much satisfaction; I firmly believed that a wise Providence was disposing every thing for the best, and I applied with great assiduity to my studies, which were classical, mathematical, and theological. These required but few books. As to experimental philosophy, I had always cultivated an acquaintance with it, but I had not the means of prosecuting it." [I-i, 34]

His theology developed radically during his three years at Needham: "While I was in this retired situation, I had, in consequence of much pains and thought, become persuaded of the falsity of the doctrine of the atonement, of the inspiration of the authors of the books of Scripture as writers, and of all idea of supernatural influence, except for the purpose of miracles. But I was still an Arian, having never turned my attention to the Socinian doctrine, and contenting myself with seeing the absurdity of the Trinitarian system." [I-i, 40]

In his research on the atonement, that Christ's sacrificial death for our sins reconciled us and God, he found " pretty numerous" passages which satisfied him that Paul's "reasoning was in many places far from being conclusive." [I-i 38] An elder scholar advised him not to publish such a radical conclusion until his reputation was established.

For instance, Paul wrote that in church, "Let the woman learn in silence with all subjection. But I suffer not a woman to teach, nor to usurp authority over the man, but to be in silence. For Adam was first formed, then Eve. And Adam was not deceived, but the woman being deceived was in the transgression." [I Timothy 2:11-14] Priestley appealed Paul's dictum to the judgment of women, "whether it be a sufficient reason for his peremptorily confining them to the place of hearers and learners, that Adam was first formed, and that Eve first transgressed?" [VII, 406]

Priestley was remarkably free of male chauvinism for an 18th century male. In his *Notes On All The Books of Scriptures*, published in Northumberland a year before his death, Priestley's comment on Genesis 2:21-24, that God made Eve from Adam's rib, reflects Priestley's opinion about the Christian status of women: it was probably a "figurative representation" of the close relation between males and females in order to impress Adam's mind with their equality; "whereas, it was the opinion of some Heathen nations, that woman had some different and inferior origin, that she was made, merely to be subservient to man, and not, as we here learn, a help-meet for him, or a rational associate." [XI 48]

In a funeral sermon, Priestley praised his friend's attitude toward women: "Getting over a vulgar and debasing prejudice (that women, being designed for domestic cares, should be taught nothing beyond them,)" and he educated his daughters. Priestley commented: "Certainly, the minds of women are capable of the same improvement, and the same furniture, as those of men; and it is of importance that, when they have leisure, they have the same resource in reading, and the same power of instructing by writing, that men have...." [XV 419]

Priestley wrote in his "Institutes of Natural Religion" that "marriage, at a proper time of life, whereby one man is confined to one woman, is most favorable to health and the true enjoyment of life. It is a means of raising the greatest number of healthy children, and makes the best provision for their instruction and settlement in life..." On sex in marriage, he said, "the natural passions have their proper gratifications ...the purest and most unalloyed pleasures of sense...." He added that "the most valuable happiness of a man in this world is that which arises to him from domestic relations, the society of wife and children...." [XXV 71]

How did the Priestleys, prior to modern conception control, manage to have only four children, while his father had six in as many years and his brother Timothy had thirteen? Were the extended separations of Joseph and Mary a form of conception control? Did other devoted but less scrupulous husbands accomplish the same by considerately resorting to mistresses or prostitutes? If so, this may have been the implicit ground for the double standard of sexual morality.

Priestley opposed a double standard of sexual morality and complained that young ladies "seem to have no objection to a suitor on account of his illicit amours; imagining perhaps that a reformed rake will make the best husband.... Would this amiable part of our species only do themselves the justice to insist upon the same strict chastity and honor with respect to men, which men universally insist upon with respect to them, our sex would, no doubt, be as virtuous as theirs, and they would make much better husbands and fathers than they now do." [XXV 78]

Priestley explained: "The domestic relations of life are the foundations of the strongest claim upon our benevolence and kindness. The interests of husband and wife are the same, and inseparable; and they must necessarily pass a very great part of their time together. In these circumstances, to be mutually happy, their affection must be strong and undivided." [II 34]

After three years at Needham, Priestley accepted an invitation to preach for a year-certain at Nantwich in Cheshire near the border of Wales, a more congenial ambiance; he stayed for three satisfying years in which he developed his theory and practice of education.

The congregation of sixty people at Nantwich was smaller than Needham, but they accepted his theology and appreciated his contributions. With no controversy over his doctrines, he soon opened a school for boys and girls that met from 7:00 a.m. to 4:00 p.m., followed by tutoring in a home until 7:00. Though he had a "great aversion to the business of schoolmaster," contrary to his expectations he found the greatest satisfaction in it. [I-i 41] He composed an English grammar for use in the school (later expanded and published--almost everything he composed he published sooner or later), required writing themes in English which he corrected, and bought an air pump (for creating a vacuum) and a machine for generating static electricity--both of which he used to introduce science at the grade level, and which the pupils demonstrated for their parents. He was given a telescope, hand-made by a neighboring vicar who studied science and kept a room set apart just for Priestley's frequent visits.

At Nantwich, his speech impediment increased so much that he announced that he must give up preaching and confine himself to his school. He later wrote in his memoirs: "However, by making a practice of reading very loud and very slow every day, I at length succeeded in getting, in some measure, the better of this defect, but I am still obliged occasionally to have recourse to the same expedient." [I-i, 62] He lodged with a Nantwich family in a grocer's shop where he surprised them by gaily jumping over the counter. The owner was fond of music and induced Priestley to play a little on the English flute; "though I was never proficient at it, my playing contributed more or less to my amusement many years of my life." [I-i, 44]

One of the pupils in Priestley's school was William Wilkinson whose father was manager of an iron foundry at Wrexham, about 20 miles west of Nantwich in Wales. Priestley often visited the Wilkinson home, primarily because of his attraction to their daughter Mary, whom he later married.

His time was so consumed by his school that he said he "added very few sermons to those which I had composed at Needham, where I never failed to make at least one every week." [I-i 43] And he had little leisure for Biblical criticism and theological speculation, or for making original experiments. But his experience prepared him for his next big move--six years as an outstanding educator at Warrington Academy, where he married Mary Wilkinson.

However, in time the Academy could not support his growing family and he accepted an invitation to become minister of a flourishing, long-established chapel at Leeds in Yorkshire, six miles from his childhood home, with an income exceeding that of most Dissenter ministers.

Leeds was on the northern edge of Yorkshsire in the "soft water" area of the Pennine hills, which made it attractive to weavers of wool, and a famous cloth market. In the 18th century, Leeds was dominated by manufacturers of agricultural and industrial equipment, and was a trade center with a population of about 17,000 people. Like Birmingham, the city had no separate parliamentary representation until the Reform Act of 1832. During the Civil War, the area's sympathies were with Parliament and not King Charles I, who was executed in 1649. Since the Nonconformists and Dissenters were strong in the armies of Parliament, thereafter the Royalists held the Dissenters responsible for the king's death.

In the brief period of toleration that followed Charles II's 1672 Declaration of Indulgence, which suspended all penal laws against Nonconformists, more than 120 licenses to hold their religious meetings were issued in Yorkshire. Most met in homes. [Holt 1970, 2] Within two years, the Presbyterians in Leeds had built one of the first Presbyterian chapels in England. The present handsome stone chapel, built in 1848 when the congregation of a thousand was very influential, faces the City Center square containing a life-size statue of Priestley, among other notables.

The then orthodox Presbyterian Leeds congregation was harassed from 1682 to 1687 when feelings were bitter against the Dissenters: the minister was put into Newgate prison for six months, the chapel was closed and attempts to hold services in homes were broken up by the authorities.

Priestley's predecessor in the Leeds pulpit, Thomas Walker-- his friend since their conversations at Aunt Sarah's in his youth-- abandoned orthodox Calvinism; he was an anti-trinitarian who doubted the doctrines of the atonement and the innate depravity of human nature. He lost many members from his congregation but built "the liberal, friendly, harmonious congregation that welcomed Priestley." [Holt 1970, 42]

Beginning in Leeds and thereafter, Priestley was a practical and successful minister, contributing to the theory and practice of congregational organization and public worship. Christianity was founded on miracles, he said, but it must now support itself by transmitting the evidence of the miracles and by "the wise constitution of its churches."[XV61] He was distressed that liberal churches had become mere preaching stations instead of religious communities: a minister among the less orthodox "rational Dissenters, begins now to be considered as a person who is paid by his hearers for haranguing them once a week," and "the performance of the minister being the only object of attention, if they dislike his sentiments or delivery," they go elsewhere. [XXI 405] The lay responsibility for administering Dissenter societies through "elders" had been abandoned with the consequence, said Priestley, "that our congregations have become mere audiences, the members having little attachment to each other except in their preference of the same preacher...." [XV 52]

With psychological prescience, two centuries before "group dynamics" became a science, Priestley observed that in order to engage loyal support in an association, "if we consult human nature," the members must be involved: "Was it ever known that any man became attached to any kind of society in which he was a mere cipher, in which he had no sphere of action, and when nothing that he did had any chance of being heard of, or of being mentioned to his praise, either in the society or out of it?" [XV 52]

Priestley understood the dynamics of his Puritan heritage of congregational polity, a democratic decision-making process by majority vote of a congregation. He advocated the same principle of social organization for government institutions.

He took the New Testament churches as his basic model for administration and proposed restoration of the office of elders elected by ballot: "Let these elders, with the minister at their head, (but with no more power than any other of them,) form a consistory [now called a "board of trustees"] and meet about once a month, (but to be assembled by the minister on any other particular occasion,) to consult together concerning the state of the church, and the best method of promoting its real interests; but let them have no power to proceed farther than an admonition, without the consent of the people at large." [XXI 425] A record was to be kept of the public proceedings, and included the names of church members. "Deacons" were younger men who served communion and took up collections to relieve "the industrious and helpless poor," including the old. Priestley received the enthusiastic consent and support of his congregations in Leeds and Birmingham for this plan of church organization.

Like the New Testament churches, but unlike established churches, Dissenter chapels were supported entirely by voluntary contributions of their members--as Priestley thought all churches should be supported.

Dissenter chapels were autonomous, practicing "congregational polity"--the majority vote of the members in meeting assembled was their ultimate authority. Hence, Priestley noted, "every single society may improve their sentiments and discipline as much as they please, without troubling themselves, in the least, about the opinions or practices of others." And having subscribed to no creeds, Dissenters were free to "call in question received opinions," which facilitated continued reformation. [XXI 252]

A minister was not a "pastor" to a flock of sheep, explained Priestley: "those only can be considered as shepherds, who are in circumstances in which they can assume the power of shepherds, and act as such; which cannot in reason be expected of those who are called ministers among the Dissenters." [XXI, 439]

Ministers, he said, should be learned in the languages of the Bible, in liberal science, in modern literature, in moral and metaphysical subjects, in the composition of sermons, and in public speaking.[XXI, 418] The only distinction of a minister, in Priestley's view, was such training, not apostolic authority conferred by the laying on of hands or other forms of ordination. The sermon was not essential to public worship: reading the Scriptures, praying, and singing were important because they were more emotionally motivating, he said, and required no learned leader. [XXI, 415] Hence, able laity were just as authorized to preside at public worship services, baptisms, and funerals as ministers. He later urged Unitarian laity to organize a church in Philadelphia and preside in it themselves, including preaching--thus the first lay-led Unitarian Fellowship in America was organized.

Group reinforcement made preaching to a congregation more effective than individual instruction, he said: "If any impression is to be made upon the heart and affections; if men are to be led to feel, in order to determine and act, the discourses will be delivered to much greater advantage to a society than to separate individuals....every individual of the audience will feel the force of the exhortation much more sensibly himself, when he perceives the effect upon others." [XV 465]

However, people were not to be passive listeners but charitably critical and active responders. Members of the congregation were "to attend, and to judge with candor, to embrace the truth whenever you perceive its evidence, and to exercise forbearance towards myself, as well as towards all other Christians, whenever you see reason to withhold your assent." He added that mere assent was not enough: "our greatest duties relate not to speculation, but to practice. We are all hearers of the word; but the greatest article of all is, to be doers of work assigned us by God to do." [XV 474] Works were more essential to salvation than faith in doctrines.

For the rest of his ministry, Priestley was loved and appreciated, even when he became a Unitarian Christian in Birmingham. But in England Unitarianism had been suppressed as odious for a century before Priestley came to its defense, and the orthodox were alarmed by its re-emergence under his leadership.

IV

"NO MAN LIVETH TO HIMSELF"
"Distrust all those who require you to abandon reason."

In Priestley's rational defense of historic Christianity, he was engaged on two fronts--the Christian corrupters and the Deist unbelievers. Historian Edward Gibbon, a Deist, remarked that Priestley "must shoot a double-battery against those who believe too little and those who believe too much."

Deism was expounded by Lord Herbert of Cherbury in early 18th century England as a natural religion that rejected biblical revelation. Priestley referred to its devotees as "unbelievers" and was more distressed by their "infidelity" than he was by the orthodox corruptions of Christianity.

Deists held a belief in the innate ideas of a Supreme Being, a benevolent God whose existence could be rationally proved by analogy with a watchmaker--God had originally made the universe and set it running without further interference; in a virtuous life as the best form of worship; in retribution in the immortal next life for good or evil done in this life; and opposed intolerance, fanaticism, and emotionalism in religion. Voltaire, after a visit to England, returned to France to carry the Deist attack on the established Catholic Church. Deism never organized an institution and dwindled away by the end of the century.

Priestley shared many of the Deist's beliefs, plus faith in biblical revelation, and was often denounced as an heretical Deist for his attacks on orthodoxy.

With the liberal and harmonious Leeds congregation, Priestley was free to resume his satisfying application to speculative theology. He became uneasy with the Arian theology he had adopted in college because it assumed that Christ had pre-existed with God as a spiritual soul.

Arianism was an anti-trinitarian Christian theology popularized by Arius in the 4th century that identified Christ with the Logos, which Priestley claimed was an early corruption of Christianity that could not be justified historically. Priestley sometimes amused himself "with tracing the rise and progress of particular opinions: for these things have their causes and consequences, as well as every thing else in the general system of nature, and therefore are proper subjects of philosophical inquiry." He concluded that Arianism originated with the "Platonizing" claim that Christ had pre-existed as a specially created soul or Logos, the agent of God in making the visible creation, and was incarnated in Jesus. [Rutt VII, 477]

Priestley read with care a book by his old friend Nathaniel Lardner, a respected biblical scholar on whom he always called when in London. Lardner had published his *Letter on the Logos* anonymously--to avoid persecution for his heretical opinions. "Logos" in Greek means "the divine word" or "creative reason," identified with Jesus as the pre-existence Creator and God- incarnate redeemer in "The Gospel According to John."

Lardner accepted the authority of the Bible but refuted the Arian hypothesis that Christ pre-existed, claiming that he had a human soul and was exalted as the Son of God because of his human suffering. Lardner cited many scripture passages in support of the humanity of Jesus and the unity of God, and refuted the texts advanced by defenders of the Trinity. [Holt 1970, 43] As usual, Priestley went beyond his mentor Lardner, who still presumed a human soul, and finally rejected not only the concept of soul, but also of spirit, and became a Socinian.

Though some of his best friends were Arians who considered themselves Unitarians, Priestley later wrote: "in my opinion, those, who are usually called Socinians (who consider Christ as being a mere man) are the only body of Christians who are properly entitled to the appellation of Unitarians...." [VI, 48]

When Thomas Belsham, Priestley's disciple and successor in his last pulpit in England, drew up the preamble in 1791 for the formation of the "Unitarian Society for the Promotion of Christian Knowledge" (which in 1825 merged in the "British and Foreign Unitarian Association"), Belsham unsuccessfully tried to exclude

Arians and to stigmatize the worship of Christ as idolatrous. [Holt 1952, 313] Arian Richard Price defiantly joined.

However, Priestley did not wish to excommunicate Arians; he only wished them to enter the dialogue in the quest for truth. He wrote, "My Arian friends ... will think that ... I bear peculiarly hard upon them; and I frankly acknowledge it. I think theirs to be an hypothesis equally destitute of support in the Scriptures, in reason, and in history." [VI,7] He regretted that "no Arian has yet appeared" in print to discuss "the state of opinions in the primitive times, as one means of collecting what was the doctrine of the apostles, and the true sense of scripture on the subject" of early opinions concerning Jesus. [I-i, 341]

The Socinian theology with which Priestley identified in Leeds was a Polish Renaissance religious movement that had spread in Europe through its publications, and the emigration of its persecuted believers.

In 16th century Poland, the intellectual and religious tolerance of the ruling nobility had permitted the emergence of an anti-trinitarian religious movement in which Laelius and Faustus Socinus (uncle and nephew) became leaders of a simplified and rationalized ethical Protestantism. They were Renaissance humanists and scholars of a patrician Italian family, noted for its advocacy of freedom of thought, who emigrated to Poland where their influence gave the name "Socinian" to the religious reformation. Faustus, the most prominent theologian in the group, was concerned with the rational basis for the ethical teachings of Christianity. He helped write the Racovian Catechism that defined the Socinian doctrines: Christianity was defined as a practice of moral conduct based on the teachings of Jesus, which were attested by miracles, interpreted by human reason (reason and revelation coincided), and issued in eternal life; God was one person, revealed by a divinely inspired but human Jesus who ought to be continually adored by prayers addressed to him (such address Priestley later rejected); people were not born with original sin; adult baptism by immersion was a rite of initiation into a church; the Lord's Supper was purely a memorial celebration; churches cared for their poor; and each church was supervised by chosen elders. The Socinians intended to restore the primitive Christian church and its doctrines as a rational faith, which was also Priestley's intention.

The Socinians, many of whom were wealthy landowners and nobles, became influential in Poland and in Hungary. But in the 17th century, resurgent Catholicism led by the Jesuits (and at first sup-

ported by the orthodox Protestants until the Catholics were powerful enough to turn against them) began to suppress the Socinians in
Poland. The Socinian meeting house in Krakow was destroyed by
a mob. Three years later, Faustus Socinus was attacked on the
streets. When his book on Jesus was published, an inflamed mob
broke into his home, dragged him from his sick- bed, burned his
books and manuscripts, and threatened him with death unless he
recanted. He refused, was rescued by Catholic university professors
and died a few years later. Socinians were persecuted and banished
from the country. With great hardship, some of the Socinians took
refuge among the organized Unitarians in Transylvania; others fled
to Prussia and ultimately to tolerant Holland and England. [Wilbur
1925, 164 ff] This was the religious tradition that Priestley identified
with in Leeds.

Priestley was loved by his congregations especially for his
religious education of young people. The religious opinions of
elders could not be easily influenced, wrote Priestley, "But, in youth,
the mind is flexible, opinions are unfixed, and habits not confirmed,"
so the minister's attention should be fixed "upon the younger and
more teachable part of his congregations." [II, xxvi] He warned,
"Care, however, must be taken lest, by making religious exercises
too rigorous, an early aversion is excited, and so the very end we
have in view is defeated." [XXV, 52] He suited his courses to the age
and interest levels of youth.

Priestley shared the opinion of his contemporaries, including
some Anglican clergy, who lamented that English society was deca-
dent: "The great profligacy of the present age being manifestly
owing to a want of moral and religious principles, imbibed in early
years,... I formed, and have carried into execution, a pretty extensive
plan of Religious Instruction, advancing in a regular progress, from
infancy to years of perfect manhood." [XV, 20] He pioneered in the
establishment of such Sunday schools in England.

Religious disenchantment in the 20th century makes religious
education no more difficult than in Priestley's age of the Enlightenment. He commented: "The superficial knowledge, or rather the
extreme ignorance of the generality of youth in the present age, with
respect to religion," is "in part, the natural effect of the moderation
of the present times" and of "the little care that is now taken by
parents in the religious instruction of their children." [II, xxii]

True religion did not come naturally: religious instruction was
necessary, he said, because "the mind of man can never be wholly
barren. Through our whole lives we are subject to successive impressions; for either new ideas are continually flowing in, or traces

of the old ones are marked deeper. If, therefore, you be not acquiring good principles, be assured that you are acquiring bad ones." [II, xv] Hence, he said, "A man has no choice, but whether his child shall imbibe the principles of true or false religion, i.e., what he himself shall deem to be so; as it is impossible to keep the minds of his children free from all impressions of this kind, unless they converse with nobody but himself." [XXV, 48]

Children could not be left to their own resources to develop a personal religion, he said, "Because common sense is a sufficient guard against errors in religion, it seems to be taken for granted, that common sense is a sufficient instructor also; whereas, in fact, without positive instruction, men would naturally have been mere savages with respect to religion; as, without similar instruction, they would have been savages with respect to the arts of life and the sciences. Common sense can only be compared to a judge; but what can a judge do without evidence, and proper materials from which to form a judgment?" [II, xxiv]

Religious and secular education should present information in an environment where questions and disagreements could be freely expressed and discussed. Religious education was not simply indoctrination of a creed. As a Dissenter, Priestley was opposed to creeds: "Can we think that wisdom will die with us? No, our creeds, could we be so inconsistent with ourselves to draw up any, would ... be rejected with equal disdain by our posterity." [XXII, 126]

To discuss and question religion required freedom, so Priestley's primary concern in education was to instill a zeal for liberty: "Religious rights, and religious liberty, are things of inestimable value. For these have many of our ancestors suffered and died; and shall we, in the sunshine of our prosperity, desert that glorious cause ...? Let us consider it as a duty of the first rank with respect to moral obligation, to transmit to our posterity...that generous zeal for religion and liberty." [II, xvii]

Priestley's moral instruction did not teach a cloistered virtue: "In general, I would neither conceal from young persons the knowledge of vice, nor deny that temporal advantages and pleasures may attend vicious indulgences; but let them always be given to understand, that those advantages and pleasures are dearly bought." [XXV, 34] He also taught comparative religion, explaining that "the man who has not been permitted to know any other religion but his own, is generally made the greatest bigot...." [XXV, 65]

Children learn more from example than from precept he wrote; the parents exemplary conduct alone does "half the business...." [XXV, B2] Also, if parents and other adults discussed with youth what they had learned, interest and reinforcement would be added to the subject.

Reason was required to acquire truth in religion, as in any other field of inquiry, Priestley admonished "My Young Friends" in Leeds: "It is only by the help of that faculty which we call reason, that we can distinguish between any two systems of religion that may be proposed to us....and also of the positive evidence that is produced in favor of them." [II, 117] He also advised adult "serious and candid professors of Christianity" that, in studying the Scriptures, "Searching must imply an earnest endeavor to find out for ourselves, and to understand the truths contained in the Scriptures; and what faculty can we employ for this purpose, but that which is commonly called reason, whereby we are capable of thinking, reflecting, comparing, and judging of things. Distrust, therefore, all those who require you to abandon it, wherever religion is concerned. When once they have gained this point with you, they can lead you whither they please, and impose upon you every absurdity which their sinister views make it expedient for them that you should embrace ..." [II, 384]

To Priestley, there was only one way of knowing, of validating truth-claims in religion as in science: the use of intelligence to note analogies and differences, to compare and contrast the known with the unknown. The ultimate confirmation of the reasoning process was empirical--your own experience by observation or experiment, or by other's credible testimony of their experience. Priestley put his religious education theory into practice for 19 years of his active ministry in his last three chapels in England. In addition to preaching twice on Sunday, he personally taught three Sunday school classes nine months of the year. He offered a class to children ages 5 to 12 before the morning service, to young people 10 to 18 in the afternoon, and to youth from 18 to 30 after the evening service. Priestley thought children should be obliged by their parents, reinforced by the Elders, to attend their classes, but young people over 18 should make their own decision to attend, only advised by their parents.

Priestley wrote, "I had more satisfaction in attending these classes than in any other part of my ministerial duty, seeing the progress my pupils made in religious knowledge." [XV, 461] He was so successful that, after he was driven from Birmingham, the young men who had been his former pupils assumed responsibility for teaching the Sunday School of 195 children, with the support of a committee appointed by the congregation to help manage the school. [XV, 461]

During his six years in Leeds, Priestley published ten religious and political books, pamphlets and journals, including three which at age 36 were his first publications in religious controversies. One was a response to "most injurious reflections"on Dissenters, which justified continuing old restrictive laws against them, by Dr. William Blackstone in his *Commentaries on the Laws of England.* Blackstone agreed to modify his strictures on Dissenters in subsequent editions, as the passage was "somewhat incorrect and confused." [XXII. 303] Meanwhile, in Leeds Priestley continued his experiments with electricity, satisfying himself that it was not a fluid as then popularly believed--he recorded his experiment only in a letter [Schofield 1966, 58]--and published a popular book on the study of electricity, based on his classic *History of Electricity* .

Then his interest was drawn to experiments with the chemistry of gases, or "airs" as they were then called, as he explained: "This last I was led into in consequence of inhabiting a house adjoining to a public brewery, where I at first amused myself with making experiments on the fixed air [carbon dioxide] which I found ready made in the process of fermentation. When I removed from that house I was under the necessity of making the fixed air for myself; and one experiment leading to another...I by degrees contrived a convenient apparatus for the purpose, but of the cheapest kind." [I-i 75] His inexpensive contrivance for carbonating water was a popular invention as it added fizz to drinks--the carbonated soft-drink industry owes its origin to Priestley.

If he had exploited his discoveries, Priestley might have become independently wealthy. Of his improved apparatus for making carbonated water, which physicians thought had medicinal value, Priestley commented, "I could have become a quack." He could also have exploited his incidental cure of a disturbed lady in Leeds with his electrical machine. The story about the incident, told by Priestley at a Birmingham dinner, was recounted by W. Matthews (the same young man who also recorded his impressions of Priestley's Sunday afternoon religious education lectures): "A poor woman unfortunately imagined herself to be possessed by a devil, and having heard that Dr. Priestley was a great philosopher, who could perform miracles, she applied to him to take away the evil spirit that tormented her. The doctor attentively listened to her statement, and being aware of her delusion, with his usual mildness and benevolence, he endeavored to convince her that she was laboring under a mistake. However, all his efforts proved unavailing, for the poor creature still persisted that the fact was as she stated; in order, therefore, to ease her mind, the doctor good-humouredly told her to call upon him the next day, and in the meantime he would consider her case."

"Agreeable to his request, the unhappy woman was punctual in her attendance, when the doctor, with a smile, informed her that he truly pitied her situation, but he hoped that he should be able to afford her some relief. His electrical apparatus being in readiness, with great gravity he desired the woman to stand upon the stool with glass legs, at the same time putting into her hand a brass chain connected with the conductor, and having charged her plentifully with [static] electricity, he told her very seriously, to take particular notice of what he did. He then took a discharger, and applied it to her arm, when the escape of the electricity gave her a pretty good shock. 'There,' says she, 'the devil's gone; I saw him go in that blue flame, and he gave me such a jerk as he went off. I have at last got rid of him, and I am now quite comfortable.'" [I-ii 111]

Priestley did not believe in devils or evil spirits, and he understood the psychological dynamics that eased her mind, but did not try to set himself up in the business of quack electrical cures, as did Franz Mesmer in France who was claiming to heal hysterical women by the "animal magnetism" emanating from his hands. Benjamin Franklin was at the time a member of a French government commission of physicians and scientists which found that Mesmer's claims of healing was really due to some as yet unknown physiological cause.

Priestley's method of manufacturing carbonated water, thought to be an antidote to scurvy, had been recommended to the organizers of Captain Cook's second voyage to explore the Pacific. But Priestley's heterodoxy lost him the opportunity to join Cook's voyage. He had written: "I wish all the incorporated philosophical societies in Europe would join their funds ... to fit out ships for the complete discovery of the face of the earth, and for many capital experiments, which can only be made in such extensive voyages." [XXV, 349] Priestley received a proposal that he be the astronomer on the exploration "with a handsome provision secured to me and my family," and made arrangements with his church in Leeds for an extended leave of absence. A few weeks later, he learned to his embarrassment that clergy on the Board of Longitude had blackballed his appointment, objecting to his religious opinions.

Priestley's lack of formal education in chemistry was no handicap. He said: "When I began these experiments, I knew very little of chemistry.... But I have often thought that upon the whole this circumstance was no disadvantage to me; as in this situation I was led to devise an apparatus, and processes of my own, adapted to my peculiar views. Whereas, if I had been previously accustomed to the usual chemical processes, I should not have so easily thought of any other; and without new modes of operation I should hardly have discovered any thing materially new." [I-i, 76] Thus he accounts for his creativity in the infancy of chemistry; his mind was open to chance occurrences and new phenomena. He claimed that the same freedom from established procedures and expectations helped his theological and biblical studies; for instance, he consulted Bible commentaries to check his interpretations only after he had completed his own research.

There were some practical spin-offs of his scientific activities. He had designed an improved electrical machine for generating static electricity that he had his brother Timothy, who was handy with tools for working brass and wood, manufacture and sell in order to help him with the expenses of his large family. [Priestley, Timothy 1804, 42]

In the process of writing his textbook on the study of electricity, Priestley was unable to secure an illustrator. He taught himself to draw and did his own competent illustrations. [XXV, 358] Finding that the printed resources on perspective were inadequate, he published what he had learned in *A Familiar Introduction to the Theory and Practice of Perspective*, popular with artists for over 30 years. In the introduction to the book, he recommended congealed latex (newly imported from Central America) as a better eraser of pencil marks than bread crumbs, and named it "rubber."

When Priestley was at Calne in 1774, he used a large "burning glass" (a large lens--laboratory gas Bunsen-burners were not yet invented) to focus the heat of the sun on mercuric oxide and thus obtained a new kind of gas that he called "dephlogisticated air." A candle burned in it "with a remarkably vigorous flame" and when he breathed this "pure air" his "breast felt peculiarly light and easy for some time afterwards. ... Hitherto only two mice and myself have had the privilege of breathing it." He correctly speculated that this "pure air" might be helpful to people with "putrid lungs"--a contribution to medicine.

A few months after he had published his discovery of dephlogisticated air, Priestley visited Paris with his employer Lord Shelburne. News of Priestley's discovery had preceded him and he gave an account of the experiment to Antoine Lavoisier, a leading French chemist who was also a financial officer in Louis XVI's government and was guillotined in 1794 during the revolutionary Reign of Terror. Lavoisier repeated Priestley's experiment, without acknowledging its origin, named the new gas "oxygen," and incorporated it into his new system of chemistry, which soon was accepted by most of the chemists in Europe and America.

Priestley defended the phlogiston theory the rest of his life, mistakenly but not unreasonably. His difference with Lavoisier was basically theological. The premise of Priestley's drive to understand the structure and dynamics of creation was the radical assumption that all substances were ultimately composed of the same homogeneous particles, differently arranged--a materialistic monism that got him into a theological dilemma. Lavoisier proposed that chemical phenomena could be explained as combinations of a multiplicity of distinct elements. Priestley's theology and his science were so intimately interwoven that Lavoisier's chemistry was a challenge to Priestley's entire world view. (Schofield 1983, 79) Priestley was interested in causal agents, the dynamics of relationships, while Lavoisier was interested in quantification, the proportions of constituent elements. [McEvoy 1975, 138] Priestley was concerned with energy, Lavoisier with weight. [Lesser 1974, 141] God-believer Priestley wanted to understand the unified universe in order to live in harmony with it; unbeliever Lavoisier wanted an exact science in order to manipulate its elements. Lavoisier founded an advance in chemistry, but Priestley was ultimately right. In spite of the table of Chemical Elements, the ultimate elements in the universe are matter and energy, differently arranged. Not merely quantities of elements in a mixture, but the sequence in which they were added and the patterns of relationships are fundamental. Priestley was not just stubborn in rejecting Lavoisier's new chemistry; he was working in a different frame of reference. Priestley was not merely dabbling in science as a hobby; he believed that the only way to understanding in theology as in science was by observation and experience, so he turned to science for answers to theological questions. He wanted to know how creation worked.

He wondered how common air, made unfit for respiration by continuous breathing and combustion, was restored--and discovered photosynthesis. At Leeds he had noticed that the purity of air bubbling in the water of a local reservoir was related to a green substance growing on its sides. [McEvoy 1975, 194] He did a series of experiments, sealing various plants in bottles of noxious air and found that the air was purified. In 1772 he wrote to Benjamin Franklin in London (who had recently visited him in Leeds), "I have fully satisfied myself that air rendered in the highest degree noxious by breathing is restored by sprigs of mint growing in it." [Schofield

1966, 104] He continued his experiments with many plants. "I am not botanist enough to know their names," he wrote to an Italian scientist, and added, "Nothing can be more beautiful than the experiment." [Schofield 1966, 176] He soon learned that sunlight was necessary to the process of purifying air by plants.

However, Jan IngenHousz, a Dutch physician who later settled in London and was elected to the Royal Society, was first to publish his discovery of the role of light in photosynthesis (London, 1779), which Priestley read only after he had arrived at the same conclusion. He graciously acknowledged IngenHousz' priority: "The same summer, and the same sun, operated for us both, and you certainly published before me." [Schofield 1966, 248] IngenHousz succeeded Priestley in Shelburne's patronage. [Schofield 1966, 360]

At the time he discovered photosynthesis, Priestley continued to call the resulting purified air "dephlogisticated air." When he began experimenting with gases, the generally accepted theory was that common air became noxious by the accumulation of "phlogiston," and salubrious air was "dephlogisticated." The reverse is now believed: respiration, combustion and oxidation absorb oxygen from the air, and when the oxygen is consumed, the air is noxious.

Priestley believed that photosynthesis, the restoration of air by a natural process, illustrated how Divine Providence worked. He defined "Providence" as a system of causes governed by natural laws instituted by the "Author of nature." [XV, 83] Providence did not mean a capricious intervention in history by a supernatural power: nowhere in his voluminous publications is there a single reference to God as "supernatural." The Creator established the process but thereafter it operated without further Divine intervention.

Priestley believed that human beings were "instruments of Divine Providence in everything respecting man." [XV, 420] "We ourselves, complex as the structure of our minds and our principles of action are, are links in a great connected chain, parts of an immense whole, a very little of which only we are permitted to see, but from which we collect evidence enough that the whole system (in which we are, at the same time, both instruments and objects) is under an unerring direction." [III, 450]

"Theodicy"--the question of why a good and all-powerful God permits suffering--was not a problem for Priestley in his frame of reference. Suffering, he thought, arises "from natural causes; and by natural causes also, and the use of human endeavors, it has pleased ... Divine Providence, that they should be rectified. [XV, 62] Priestley was charged with being a "Deist" (atheist) because of his belief that

God did not constantly supervise the world, but had pre-established the natural laws by which it continued to operate, sometimes painfully for humans.

Priestley did not think that we lived in an ideal world; he was an "existentialist" before the term was invented, believing that creation was real prior to ideas about it, that existence preceded Platonic ideals or "essences."

But he did believe we are part of a system that, taken on the whole, was the best of all possible worlds. He wrote: "There are many things in the system of nature, as tempests, lightening, diseases and death, which greatly terrify and annoy us, and which are often the occasion of much pain and distress; but these evils are only partial; and when the whole system, of which they are a part, and a necessary consequence, is considered, it will be found to be, as far as we can judge, the best, and the most friendly upon the whole; and, that no other general laws, which should obviate and exclude these evils, would have been productive of so much happiness. And it should be a rule with us, when we are considering any particular thing in the system of nature, to take in every thing that is necessarily connected with it, and every thing that we should lose if we were deprived of it; so that if, upon the whole, we should in that case, gain more than we should lose, we must pronounce the thing complained of to be beneficial to us, and should thankfully bear the evil, for the sake of the greater good that accompanies it. Fire, for instance, is the occasion of a great deal of mischief and distress in the world, but is not to be compared with the benefits that we derive from the use of that element." [II, 9]

"Farther, all the evils we complain of are the result of what we call 'general laws,' in consequence of which the same events invariably follow from the same previous circumstances; and without these general laws, all would be uncertainty and confusion. Thus, it follows from the general law of gravitation, that bodies heavier than air will, when unsupported, fall to the ground. Now, cannot we conceive that it is better, upon the whole, that this law of nature, which is productive of a thousand benefits every moment, and whereby the whole earth, and probably the whole universe is held together, should be preserved invariably, than that it should be suspended whenever any temporary inconvenience would arise from it; as whenever a man should step from a precipice, to prevent breaking his bones, or being dashed to pieces?" [II, 11]

Thirty-six years earlier Bishop Joseph Butler, a champion of orthodoxy, had declared that nature was an organized whole working according to general laws without regard to particular persons; on the whole, he said, it was friendly, though a man could not step off a cliff, or violate moral laws, with impunity. This optimism was supported by the biblical story of creation: "And God saw every thing that he had made, and, behold, it was very good." [Genesis 1:31]

At the turn of the 18th century the German philosopher Leibnitz had asserted that this is the best of all possible worlds, as did the French author and Deist philosopher Voltaire a few years later. Priestley twice quoted the same passage from *Essay on Man*, written a century earlier by his favorite poet Alexander Pope, a persecuted Catholic:

All nature is but art unknown to thee:
All chance, direction, which thou canst not see;
All discord, harmony, not understood;
All partial evil, universal good;
And, spite of pride, in erring reason's spite,
One truth is clear, whatever is, is right.

Some people were not comforted by Priestley's adoption of the phrase "partial evil": Dr. Erasmus Darwin excused his absence from a Lunar Society meeting because he was treating children for measles complicated by pneumonia and added, "Surely the Lord could never think of amusing himself by setting nine innocent little animals to cough their hearts up. Pray, ask your learned Society if this partial evil contributes to any public good...." [Holt 1970, 129] Priestley would have responded that suffering children contributed to no public good, but that, though we were exposed to diseases, the generally salutary nature of our bodies outweighed the pain of illness.

Priestley gave many examples of the providential long-range benefits of "partial evils": the Birmingham Riots exposed the Christian conduct of the Dissenters and the malignant and disordering tendencies of their adversaries' principles. The riot made him suffer but it also reconciled him with his brother-in- law William. Critics of Christianity helped purify it of its corruptions by promoting discussion.

He thought that great events were often initiated by small causes: if Henry VIII's letter to the Pope had not been delayed, Pope Clement probably would have consented to Henry's divorce, and thus avoided the English break with Rome; and if English persecution of Nonconformists had not driven them to New England, where they established their language, institutions and religion, the conquistadors and Catholic missionaries would have established Spanish institutions on these shores. Such historical events were providential in Priestley's view-- good coming from evil.

Even wars, he thought, could be providential: when the Turks invaded Constantinople, the learned men took refuge in Italy and there revived the ancient learning of Greece and Rome, initiating the Renaissance. The Crusades were calamitous, acknowledged Priestley, "But it should be considered that it was a great means of establishing the liberties of the lower orders of men, dispersing the wealth and breaking the power of the great barons, of bringing Europe acquainted with the Eastern world, and of introducing much useful knowledge, in which this part of the world was greatly deficient." [XXIV, 438]

Death was providential, said Priestley: "It is an important part of the present system, that men, as well as other animals, should live in succession, and that the individuals should not continue upon the stage beyond a limited, though uncertain, time. By this means the improvement of the whole species, and of the world, is provided for." For the old become set in their ideas, while the young more readily discover and accept new ways of thought and action. [XV, 412] "It is happy for the cause of truth, as well as other valuable purposes, that man is mortal.... For otherwise the whole species would soon arrive at its maximum in all improvements, as individuals now do." [XVIII, 39] Besides, he said, who would not wish by death to be rid of the pains, infirmities, and bodily and mental imperfections of old age-- especially the Christian who believes death is a passage to a new and better life. [XV, 429]

Faith in this kind of providence, Priestley claimed, gave anyone peace of mind in spite of personal and social problems: "It contributes greatly to the enlargement of the mind of man, extending our views beyond what we immediately see and hear around us. Without this, man is comparatively a being of narrow views, ... and has but little motive to attend to any thing beyond himself, and the lowest gratifications. Without this faith he must be liable to be disturbed and unhinged by every cross event." [XV 200] "It enlarges his view of the system of nature, of which he is a part. It discovers to him his connection with, and his interest in, other beings, and other things." [XV, 24]

For instance, Priestley delivered a sermon *On The Duty of Not Living To Ourselves* to an assembly of Dissenter ministers that illustrates the practical application of his theology in sermons. It was not simply a Christian exhortation to love our neighbors as ourselves, but in a declarative mood expounded the integrated world and our mutual dependence in it. The popular sermon was printed by request, and is included in Henry Ware, Jr.'s 1834 Boston publication of some of Priestley's works.

In the sermon, Priestley's theme was the interdependence of all human beings with each other and with all other forms of life. After claiming that human beings were the highest form of life, he added: "The situation of man in this world, or the external circumstances of human nature still oblige us to assert with Paul, that 'no man liveth to himself, and no man dieth to himself.' Man himself is but a link, though the highest link of this great chain, all the parts of which are closely connected by the hand of our Divine Author. Nay, the more various and extensive are our powers, either for action or enjoyment, on that very account, the more multiplied and extensive are our wants; so that, at the same time that they are marks of our superiority to, they are bonds of our connection with, and signs of our dependence upon the various parts of the world about us, and of our subservience to one another." [XV, 124] He did not share the orthodox Christian belief, based on the Genesis story of creation, that human beings had "dominion over ... every living thing that moveth upon the earth."

Nor did human beings have dominion over each other: "In general, nothing can be more obvious than the mutual dependence of men on one another. ... This dependence is more sensible, indeed, in a state of infancy, when the least remission of the care of others would be fatal to us; but it is as real and necessary, and even vastly more extensive, though less striking, when we are advanced in life, especially in civilized countries. And the more perfect is the state of civil society, the more various and extended are the connections which man has with man, and the less able is he to subsist comfortably without the help of others."

He continued: "The business of human life, where it is enjoyed in perfection, is subdivided into so many parts, (each of which is extended by different hands,) that a person who would reap the benefit of all the arts of life in perfection, must employ, and consequently be dependent upon thousands; he must even be under obligations to numbers of whom he has not the least knowledge."

"These connections of man with man are every day growing more extensive. The most distant parts of the earth are now connected: every part is every day growing still more necessary to every other part; and the nearer advances we make to general happiness, and the more commodious our circumstances in this world are made for us, the more intimately and extensively we become connected with, and the more closely we are dependent upon one another." [XV, 125]

Thus,he said, no one can live for self alone: "In order to preserve mutual connection, dependence and harmony among all his works, it has pleased our Divine Author to appoint, that all our appetites and desires ... should point to something beyond ourselves for their gratification; so that the idea of 'self' is not the least necessary to a state of the highest enjoyment." [XV, 129]

Criticisms of Christianity by outsiders, such as Deists and atheists, were ignored by the Established Church; animosity was focused on Priestley because he was an insider, a Christian minister attacking the corruptions of Christianity. When the Boston Association of Unitarian ministers met in 1843 to consider expelling Theodore Parker from membership for bringing orthodox odium on their movement by his sermon, "The Transient and Permanent in Christianity," the Reverend Mr. Frothingham charged: "He that rejects the church must not belong to it. If he wishes to throw stones at the windows, he must go outside." [Commager 1947, 88]

Some of Priestley's theological views were so quaint--how could such a sophisticated son of the Enlightenment hold such outlandish ideas--that his theories have been ignored by liberals of later generations. On the other hand, scientists evaluating Priestley's contributions make allowances for the state of science in his time. In a report to the British Association for the Advancement of Science in 1831, Dr. William Moore wrote: "To estimate, justly, the extent of Priestley's claim to philosophical reputation, it is necessary to take into account the state of our knowledge of gaseous chemistry, at the time when he began his inquiries." [Henry 1831, 61] Likewise, to recognize Priestley's innovative contributions to theology, we need to take into account the state of theology in his time; then we can appreciate his prophetic contributions. Priestley believed in miracles--divine intervention in the laws of nature--such as the resurrection of the body on Judgment Day and the establishment of the Kingdom of God on earth with the Second Coming of Christ, but he did not believe in the "great miracle" of Original Creation.

He had concluded that the Genesis story of creation was not "literally true" since six days were not enough time to allow for "the operation of the regular laws of nature." Creation could not have been a miracle since "so much of interposition, and deviation from regular laws, was ... improbable, considering the slowness with which the course of nature proceeds." [VII, 305] He assumed that "the creation, as it had no beginning, so neither has it any bounds;

but that infinite space is replenished with worlds...." [II, 5] Creation was as eternal as the Creator, said Priestley: "The probability will be, that his works, as well as himself, occupy the whole extent of space, infinite as it must necessarily be, and that as he could have no beginning, so neither had his works." [IV, 341]

The resurrection of the body was essential, on practical grounds, to Priestley's theory of the moral function of religion: the certain knowledge of a resurrection and retribution in a future life for good or evil in this life is "the only great and powerful sanction to virtue, and which alone can enable a man to bear the trials of life, and die with hope and joy." [XVIII, 570]

Assurance of a future life, he claimed, was founded on revelation; "the historical evidence of the miracles, of the death, and of the resurrection of Christ" [which was the fundamental miracle], was based on the credible testimony of contemporary witnesses, as recorded in the New Testament. That account, Priestley believed, was circumstantial and "perfectly credible, according to the most established rules of evidence." [VII, 65] He argued that we accept the testimony of witnesses to other historical events, as well as the contemporary reports of scientists.

David Hume objected that miracles were incredible because they could not be corroborated by personal experience. Now it is a maxim of science that a conclusion to be valid must be falsifiable by repetition of the experiment or observation. Though Priestley believed the only way of knowing was by observation or experience, and carefully recorded the procedures of his scientific experiments, whether they led to discoveries or not, so they could be repeated by others, he could not apply the same principle to "revelations" that were essential to his faith. Priestley's faith in a future life, in some form or other, was shared not only by the orthodox but by Deists and skeptics in his time. Priestley was imprinted with faith in an after life as his mother's compensation for her suffering in this life, and as a necessary sanction for morality.

However, Priestley's personal faith in the resurrection of the body at a future Day of Judgment rejected the popular belief in an immortal, spiritual soul that on death flew immediately to a "local heaven," or to a hell in the bowels of the earth, according to its just deserts, which he claimed was a later innovation. Instead, he returned to the biblical doctrine of the resurrection of the body at the Second Coming of Christ; he incongruously explained that this would "require a miraculous interposition of the Divine power" to reconstitute the particles of matter in their previous bodily form and mind. [IV, 50]

He accepted miracles only at the beginning and end of the Christian dispensation; the rest of history was subject to divinely appointed laws of nature. His integration of science and theology did not extend to the integration of empiricism and Christian revelation. But, just as his discoveries in chemistry undermined his own chemical theories, so his theological speculations undermined his Christian assumptions.

Priestley was not daunted by change; he thought it was an elemental movement toward the improvement of the world. He wrote: "Let us examine every thing with the greatest freedom, without any regard to consequences, which, though we cannot distinctly see, we may assure ourselves will be such as we shall have abundant cause to rejoice in. ... We scruple not to plant trees for the benefit of posterity. Let us likewise sow the seeds of truth for them.... I do not write this from a persuasion that every thing that I have myself contended for is indisputably true. On the contrary, I have for the sake of discussion, hazarded many things, and shall probably hazard many more; and I have actually changed my opinions, theological as well as philosophical, which I have advanced since I was a writer." [XVIII, 549]

He kept on changing his opinions, sowing seeds of truth for the future, which made him more odious to many of his contemporaries--and more appreciated in the 20th century.

V

"ODIUM THEOLOGICUM"
"Semper Reformada"

During the 18th century Enlightenment, many people quietly left the churches and became skeptics or Deists, but retained a belief in an afterlife. Priestley remained faithful to his Christian heritage but used his enlightenment to reform Christianity, seeking to purify orthodoxy of its corruptions of the original gospel, corruptions he thought were the source of disbelief. His arguments were hard to refute as he substantiated his opinions about "pure Christianity" with scholarly biblical criticism and historical research in the opinions of Christian writers of the first three centuries. He was both a son of and contributor to the Enlightenment.

The Enlightenment emerged from the 17th century Age of Reason when the burgeoning science of Galileo Galilei and Johann Kepler had demonstrated that the earth was not the center of the solar system; Isaac Newton in a triumph of mathematical reason explained the solar system as the operation of the universal law of gravity; Francis Bacon systematized science as a way of knowing, testing hypotheses by experiment and inductive reason; and John Locke maintained that the data of experience tested by reason were the only source of knowledge. The power of human reason to discover answers to questions was validated. The autonomy of human reason was hailed by some as the criterion of even religious truths.

However, in the 17th century, two definitions of "reason" developed: "practical" reason and "pure" reason, each with a different epistemology. In addition to the scientist's practical reason based upon empiricism whereby the mind in all inquiries compared and contrasted data the senses provided, the pure reason of the Neoplatonists arrived at moral and religious truths, or ideals, by direct perceptions of the spiritual soul, with no confirmation by evidence.

Pure reason in 17th century England was the theory of knowledge about eternal, unchanging religious and moral truths developed by the Neoplatonists. Plato had assumed that eternal truths, beyond change, could not be derived from experience as information derived from the senses always was changing. Eternal truths could be realized only in the spiritual realm beyond changing matter, in the divine mind of the "One" or the "Good."

For the Neoplatonists, knowledge of the transcendent "first principle" was different from other kinds of knowledge in the world of time and change. Eternal truths could be known only when the spiritual mind or soul was raised to union with the spiritual "Eternal"--Ralph Waldo Emerson's "Oversoul." Pure reason was a form of "rationalism"--human reason alone could arrive at objective truth, without confirmation by experience. Those with the spiritual capacity for intuitive thought perceived innate ideas of the Supreme Being and of eternal ethical principles. The Scottish "Common Sense" philosophers adopted this theory, to Priestley's dismay. So did Priestley's colleague Richard Price. Epistemological rationalism as the only source of spiritual truth was criticized by John Locke and David Hume, as well as by Priestley.

Neo-Platonism flowered by the end of the 18th century in Romanticism, a protest in the arts against the Age of Reason, which also threatened the orthodox Christian perception of the world. The poet Samuel Taylor Coleridge, an erstwhile admirer of Priestley, played an important role in the transition from the Enlightenment to 19th century Romantic Idealism in England and in America. He had become a Unitarian while a student at Cambridge and was at Cambridge in April 1794 when Priestley and his wife fled England to join their sons in Pennsylvania. Among the farewell tributes Priestley received was an elegant silver inkstand presented by three young gentlemen and inscribed: "To Joseph Priestley, LL.D., &c. on his departure into Exile, from a few members of the University of Cambridge, who regret that expression of their Esteem should be occasioned by the ingratitude of their country." [Smith 1920, 13] The following Christmas-time, after dropping out of Cambridge without a degree, the 22 year old Coleridge wrote in "Religious Musings":

Lo! Priestley there, Patriot, and Saint, and Sage

Whom that my fleshly eye hath never seen
A childish pang of impotent regret
Hath thrilled my heart. Him from his native land
Statesmen, blood-stained, and priests idolatrous
By dark lies maddening the blind multitude
Drove him with vain hate. Calm, pitying he retired,
And mused expectant on these promised years.

In January 1798, Coleridge wrote, "I regard every experiment that Priestley made in chemistry, as giving wings to his more sublime theological works." [Schofield 00, 13] He also wrote, "In order to explain thinking, as a material phenomenon, it is necessary to refine matter into a mere modification of intelligence....Even so did Priestley....He stript matter of all its material properties; substituted spiritual powers." [Schofield 00, 13]

Coleridge, who thought of becoming a minister in order to gain financial security, was briefly an unsuccessful lay Unitarian preacher. [Schofield 00, 12] However, Tom Wedgwood and his brother Josiah, his friends and patrons, gave him an unconditioned allowance--which for years supported Coleridge's wife and children. Coleridge went to Germany with his intimate friends William Wordsworth and his sister Dorothy, and spent ten months learning the language and for a time studying at Gottingen University. He returned to England with a "glowing enthusiasm" for the transcendental idealism of Immanuel Kant. [Schofield 00, 1] Coleridge already in England knew Kant's works, and had been prepared for that philosophy by the idealist strain of Cambridge Neoplatonism in British thought. [Schofield 00, 9]

As Coleridge developed his own idealism, he criticized Priestley for offering a "compendious philosophy, which talking of mind, but thinking of brick and mortar, or other images equally abstracted from body, contrives a theory of spirit by nicknaming matter." [Schofield 00, 15] Coleridge espoused "pure reason," by which he said he meant "the power by which we become possessed of principles." He is credited with introducing German transcendentalism in England. He rejected some of Priestley's fundamental ideas such as materialism, utilitarianism and empiricism, and helped set the romantic tone of the 19th century, which would have little interest in Priestley's thought. When the government Reform Bill, which Priestley had earlier advocated, was enacted in 1832, Coleridge opposed it.

Priestley wrote to a friend: "My case is singularly hard. The greater part of my philosophical acquaintances ridicule my attachment to Christianity, and yet the generality of Christians will not allow me to belong to them at all." [French 1984, 43]

Priestley experienced the incredulity of his "philosophical acquaintances" especially in Paris when touring Europe with Lord Shelburne, then a widower.

On the tour, Priestley wrote long letters to Shelburne's two sons, whose education he supervised, with his observations on dress, architecture, paintings, crops, soil, the churches he attended, the character of the people, the beauty of the countryside, and the political situation.

His tour, said Priestley who spoke some German and French, "was extremely pleasing, especially as I saw everything to the greatest advantage, and without any anxiety or trouble, and had an opportunity of seeing and conversing with every person of eminence, wherever we came; the political characters by his lordship's connections, and the literary ones by my own. I was soon, however, tired of Paris and chose to spend my evenings at the hotel, in company with a few literary friends." ["Lord Shelburne carried the Doctor to public spectacles, and the assemblies and routs of the great; but these things were very insipid and irksome to him," explained a friend. I-i 257], He especially enjoyed the company of John Hyacinth De Magellan, a Portuguese Jesuit and member of many scientific societies in London who accompanied Priestley when he returned to London before Shelburne. [I-i 198]

Priestley was already known in the scientific circles of Paris from the publication of a French translation of his *Observations on Air*, which included his discovery of "dephlogisticated air." From reading that publication, the Montgolfier brothers, French paper-makers and scientists, learned that hot air was lighter than cold and got the idea of capturing some hot air in a bag and found that the bag rose; a few years later they gave the first public demonstration of a hot-air balloon.

In England Priestley could publish anything he chose, but in France he experienced censorship of the press under the "ancient regime" royal government: a paragraph was deleted in the preface to his *Observations on Air*, which said that a consequence of the spread of knowledge was the reformation of religion. And a translation of his *Essay on the First Principals of Government* had to be printed in Holland and smuggled into France--where Priestley became known for his contributions to democratic political theory and was made an honorary citizen after the Birmingham Riot, at the same time as George Washington. [I-i 256]

Priestley wrote that all the scientists he met in Paris were unbelievers, or atheists. As he always affirmed that he was a believer, he was told by some of them that he was the only person, whose opinions they respected, who professed a belief in Christianity. "But on interrogating them on the subject, I soon found that they had given no proper attention to it, and did not really know what Christianity was." [I-i 198] He told them that he "could easily account for their infidelity by the very corrupted state of their established religion...." [I-i 255] He concluded that in order to defend Christianity's "genuine principles" it was necessary to "free it from those corruptions which prevent its reception with philosophical and thinking persons." That was the theme of his *Letters to a Philosophical Unbeliever* that he began writing soon after his return to England: "Having conversed so much with unbelievers, at home and abroad, I thought I should be able to combat their prejudices with some advantage...." [I-i 198]

In his *Letters to an Unbeliever*, Priestley first formulated the ideas that he later developed in his most controversial work on the corruptions of Christianity and on early opinions concerning Jesus that so alarmed English churchmen. He could be ignored so long as he tried to convert unbelievers, but not when he turned the same polemical guns toward the established citadel of orthodoxy.

To the philosophical unbelievers he wrote that disbelief was caused by the corruptions introduced by the pagan philosophy of early Greek converts--the Platonic dualism of a mortal physical body and an immortal spiritual soul--and added "That philosophy has been exploded, but the remains of it, in the christian system, are still but too apparent; and being manifestly absurd, they expose it to many objections. The principal of these ... are ... the trinity of persons in the godhead, original sin, arbitrary predestination, atonement for the sins of men by the death of Christ, and (which has perhaps been as great a cause of infidelity as any other) the doctrine of the plenary inspiration of the Scriptures."

On the other hand, Priestley wrote, the essentials of Christianity were "the great historical facts recorded in the Old and New Testament, in which we are informed concerning the creation and government of the world, the history of the discourses, miracles, death and resurrection of Christ, and his assurance of the resurrection of all the dead in a future life of retribution...." [IV466]

Priestley's basic biblical assumption was the significant affirmation that Christianity was an historical religion based on events, not on philosophical speculation. This meant that the facts could be checked both with other known facts and with what was reasonable, though Priestley exempted the special revelation of the Second Coming of Christ. It also meant that Christianity as an historical religion could improve with time. This was a contribution of Judaism--the concept that history moved forward, in contrast to the Greek assumption that history was circular, endlessly repeating past failures. If religion was "once and for all revealed to the saints," it could not benefit by experience and new understanding. That religion, as well as society, could improve over time was the ground of Priestley's optimism.

Renaissance humanism from the 14th to the 16th century believed that the golden age was in the past, the flowering of antiquity in Greece and Rome. In contrast, Francis Bacon in the 17th century claimed that antiquity was the youth of the world, while his generation was the heir of accumulated knowledge and could look forward to greater conquests of nature: the world was progressing toward perfection, a belief shared by Priestley and Franklin. [Now we are learning that the reckless conquest of nature can be disastrous.]

Unitarianism in the 18th century was a "sect everywhere spoken against." [McLachlan 1951, 2] Denying the Trinity was still legally punishable by the confiscation of goods and imprisonment for life, though not enforced. The law was not repealed until 1813. Nonetheless, in Birmingham Priestley became outright and exclusively Unitarian in the late 16th century tradition of Francis David. He had moved on from Arianism because of its doctrine of Christ's pre-existent soul, and then from Socinianism because it worshiped Christ--though both positions were anti-trinitarian. And his congregation through 11 years moved theologically with him.

Francis David was a well-educated and open-minded Catholic priest in Kolozsvar, capital of Transylvania, in the century of the Protestant Reformation. As the successive missionaries for religious reforms came to Transylvania, David debated with them and changed his opinions. He became minister of the largest Lutheran church in Kolozsvar, and then was won to Calvinism, carrying his church with him. As a leader of the Calvinists, he converted young King John Sigismund and other leaders. He was made court preacher and bishop of the new Reformed Church in Transylvania.

Then David was confronted with Socinianism by Georgio Biandratta, a friend and court physician, and again changed his opinion without estranging his church. Biandratta was an anti-trinitarian who had fled from Calvin in Switzerland, where Michael Servetus, a physician and anti-trinitarian, had earlier been burned at the stake for his heresy. In Poland, Biandratta became a leader in the Socinian movement and then was invited by King John to Transylvania as court physician. Biandratta debated his anti-trinitarian views with David, who was won over. While Biandratta's experience had taught him to move carefully and slowly in refor-mation, David was bold and fearless, openly speaking against the trinity and for the unity of God from his Kolozsvar pulpit, foment-ing controversy with the orthodox Catholics and Protestants.

Fortunately, King John's queen mother, while earlier regent, had decreed legal toleration for Catholics and Protestants "in order that each might hold the faith which he wished, with new rites as well as with the old, that this should be permitted him at his own free will." Still, the religious controversies became so heated that King John feared they would disturb the peace of the state and called a series of synods to try to restore harmony, to no avail.

At the Diet of Torda, convened by King John in 1568, David made an eloquent plea for religious toleration: "There is no greater piece of folly than to try to exercise power over conscience and soul, both of which are subject only to their creator." After the debates between David and Catholic, Lutheran and Calvinist speakers had petered out, with David pre-eminent but no agreements, King John Sigis-mund renewed and amplified the earlier edicts of toleration; he decreed "that preachers shall be allowed to preach the Gospel everywhere, each according to his own understanding of it. If the community wish to accept such teaching, well and good; if not, they shall not be compelled, but shall be allowed to keep the preachers they prefer. No one shall be made to suffer on account of his religion, since faith is a gift of God." [Wilbur 1925, 224] That edict gave David's followers the right to be in their own churches without molestation, though it did not ultimately save David from martyr-dom.

In the period when King John decreed total religious toleration in his land, the Inquisition in Italy instituted a "reign of terror" to stamp out Protestantism; in the Netherlands, Alva was putting Protestants to death by the thousands; in Portugal, the Inquisition against Jews drove them from the country; in Spain, the Inquisition continued for more than two centuries; in France, the St. Bartholomew mas-sacre of protestant Huguenots took 20 to 30 thousand victims; and in England, anti- trinitarians were still burned alive. King John was persuaded by David's arguments for the unity of God. To settle the hotly debated question of the Trinity, he convened a synod of ministers from Hungary and Transylvania in the great hall of his palace to debate before the King, court, and a throng of ministers and nobles. David, who led the five unity-of-God debaters, referred only to the authority of the Bible, while the bishop, who led the six Calvinist debaters, referred also to creeds and orthodox theologians. The debate in Latin lasted ten full days when, as agreement was not being reached, the King ended it. It was considered a complete victory for David's unity-of-God views. [The proper name "Unitarian" was not yet used to designate converts to the unity-of-God concept.]

On David's return to Kolozsvar, the streets were crowded with supporters who hailed his victory. The city became practically unitarian, as all its churches and schools were followers of David, as were all the members of the City Council and higher officials. [Wilbur 1925, 226] After another debate, the King was won to David's views, and henceforth the King clearly accepted the unitarian faith, followed by his court. The only unitarian king in history did not use his authority to oppress other churches or to secure special privileges for his own, but insisted on equal rights and privileges for all.

Soon, there were over 300 unitarian churches in Transylvania and neighboring Hungary. Unitarianism was taught in thirteen higher schools or colleges, and the doctrine was spread by the unitarian press which published books in Latin for scholars and in Hungarian for the common people. [Wilbur 1925, 228]

King John died at age of 30 in 1571, leaving no heir to the throne. The nobles then elected as king a Catholic, who swore to protect the rights of the four recognized religions, including unitarian. But the unitarians had opposed his election and he proceeded to remove all of them, except Biandratta, from court and high public offices. David was displaced by another as court preacher. The unitarian printer was exiled, terminating unitarian proselytizing by publications.

The Diet decreed that any "innovators" who introduced further reforms in religion would be banished, imprisoned, or put to death for blasphemy, at the discretion of the king. The unitarians revolted; many were killed in battle, nobles were executed as rebels or their estates were confiscated, and unitarians activities were restricted.

The king invited Jesuits to come help him restore the influence of the Catholic church, which they did so energetically that the nobles, alarmed at their interference in all policies of state, in the Diet voted unanimously to expel the Jesuits from the land, which ended their domination.

Though the unitarians no longer believed that Christ was part of the Godhead, they had retained from their past experience in Catholic and Protestant churches the habit of praying to Christ, which the Socinians thought was essential to Christian worship. However, some unitarian scholars believed that the practice was not taught in Scripture and should be given up. It was widely discussed among unitarians without serious objection, and David supported the idea. At a unitarian synod, he publicly opposed the worship of Christ ("Non adoramus") as well as infant baptism, as unscriptural--always reforming ("Semper Reformada"). The Jesuits urged that David be prosecuted for "innovation."

Biandratta at Court realized that there was great danger that the Jesuits would use the charge of blasphemy to have all unitarians banished from the country. He urged David to keep quiet, which David said would be hypocrisy. Biandrata invited Faustus Socinus, who defended worship of the human Christ, to come from Poland to reason with David on Biblical grounds. Socinus lived with David for months, at Biandratta's expense, and unsuccessfully carried on a running discussion about the worship of Christ. After Socinus' arguments failed to change David's mind, Biandratta informed David that he could no longer protect him in the Court.

David was ordered removed from his pastorate and kept under house arrest. David was ill but the next day being Sunday, he preached in two Kolozsvar churches, defending the unitarian doctrine and declaring that the worship of Christ was just the same as invoking the Virgin Mary or the saints. He concluded, "Whatever the world may say, it must sometime become clear that God is one." It was the last sermon he ever preached.

The angry King had David, sick and too weak to stand, arrested and brought to trial before him for "innovation." A Unitarian in Transylvania wrote that David, "Far from denying the doctrines he preached, he boldly maintained their scriptural truth, and, instead of new innovations, declared them to have been long known to, and believed in, by the Unitarians of Transylvania." [Beard 1846, 302] He was found guilty and sentenced to imprisonment in the castle at Deva, where he soon died a martyr in 1579.

The name "Unitarian" was bestowed by its opponents and first appeared in records in 1600; it was formally adopted by the followers of David in 1638. [Wilbur 1925, 229] In 1968 the 120 Unitarian churches with 80,000 members in Transylvania, now part of Romania, celebrated the 400th anniversary of their founding by Francis David after the declaration of religious freedom at the Diet of Torda.

Unitarianism had antecedents in 17th century England, based on independent studies of the Bible. When Socinian publications reached England, they reinforced the anti-trinitarian theology already developed by John Biddle and others. Biddle died in prison of "odium theologicum"--hatred toward those who advance new theological ideas which threatened cherished doctrines or ecclesiastical authority.

A century later, Samuel Johnson of English dictionary fame who once dined with Priestley, explained why theological reformations provoked such odium: "Every man will dispute with great good humor upon a subject in which he is not interested" or if he is "not in earnest as to religion." But when an accepted religion gives meaning and value to life, said Johnson, "every man who attacks my belief, diminishes in some degree my confidence in it, and therefore makes me uneasy."

John Biddle made many uneasy. He was the son of a dealer in woolen cloth and was such a good student that a neighboring nobleman made an annual substantial contribution toward his education. He graduated from Oxford in 1638 with a reputation as a scholar, became a tutor and earned a Master's degree, and was appointed master of a school in Gloucester. He could quote from memory most of the New Testament in Greek and in English. As a Bible scholar, he concluded that it did not teach the unreasonable doctrine of the Trinity, though Christ was to be worshiped. In that Age of Reason, the Bible was to be interpreted by reason, not by tradition. When he showed some friends a manuscript arguing that the Holy Spirit was not a Deity, one of them reported his heresy and he was sentenced to jail. As he persisted in expounding his ideas, he spent most of the rest of his life in prison or exile, except for interludes of freedom secured by his influential friends, such as Thomas Firmin, a wealthy philanthropist. He published a pamphlet opposing the Trinity that was found so blasphemous the hangman was ordered to burn it, and on the Continent four fat books were written to refute it.

Finally, he was released from prison when Parliament passed a general Act of Oblivion remitting punishment for offenses. He returned to London and held meetings with his supporters who organized an independent congregation. He preached that faith was not a gift of God but could be acquired by people's natural abilities, that faith could not believe "anything contrary to or above reason," that there was no "original sin," and that the authority of church Fathers or Councils did not determine matters of faith. He advised that people had only to consult the Bible "to reduce our Religion to its first principles." He became familiar with Socinian publications and published a Catechism which was regarded as a dangerous form of Socinianism. Three years later he was brought before Parliament and charged with promulgating scandalous teachings. All copies of the book were ordered burned and he was jailed, but Parliament dissolved without bringing him to trial and he was again released.

Instead of avoiding further trouble by being silent, he went back to preaching. The orthodox challenged him to a public debate in which the first question was whether any one present denied that Christ was God. Biddle responded that he did. Before the debate was finished, he was arrested to be tried for his life, which aroused great public interest. Oliver Cromwell, then head of the Commonwealth government with Presbyterians in the ascendancy, wished to avoid a furor and banished Biddle to the Scilly Islands and granted him a pension.

Two years later, friends secured a write of habeas corpus that set him free. He returned to London and continued preaching until Charles II came to the throne and a new Act of Uniformity was adopted, making it a crime to hold public worship except with the forms of the Church of England. Biddle held private services but was spied upon; he and his friends were imprisoned. Biddle was ordered to lie in a foul prison until he could pay an excessive fine; he died a month later, in 1662, of "odium theologicum"--a theology exciting hatred. Priestley a century later identified himself with a radical religious tradition that was already odious.

In his *History of the Christian Church*, Priestly included a brief biography of Biddle, including: "Mr Biddle, a man of great learning and piety, who, without having read any of the Unitarians, but from his study of the Scriptures, embraced their sentiments...." [X, 360]

During Biddle's lifetime, anti-trinitarians were called Arians or Socinians. Ten years after his death, his friend and supporter Henry Hedworth, in a controversy with Quakers, issued a pamphlet which contains the first known use in English print of the name "Unitarian." In Holland, Hedgworth had known and helped Transylvanian Unitarian refugees and adopted the name for his own position. [Wilbur 1978, 199] In 1691, Biddle's friend and supporter Thomas Firmin (who never withdrew from the Church of England) persuaded a Unitarian clergyman to prepare *A Brief History of the Unitarians, called also Socinians*, which Firmin had published along with other Unitarian tracts, including three by Biddle. Subsequent Firmin publications, five volumes in all, contained many tracts by Arian clergymen of the Established Church, which stirred up a Trinitarian controversy in the Church of England. [Wilbur 1925, 310]

Unitarians in the 17th century established no permanent religious institutions, and the movement, constantly threatened by government persecution, died out. Priestley revived the tradition, not only in his Birmingham chapel but among many Dissenter ministers and congregations. Though he had inadvertently become odious years before as a result of his speculations about human nature and the substance of the cosmos, it was as an avowed Unitarian in Birmingham that Priestley became involved in an inflaming controversy.

VI

HOW DO WE KNOW WHAT IS TRUE?
"A great probability"

Priestley sought answers to questions in science and in theology with a unified epistemology (how we know what is true or real--the "real" continues to manifest itself regardless of what we think about it), which engendered a radically different world view than had most of his contemporaries, but which is more congenial in the 20th century.

His epistemology started off on a different track when he began to develop "more rational notions of religion." Until opponents in a discussion agree on an epistemology, he thought the discussion was fruitless. Priestley applied himself to the question of epistemology in reaction to the epistemology of the emerging Scottish school of "Common Sense" philosophy. He rejected all dualistic theories of knowledge and of reality. He became a consistent "monist," integrating reason and intuition, science and religion--with exceptions, body and soul, matter and spirit, and progressively rejected cherished doctrines of orthodox Christianity in favor of a rational affirmation of "pure" historical Christianity that he claimed was unitarian-- while retaining a belief in some biblical revelations.

Priestley's critique of Common Sense--a school in a long Platonic tradition of intuitionism and innate ideas--was significant because the assumptions of Common Sense are still implicit, under other names, in the epistemology of people all over the world.

The Age of Reason and the Enlightenment in the seventeenth and eighteenth centuries had produced a conflict between orthodox

Christianity and the epistemology of science, supernaturalism and naturalism, and revelation and reason. Priestley explicitly set himself the task of resolving the conflict. [Rice 1975, 3] He was an outstanding representative of the English thinkers who sought to maintain the "holy alliance" between the most advanced scientific views and Christianity. [Chapin 1967, 36] Religion and science were compatible domains for Priestley: "the scientific discovery of the works of God in nature were inherently in harmony with an historically sound interpretation of the word of God. Between the 'word of God' and the 'works of God' there was for Priestley just a natural partnership." [Hiebert 1980. 29]

Priestley thought that science and religion were too much separated. He pursued his interests in both theology and science: "These pursuits, different as they are, are far from being at variance. On the contrary, they perfectly harmonize with, and promote, each other." [XV, 30] He wrote: "The importance of these inquiries must be evident to any person who attends to the progress of knowledge and good sense in the world. For if the general body of Christians retain any doctrine as essential to revealed religion, which true philosophy [science] shall prove to be actually false, the consequence will be, that the whole system will be rejected by those who consider that tenet as an inseparable part of it. So greatly doth it behoove us, that Christian knowledge should keep pace with philosophical." [III, 388] "If what is called a mystery in Christianity, be really a falsehood in philosophy," wrote Priestley, "the belief in it must be abandoned altogether, at any hazard." [Hoecker 1978, 45] The findings of science overruled the alleged truths of revelation for Priestley, except the ultimate resurrection of the dead.

On the title page of his 1774 first volume of *Experiments and Observations on Different Kinds of Air*, Priestley had printed his translation from Latin of a paragraph by his seventeenth century philosophical predecessor Francis Bacon:

"So if there is any humility towards the Creator, any feeling of awe and praise for his works, any love for men, any concern to relieve human need and hardship; any love of truth and hatred of obscurity in the things of nature, any desire to make the mind pure; men should be asked over and over again, to dismiss trivial and absurd philosophies which have put thesis before hypothesis, and have led experience captive, and triumphed over the works of God; and to approach with a certain reverence to unroll the book of the Creatures. They should not delay over this, but think deeply, and speak uprightly and honestly, free and untouched by prejudice. ... In searching out the interpretation of Nature, let them spare no effort,

but go on with energy, fix their minds on it, and never hang back."
[McEvoy 1975, 17] Priestley accepted Bacon's challenge.

Priestley was editing for publication his rational systematic theology, *The Institutes of Natural and Revealed Religion*, when he was disconcerted to learn of the existence of works by three Scottish "Common Sense" philosophers. He said, "If this new scheme of an immediate appeal to 'common sense' upon every important question in religion (and which superseded almost all reasoning on the subject) should take place, the plan of my work, with which I had taken some pains, ... was absurd from the very beginning." [III 5] He turned his attention to Common Sense, reading Dr. Reid's *Inquiry*, Dr. Beattie's *Essay*, and Dr. Oswald's *Appeal*, and wrote a critique to defend his own epistemology.

In his *Institutes*, Priestley had written: "Reason, whereby we are capable of thinking, reflecting, comparing, and judging of things" in nature should be used as well in understanding religion, for both reason and religion "proceed from the same God.... They cannot, therefore, be contrary to one another, but must mutually illustrate and enforce one another. Besides, how can we distinguish one scheme of religion from another, so as to give the preference to that which is most deserving of it, but by the help of our reason and understanding?" [II, 384]

"Reason" in the eighteenth century was appealed to with different meanings in diverse theories of knowledge and of reality. Priestley opposed the ancient school of "pure reason", renamed "common sense" by the Scottish philosophers, with the "natural reason" that he had adopted from the Enlightenment.

"Pure reason," a function of the soul, or spiritual mind, philosophized with its own innate axioms without reference to reality. In fact, in the tradition of Platonic "idealism," ideas were more real than the physical universe, universal principles than sense objects. Suprasensible universal truths were apprehended by pure reason--a function of the spirit--in contrast to particulars apprehended by the senses. Truth perceived by the "light of reason" was self-evident and could not be falsified by experience, claimed the tradition of Plato, Descartes and the Scottish philosophers.

"Natural" reason by the physical mind verified ideas or principles by comparing them with facts observed or experienced by the senses. Theories or principles were inferred from particulars. Truth was contingent upon "matters of fact," empirical in proof and pragmatic in meaning. Priestley's empirical epistemology could begin with an intuited hypothesis, but its truth was not known until it had been tested by observation or experience. Reason compared an insight with facts. Newton wrote, "Tell me your experiments; if not, your opinion is precarious. Reasoning without experience is very slippery." [Merchant 1883, 284]

Common sense epistemology began with an intuited hypothesis or "first principle" which could be tested for truth only by its logical consistency with other eternal truths, a purely intellectual exercise with no reality test. It was claimed to be self-evident.

In his *Examination* critical of Common Sense, Priestley wrote with such asperity that, chastened by his friends, he rued his style. Mrs. Theophilus Lindsey, whose criticisms Priestley sought and valued, wrote to Mr. Turner that a young lawyer, "just come from Edinburgh, had been with Dr. Robertson and Hume at the time they had read our friend's book [Priestley's *Examination of Common Sense*], and they both declared that the manner of the work was proper, as the argument was unanswerable. I own, had I seen it in MS, I should have wished to have softened a few things; but I think there is no room for any great censure." [I-i, 252]

Common sense was in turn a reaction to the Scottish philosopher David Hume's epistemology that led to skepticism. He claimed that religious and moral convictions and convictions about the facts of reality were separate domains with different epistemologies--a multiverse instead of Priestley's universe. Moral convictions were based only upon "sentiment." His theory of knowledge undermined traditional certainties about the soul, God, nature, causation and miracles. [Willey 1977, 110] Hume's religious skepticism, which Reid complained "leaves no ground to believe any one thing rather than its contrary," led Reid to ground certainty of moral conviction on common sense." [McEvoy 1975, 358] Common sense meant what was commonly believed.

Dr. Thomas Reid, professor of moral philosophy at the University of Glasgow,wrote that common sense was the faculty of all rational beings to directly perceive self-evident truths, or "first principles," including axioms of morality, metaphysics, mathematics and logic. The capacity to perceive the truth of first principles was innate and instinctive; it could not be taught. Dr. James Beattie wrote, "A man defective in common sense may acquire learning, he may even possess genius to a certain degree, but the defect of nature he never can supply." [III, 75]

Priestley was most distressed by such a dismissal of the efficacy of education to improve moral and religious principles-- education was the hope of improving the human race. His innovative theory and practice of education was denied by common sense philosophy any contribution to progress in religion or morality.

Beattie, a Scotch writer and Reid follower who bitterly railed against those who differed with him (he was popular with King George III who awarded him a generous pension), defined common sense as "that power of the mind which perceives truth or commands belief, not by progressive argumentation, but by an instantaneous, instinctive and irresistible impulse, derived neither from education nor from habit, but from nature, acting independently on our will, ... and acting in a similar manner upon all, or, at least, upon a great majority of mankind, and therefore properly called common sense." [III, 73] The authority for such determinations of truth, wrote Beattie, is feeling: "All that we know of truth or falsehood is that our constitution determines us in some cases to believe, in others to disbelieve; and that to us is truth which we feel that we must believe; and that to us is falsehood which we feel that we must disbelieve." [III, 72] Whatever was generally believed must be true, he said.

Such subjectivism, said Priestley, "makes all truth ... relative to ourselves only," while John Locke's empiricism, which Priestley espoused, "makes truth depend upon the necessary nature of things" as observed. Common Sense as an instinct "admits of no appeal to reason" by which the agreement or disagreement of ideas and facts can be investigated and judged, as Locke had advocated. The instinctive feeling of truth, "if strictly analyzed, ... might appear to be mere prejudice," suggested Priestley. He was concerned that it "leads to great arrogance and insolence with respect to our opponents in controversy, as persons defective in their constitution, destitute of common sense, and therefore not to be argued with, but to be treated as idiots or madmen." [III, 70] Priestley feared that such an attitude would preclude discussion or friendly arguments that he believed facilitated the discovery of new truths.

Beattie believed that persons were born with a degree of common sense as part of their mental constitution that could not be altered by education [III, 75], while Priestley believed that any person could by study acquire "as good a power of distinguishing truth from falsehood as his neighbors" and "is encouraged to indulge a freedom of inquiry, and to persist in his investigations." [III, 74]

Priestley was unjustifiably alarmed that common sense taught every man "to think himself authorized to pronounce decisively upon every question according to his present feeling and persuasion, under the notion of its being something original, instinctive, ultimate and uncontrovertible." [III, 71] Actually, Beattie restricted the application of common sense to the recognition of self-evident religious and moral "first principles," urging the patient investigation of man and nature by "rational inquiry," with "liberty of speech and writing" and no restrictions by the civil power. [McEvoy 1975, 106]

However, Priestley feared that common sense would implicitly sanction authoritarianism: "I am afraid we shall find these new principles extending their authority farther than the precincts of metaphysics, morals, religion, Christianity and Protestantism, to which they have been confined. Papists may begin to avail themselves of them for the support of all those doctrines and maxims for which the powers of reason had proved insufficient; and politicians also, possessing themselves of this advantage, may venture once more to thunder upon us their exploded doctrines of passive obedience and non-resistance. ... The whole business of thinking will be in a manner over, and we shall have nothing to do but to see and believe." [III, 101]

Priestley most objected to innate "first principles" intuited by common sense because they restricted human improvement in morals and religion, just as did the authority of traditional orthodoxy. His defense of pure Christianity against both orthodox corruptions and philosophical unbelievers required, he said, that "Christianity, besides being proved to be true, and, indeed, as a necessary step in the proof of its truth, must be shown to be rational, such as men of good sense can receive without abandoning the use of their reason, or making a sacrifice of it to what is called faith." [XVI, 477] Credulity was no more warranted in religion than in science. Priestley believed that "It is the glory of human nature, that the operations of reason, though variable, and by no means infallible, are capable of infinite improvement." [XXII, 47]

Common sense precluded the moral improvement of human beings by education, while Priestley believed in the progressive development of human nature by the transmission of information about successful living from one generation to the next. Moral and religious principles, as well as secular information, had to be learned by personal experience, imitation, or instruction. Systematic teaching speeded up the process of learning: "Every addition that is made to the common stock of art or science is the effect of slow trial and experiment, but what a man attains to by the study and labor of his whole life he may communicate to another in a few days or hours." [XXV, 11]

Beattie had claimed that he inherently knew the proper mode of conduct, "Because my conscience tells me so." [III, 85] The conscience to Priestley was not innate but was the value system developed in an individual and available for immediate response, without deliberation, when confronted with a decision or choice. [II,

25] It was not imparted at birth but was informed by the happy or painful consequences of experience, either personal or learned from the example of others, said Priestley. [III, 477] In the process, "the two great principles which comprise the whole of the moral law, the love of God, and of our neighbor, will in due time appear, and it will produce all the fruits of righteousness...." [XVI, 23] Therefore, Priestley felt it was his duty with zeal "to enlighten the minds of my friends, my countrymen, and mankind in general" with biblical moral principles. [VII, 74]

"This opinion of the gradual formation of the ideas of moral right and wrong, from a great variety of elements," said Priestley, "easily accounts for that prodigious diversity in the sentiments of mankind respecting the objects of moral obligation; and I do not see that any other hypothesis can account for the facts." Moral principles are culture-specific and vary from culture to culture according to circumstances and instruction. If they were "simple ideas" of the uninformed conscience, Priestley said, they would be more universal, "invariable as the perception of colors or sounds." [III, 195] Different circumstances, including education, also accounted for the variety of individual moral norms within cultures.

"Circumstances" were a crucial variable in Priestley's theory of knowledge, accounting for the variety of opinions of people. An awareness of the effect of circumstances engenders both humility and compassion. In humility, Priestley was grateful "to that good Being who has brought me hitherto" for the circumstances of his own life: "the blessings of a religious and liberal education," and "a happy temperament of body and mind, both derived from my parents...." Though his health was "far from robust," it was "excellently adapted to that studious life which has fallen to my lot." [I-i, 342]

Circumstances included states of mind, mental hypotheses and presumptions: "In what different lights may the same thing be seen by different persons, according as their different hypotheses incline them to regard it." [III, 55] Circumstances also included "prejudice." He recognized its influence in his scientific experiments: "The force of prejudice ... biases not only our judgments ... but even the perceptions of the senses ... that the plainest evidence of sense will not entirely change." [Schofield 1978, 348] Priestley thought these circumstances should modify antagonism in any differences of opinion. In controversies, he wrote with candor, except when he was denigrated.

Recognizing the influence of circumstances, he thought, also evokes forgiveness. Concerning his feelings about the Birmingham rioters, Priestley wrote: "Let us ... consider that, since our adversaries are men, as well as ourselves, of the same original constitutions, and, consequently, liable to be affected in the same manner by the same circumstances, with the same advantages with which we have been favored, they would have thought, have felt, and have acted as we do; and that, had Divine Providence so ordered it, by reversing our respective situations, we had been the unhappy persecutors, and they the persecuted. Let us ... be thereby disposed to pity and to forgive." [XV, 486] This provided the grounds, said Priestley, for adopting the precept of Jesus as he was being crucified; "Father, forgive them, for they know not what they do." [VII, 484]

In Priestley's public disagreement with *Burke's Reflections on the French Revolution*, Priestley accounted for their different opinions by circumstances: "Objects appear in very different lights to different persons, according to their respective situations, and the opportunities they have for observing them." [XXII, 163] Priestley added, "So different ... are men's feelings, from the difference, no doubt, of our educations, and the different sentiments we voluntarily cherish through life, that a situation that gives you the idea of pride, gives me that of meanness. You are proud of what, in my opinion, you ought to be ashamed, the idolatry of a fellow-creature [the French king]." [XXII, 171]

The "less controlled passions" of the well-born, Priestley had probably reflected on his intimate association with the family of Lord Shelburne, "are entitled to compassion, it being the almost unavoidable consequence of their education and mode of life." [I-i, 206] Persons of large fortunes and many engagements are seldom at home long enough to pay attention or express endearments to their children, and what is done for them is to prepare them for their station in life, and has "but little connection with the principle of disinterested love for their offspring." [XXV, 56] (If Lord Shelburne or his second wife read these observations, they cannot have been pleased, which may have contributed to their estrangement from Priestley two years later.)

Priestley thought that even mother love was a function of circumstances: "It is the constant, hourly attention a mother gives to her child, an attention that commences, on her part, even before it is born, and not anything properly instinctive ... which is the source of maternal tenderness, a kind of tenderness that the father seldom feels ... till some months afterwards, when it is acquired by the same attention." [XXV, 56]

The development of religious beliefs was influenced by circumstances, Priestley claimed: "The Corruptions of Christianity, in every article of faith or practice, was the natural consequence of the circumstances in which it was promulgated; and also that its recovery from these corruptions is the natural consequence of different circumstances...." [Parke 1957, 50]

With his monistic penchant for applying his principles in all fields, Priestley noted in the preface to his *History of Electricity* that circumstances determined the appearance of any phenomena. It is the aim of science, he wrote, to determine "those circumstances in which any appearance in nature is certainly and invariably produced." [McEvoy 1978, 31] In all his inquiries, Priestley noted the different circumstances that produced different results.

He emphasized the importance in chemistry of "different circumstances"--gases mixed in different sequences-- in producing different compounds: "as much depends upon the mode of arrangement, concerning which we know nothing at all, as upon the elements themselves. For things the most different in their properties appear to consist of the very same elements." [Schofield 1966, 274]

It was this emphasis on "mode of arrangement" that made Priestley steadfastly oppose the new chemistry of Lavoisier, which flourished by the "simple combinations of varying proportions of simple atoms" without heeding the order in which the elements were mixed. It was some time before chemists began to wonder about the "mode of arrangement" that Priestley was speculating about. He was not simply perverse in his opposition to Lavoisier's oxygen, though Priestley was mistaken in his persistent defense of the phlogiston theory. [Schofield 1966, 275]

Priestley's theory of knowledge was informed by his study as a student at Daventry Academy of the works of John Locke, who advanced empirical epistemology in the Age of Reason, and of David Hartley, who is called the father of physiological psychology. Both men were doctors of medicine, scientists.

John Locke, born the son of an English lawyer a century before Priestley, was dissatisfied with the scholastic philosophy taught at Oxford and on graduation refused holy orders. He was attracted to scientific studies by Robert Boyle (of Boyle's Law on gases and one of the founders of modern chemistry) and continued at Oxford as a Fellow studying medicine. On completing his studies, he joined the household of Lord Shaftesbury in London as family physician and confidential advisor, and was elected a Fellow of the Royal Society.

Shaftesbury led the opposition to a Catholic successor to Charles II, proposing an act of Parliament to exclude Catholics from the throne, which challenged the tradition of hereditary royal succession and the absolute rule of the sovereign without regard to law or the preferences of the citizens. The king, whose supporters were called Tories, threatened Shaftesbury and his adherents who were called Whigs. Locke had published treatises opposing the divine right of kings and ascribing the foundations of legitimate government to an implicit "social contract." With increasing royal suppression of subversive movements, Locke in 1683 took refuge for six years in Holland, supported by the inheritance from his father and an annuity purchased with the aid of Lord Shaftesbury.

The English "Glorious Revolution" of 1688 put the Crown under parliamentary control and provided more liberty. Locke returned to England in 1689 and published his *Essay Concerning Human Understanding* that he had been working on for 18 years.

Priestley adopted the epistemology of Locke, who opposed innate ideas by arguing that ideas reached the mind through sense experience and were converted into knowledge by reflection. In his essay Locke stated his thesis: "Let us ... suppose the mind to be, as we say, white paper void of all characters, without any ideas. How comes it to be furnished? ... To this I answer, in one word, from experience; in that all our knowledge is founded, and from that it ultimately derives itself. Our observation, employed either about external sensible objects, or about the internal operations of our minds perceived and reflected upon by ourselves, is that which supplies our understandings with all the materials of thinking. These two are the fountains of knowledge, from whence all the ideas we have, or can naturally have, do spring." [Locke 1977, 33]

Priestley summarized Locke's theory of knowledge: "The outlines of Mr. Locke's system are, that the mind perceives all things that are external to it by means of certain impressions, made upon the organs of sense; that those impressions are conveyed by the nerves to the brain, and from the brain to the mind, where they are called sensations, and when recollected, are called ideas; that by the attention which the mind, or sentient principle, gives to these sensations and ideas, observing their mutual relations, ... it acquires other ideas, which we call the ideas of reflection, and thereby becomes possessed of the materials of all its knowledge." [III, 26]

Priestley shared Locke's conviction that the true ground of morality "can only be the will and law of god" or the law of nature which is "not imprinted on our minds" but is "something that we ... may attain to the knowledge of, by the use and due application of our natural faculties." [Locke 1977, XV] For both, such application meant learning the moral laws revealed in the Bible.

Locke recognized the influence of circumstances when he wrote of the "shaping power of the environment;" a person might be irrational because of defective surroundings.

However, Priestley did not blindly accept Lock as an authority: some things in his theory about the mind "were not well founded; and I think he has been hasty in concluding that there is some other source of our ideas besides the external senses." [III, 27] He meant Locke's assumption that there was a soul to serve as a supplementary source of ideas. Priestley outraged many when he denied the existence of a spiritual soul.

Before Locke's death and 14 years after the publication of his *Essay Concerning Human Understanding,*the heads of houses at Oxford agreed that they would each "endeavor to prevent its being read in his College, without coming to any public censure." [XV 422] Priestley chose Locke's theory of knowledge that was shunned by the establishment in education.

Dr. Hartley took up the subject of the source of ideas where Locke left it, and followed in Locke's steps. Priestley at Daventry Academy had read Hartley's *Observations on Man,* of which he later wrote, "I can almost say, that I think myself more indebted to this one treatise, than to all the books I ever read beside, the Scripture excepted." [III, 10] Priestley and Hartley's brief correspondence ended with Hartley's death in 1757. Priestley thought an antidote to common sense, and a means "to establish the true science of human nature," was to republish part of Hartley's *Observations on Man.* [Rice 1969, 77]

David Hartley, the son of a Yorkshire clergyman, was almost 35 years Priestley's senior. At Cambridge Hartley intended to become a clergyman but "had scruples on the subject of eternal punishment" (which had also troubled young Priestley). [Willey 1977, 136] He was loath to subscribe to the Thirty Nine Articles, abandoned the clerical profession, and as a fellow turned to the study of medicine. He practiced in several towns, including London, and spent his last years in Bath.

To champion religion, Hartley tried to apply to mental phenomena the same kind of mechanical laws that Newton had applied to understanding the universe. Hartley explained: "By the mechanism of human actions, I mean that each action results from the previous circumstances of body and mind, in the same manner and with the same certainty, as other effects from their mechanical causes." He thought that by establishing such a mechanism he reconciled "the prescience of God with the free will of man." [Lindsey 1970, 33] Priestley accepted Hartley's psychology as an authority with reservations; Priestley did not accept the ideas of any of his sources, including the Bible, without modification. He explained: "Even Dr. Hartley, who ascribes so much to matter, and so little to any thing immaterial in man, ... yet supposes, that there is something intermediate between the soul and the gross body, which he distinguishes by the name of 'the infinitesimal elementary body.' But, great as is my admiration of Dr. Hartley, it is very far from carrying me to adopt every thing in him. His language, in this instance, conveys no clear ideas to my mind, and I consider both his 'intermediate body' and immaterial soul as an encumbrance upon his system, which, in every other respect, is most admirably simple." [III, 279]

Hartley's theory of the functioning of the mind,which explained how sense impressions became moral principles, was based on the "association of ideas," a concept he attributed to Locke. Pleasant associations reinforced an idea and unpleasant associations rejected an idea. Ideas or sensations were associated if they occurred simultaneously or contiguously.

"Our Passions and Affections [powerful emotions and feelings] can be no more than Aggregates of simple ideas united by Association," wrote Hartley, and out of such aggregations came the moral sense, which was not inborn but molded by circumstances. [Lindsey 1970, 34] Hartley and Priestley thought that the law of association of ideas scientifically explained the origin and synthesis of moral principles, just as Newton's law of gravity had explained the physical universe.

Priestley described how the association of ideas worked: "Till the mind has been affected with a sense of pleasure or pain, all objects are alike indifferent to it; but some, in consequence of being always accompanied with a perception of pleasure, become pleasing to us, while others, in consequence of being accompanied with a sense of pain, become displeasing; and to effect this, nothing can be requisite but the association of agreeable sensations and ideas with the one, and of disagreeable ones with the other." The association of pleasure or pain with particular experiences was "all that is requisite to the formation of all our passions or affections, or of some things being objects of love, and others of hatred to us." [III, 477] The examples Priestley gave were that a dog once burned avoided fire, or a child withdrew its hand from the pain of a candle flame but reached for things that it associated with pleasure. [III, 19]

Hartley and Priestley were among Englishmen who applied their "scientific ardor" to theological problems, confident that they were reinforcing Christianity. While in eighteenth century France most of the enlightened philosophers were unbelievers in Christianity, in England scientists such as Newton, Boyle, Locke, Hartley, and Priestley were ardent believers: "That peculiarly English phenomenon, the holy alliance between science and religion, persisted (in spite of Hume) till near the close of the century." [Willey 1977, 136] However, Priestley as the only scientist whose primary vocation was the Christian ministry, became the scapegoat of orthodox persecution.

Priestley also had misgivings about Hartley's hypothesis of "vibrations," which assumed that a subtle and elastic fluid called "ether" filled hollow nerves and transmitted the vibrations of light and sound to the brain: "no tolerable hypothesis [had] been advanced concerning the manner in which the brain is affected by this motion of the nervous fluid." [III, 175]

He dismissed not only the then generally accepted hypothesis of the existence of ether but also the hypothesis that electricity was a fluid, which was assumed by Franklin. He described in a letter, but never published, his ingenuous experiments that "make me inclined to think, there is no electric fluid at all, and that electrification is only some modification of the matter of which any body consisted before that operation." [Schofield 1966, 58] He rejected unverified hypotheses in science as he did in religion.

Priestley was years ahead of his generation in adopting Hartley's physical psychology, which he lifted from obscurity. He said that "the most important application of Dr. Hartley's doctrine of the association of ideas is to the conduct of human life, and especially the business of education." [III, 6] He proposed to make the application: "I have made many observations on human nature, with a view to the illustration of Hartley's theory. They related very much to the conduct of the mind and happiness, and they are so necessarily intermixed with observations on education, that I think it will be best to publish them altogether as one work, and consequently not very soon." [I-i, 274] His file of observations in shorthand was totally destroyed 16 years later in the riot.

Priestley believed that a shared epistemology was a precondition of constructive discussion. Then as now, few shared his theory of knowledge in religion, though many did in science. That explains why his contributions to science are still celebrated, while his contributions to religion are generally ignored. He thought that understanding and agreement were facilitated when discussants had information, rules of reasoning and grounds of verification in common. He complained of an opponent that he was "destitute of some common principles, without which it is impossible to come to any conclusion with respect to the question in debate." [XX, 252]

Knowledge, or information, was essential to sound reasoning, wrote Priestley: "A mind destitute of knowledge ... is like a field on which no culture has been bestowed, which, the richer it is, the ranker weeds it will produce. If nothing good be sown in it, it will be occupied by plants that are useless or noxious." [II, xv]

Priestley adopted Newton's rules of reasoning: "The first of these rules, as laid down by Sir Isaac Newton, is, that we are to admit no more causes of things than are sufficient to explain appearances; and the second is, that to the same effects we must, as far as possible, assign the same causes." Priestley charged that in the scientific research of nature we have observed Newton's rules, but we "have formed our notions, with respect to the most general and comprehensive [religious] principles of human knowledge, without the least regard, nay, in direct contradiction to them." [III, 221] Priestley believed that the same rules of reasoning obtained in all fields of inquiry. He reasoned that as Newton discovered the composition of white light, not by thinking about it, but by experimenting with a prism, so the composition of general principles should be discovered, not by "mental reflections," but by analyzing the origin of complex ideas from sense experience. [III, 189]

Priestley's empirical epistemology based on facts led him to mistrust a priori (before the facts) reasoning by logical deduction from unsupported hypotheses, which was mere speculation. He thought that a posteriori (after the facts) reason, arriving at conclusions by induction from facts, provided the only positive evidence for truth in science or religion: "The proper proof ... of universal propositions, such as ... that milk is white, that gold is yellow, or that a certain degree of cold will freeze water, consists in what is called an induction of particular facts, of precisely the same nature. Having found, by much and various experience, that the same events never fail to take place in the same circumstances, the expectation of the same consequences from the same previous circumstances is necessarily generated in our minds...." [III, 16] He generalized: "Particular facts are first discovered, and general propositions, or principles, are formed from them." [III, 77]

Once truths are established by induction from facts, Priestley wrote, the probable truths about other phenomena of similar circumstances can be established by analogy: "Thus if we found the milk of all animals with which we are acquainted to be nourishing, though the nature of those animals be considerably different, we think it probable that the milk of any strange animal will be nourishing." [III, 16]

Priestley was criticized by his contemporaries because his analogical reasoning concluded with "probabilities," not the syllogistically "necessary conclusions" of formal logic. He thought certainty unobtainable. For instance, he hoped that his letter in response to an inquiry about baptism would be satisfying, adding "but, in this imperfect state, we are not to expect a perfect solution of all our doubts and difficulties. We must be content with as much light as is sufficient to guide our conduct, and, in lesser things, we must often be determined by probabilities only, certainty not being to be had." [I-i 119] In lieu of absolute certainty, he called for "moral certainty which is only a great probability." [IV, 177]

Perceiving analogies is a work of the imagination, which contributed to Priestley's genius. His contemporary William Henry, M.D.,wrote after Priestley's death of the "intellectual powers" that accounted for Priestley's numerous scientific discoveries: "If we examine, with which of its various faculties the mind of Dr. Priestley was most eminently gifted, it will, I believe, be found that it was most remarkable for clearness and quickness of apprehension, and for rapidity and extent of association. On these qualities were founded that apparently intuitive perception of analogies, and that happy facility of tracing and pursuing them through all their consequences, which led to several of his most brilliant discoveries." [Henry 1831, 63] The same qualities account for his original non-scientific perceptions.

On the other hand, Henry noted the limitation of Priestley's intellectual achievements in formulating general laws or in using hypotheses to guide his research: "Quick as his mind was in the perception of resemblances, it appears (probably for that reason,) to have been little adapted for those profound and cautious abstractions, which supply the only solid foundations of general laws. In sober, patient, and successful induction, Priestley must yield the palm to many others, who, though far less fertile than himself in new and happy combinations of thought, surpassed him in the use of a searching and rigorous logic; in the art of advancing, by secure steps, from phenomena to general conclusions; and again in the employment of general axioms as the instruments of further discoveries." [Henry 1831, 65]

Still, Priestley was singularly free from the predispositions that block insights of new possibilities, as Henry explained: "This security he owed to his freedom from all undue attachment to hypotheses, and to the facility with which he was accustomed to frame and abandon them--a facility resulting not from habit only, but from principle. 'Hypotheses,' he pronounces in one place, 'to be a cheap commodity'; in another to be 'of no value except as the parents of facts'...." [Henry 1831, 67]

The low value Priestley ascribed to hypotheses, except to suggest experiments, was a consequence of his dedication to observation instead of speculation. He followed Newton who had written: "I frame no hypotheses; for whatever is not deduced from the phenomena is to be called an hypothesis; and hypotheses, whether metaphysical or physical, ... have no place in experimental philosophy. In this philosophy particular propositions are inferred from the phenomena, and afterwards rendered general by induction." [Boorstin 1983, 407]

Priestley defended his failure to relate the facts to some general theory in his *History of Electricity*: "When the facts are before the public, others are as capable of showing that connection, and of deducing a general theory from them as myself. Every fact has a real, though unseen connection with every other fact: and when all the facts belonging to any branch of science are collected the system will form itself. In the meantime, our guessing at the system may be some guide to us in the discovery of facts; but at present, ... let us mutually communicate every new fact we discover, without troubling ourselves about the system to which it may be reduced." [McEvoy 1979, 24]

Significant new observations often occur by chance, but may be obscured by prejudice, Priestley had learned. In the preface to his second volume on *Experiments and Observations on Different Kinds of Air*, Priestley described the effects of chance and prejudice on his discoveries: "More is owing to what we call chance, that is, ... to the observation of events arising from unknown causes, than to any proper design, or preconceived theory in this business. ... I will frankly acknowledge, that at the commencement of the experiments recited in this section, I was so far from having formed any hypothesis that led to the discoveries I made in pursuing them, that they would have appeared very improbable to me had I been told of them; and when the decisive facts did at length obtrude themselves upon my notice, it was very slowly, and with great hesitation, that I yielded to the evidence of my senses. And yet, when I re-consider the matter, and compare my last discoveries relating to the constitution of the atmosphere with the first, I see close connection between them, so as to wonder that I should not have been led immediately from one to the other. That this was not the case, I attribute to the force of prejudice, which, unknown to ourselves, biases not only our judgment, ... but even the perceptions of our senses; for we may take a maxim so strongly for granted, that the plainest evidence of sense will not entirely change, and often hardly modify, our persuasions...." [Holt 1931, 101]

An example of chance and prejudice in Priestley's experimenting was his 1771 chance discovery of an element, which he did not realize was new until 1774. With a large "burning glass" he focused the sun's rays on mercuric oxide and again obtained the same gas, which he called "dephlogisticated air," and which Lavoisier named "oxygen" when he heard about it.

Priestley's fundamental theological assumption was that the universe was an interrelated system as infinite as the Creator, and that finite human reason could never understand it all. But free inquiry was essential to increasing knowledge of the universe.

Inquiry was an activity of individual minds, not of authoritative groups: "For whenever numbers have truth or knowledge for their object, and act as a collective body, that is, authoritatively, so that no single person can have power to determine any thing till the majority have been brought to agree to it, the interest of knowledge will certainly suffer." (XXII, 47] He recognized group dynamics to the extent that an individual can consult with others in order to collect facts and ideas, but society should not be made an umpire of truth, "so that no opinion would be admitted without authoritative decision." [XXII, 477] Priestley concluded that "no man ought to surrender his own judgment to any mere authority however respectable." [Schofield 1966, 289]

Priestley was a "nominalist" in the 14th century tradition of William of Occam's opposition to Platonic idealism--words were abstract symbols of real things, not absolutes. Priestley wrote, "I shall never quarrel with any man for the mere use of terms, since they are, in their own nature, nothing more than arbitrary signs of ideas." [III, 71] He was concerned with the meaning of words, not the words themselves--he was semantic before that linguistic science was developed. He was also existential-- existence preceded essence or being preceded ideas--before that assumption was developed into a philosophy a century later.

Priestley was aware of his progressive penchant for changing his mind: "I have always shown the greatest readiness to abandon any hypothesis that I have advanced, and even defended while I thought it defensible, the moment I suspected it to be ill founded, whether the new facts that have refuted it were discovered by myself or others. My friends in general have blamed me for my extreme facility in this respect; and if I may judge of myself, I am just the same with respect to theology." [XVIII, 43]

His advanced epistemology led Priestley to develop a psychology and cosmology based on materialism, which outraged orthodox clergy and disturbed his Dissenter friends. In his criticism of common sense, Priestley wrote that "judging by the most obvious facts, and universal experience, nothing is more evident, than that the principle which we call 'mind,' whether it be material or immaterial, is of such a nature, that it can be affected by external objects, and that its perceptions correspond to the state of the corporeal system, especially that of the brain. ... If a due attention to these facts obliges us to alter our notions of mind and materialism, the received rules of philosophizing compel us to do it." [III, 254] He did.

VII

"NO SOUL PRIESTLEY"
"No better than an atheist"

When Priestley entered college to train for the ministry, he accepted the philosophic-idealism assumption that mind was a function of an immortal soul, which was challenged by his reading of David Hartley. He later changed his theory of the mind and, to further counter the common sense philosophy, he reprinted the section on "The Theory of the Human Mind" from *Observations on Man* by Dr. Hartley. In the preface to the reprint, Priestley casually expressed some doubt about Hartley's assumption that there was an intermediate soul that transmitted sense perceptions between the body and brain, and said that he thought man was composed of one substance; mental activities were the result of the organic structure of the brain, composed exclusively of matter. This was his most radical and disturbing proposal; it obviated Christian faith in the spiritual soul, which was the agent of the absolute free-will, and of immediate personal-immortality at death.

In his memoirs, Priestley recalled the furor in newspapers and magazines raised by his denial of the soul as the sentient principle in human beings that could survive death: "The outcry that was made on what I casually expressed on that subject can hardly be imagined. ... I was represented as an unbeliever in revelation, and no better than an atheist. This led me to give the closest attention to the subject, and the consequence was the firmest persuasion that man is wholly material.... I therefore digested my thoughts on the subject, and published my *Disquisitions Relating to Matter and Spirit*. ..." two years later.

The work contributed to a better understanding of human nature and matter about a century before Charles Darwin established the theory of evolution, Albert Einstein proposed the 2 theory E=MC, and Niels Bohr and Werner Heisenberg developed particle physics.

Priestley ignored warnings that exposing his opinions on the subject might reflect odium on his patron: "But being, as I thought, engaged in the cause of important truth, I proceeded without regard to any consequences, assuring them that this publication should not be injurious to his lordship." [I-i, 203]

It was injurious to his relation with his employer. Priestley noticed that thereafter Lord Shelburne showed "evident marks of dissatisfaction," and three years later they parted company, though Shelburne said he found no fault with Priestley's conduct and later invited Priestley to return to his service. Shelburne, a widower when Priestley entered his service, remarried shortly before their separation, which some Priestley biographers speculate was a contributing cause. Shelburne continued to send Priestley's agreed-upon annuity until shortly before Priestley's death in America.

Priestley's Unitarian colleague Richard Price, an intimate of Lord Shelburne, had recommended Priestley as librarian and literary companion to Shelburne, who knew Priestley's reputation as a scientist. Price had previously refused the same position. Though Priestley was happy in his ministry at Leeds, where his sons Joseph and William were born, he lamented that "it affords me no prospect of making any provisions for a growing family." The much better salary plus housing and a guaranteed lifetime income for himself, or for his family in case of his termination or death, tempted him to accept Shelburne's invitation.

In weighing the pros and cons, he wrote to Price: "I am so habituated to domestic life, and am so happy at home, that it is not possible I should receive any compensation for not living in my own family." [I-i,176] But later, again to Price, he wrote, "I cannot help thinking that it will put me in the way of being more useful to my family and the world than I can be in my present situation." [I-i, 185] He thought,"I do not see that I am doing more good here than another will do after me; probably less, on account of the odium of my sentiments." [I-i, 178] He had already learned, from Benjamin Franklin's inquiry to Professor John Winthrop at Harvard about a possible college position for Priestley, that "his unorthodox religious views would limit his acceptability in any American college." [Lesser 1974, 211]) He accepted Shelburne's invitation.

The position did separate him from his family for long periods: "In this situation, my family being [in a home provided] at Calne, in Wiltshire, near his lordship's seat at Bowood, I continued seven years, spending the summer with my family, and a great part of the winter in his lordship's house in London." [I-i, 197] In that period, Priestley's youngest son was born and named Henry at Shelburne's request--after his own eldest son; Priestley's father went bankrupt and then died; his wife and married daughter visited for a year in Leeds; and during his last few months in London, he was gravely ill with gall stones. While with Shelburne, explained Priestley, "I was careful not to publish any political pamphlet or paragraph whatever, lest it should be thought that I did it at his instigation, whereas politics was expressly excluded from our connection." [XXV, 396]

Lord Shelburne, three years younger than Priestley, was born William Fitzmaurice in Dublin of a wealthy, land-owning family. He was educated at Oxford and, after a distinguished career in the British army, he succeeded his father as Earl of Shelburne. He became a Whig member of the House of Commons and supported the American Colonies, the Dissenters plea for liberty from restrictions, the French Revolution, and free trade. He collected rare manuscripts and books, old masters and contemporary paintings-- to encourage the artists, all of which Priestley catalogued. In 1782, Shelburne was appointed Prime Minister in a minority government that lasted long enough for him to negotiate (with his friend Benjamin Franklin and others) the Treaty of Paris that in 1783, on favorable terms, recognized the independence of the United States.

When Priestley toured the Continent with Shelburne, where Priestley was already well known as a scientist, in Paris he related his procedure to procure "dephlogisticated air," which he had discovered a few months earlier, to Antoine Lavoisier and other noted chemists. Lavoisier repeated the experiment, named the new gas "oxygen," and with it developed a new branch of chemistry that was generally accepted. But not by Priestley, who was more interested in relations and sequences of mixing the ingredients of an experiment than in Lavoisier's quantification of the ingredients. Priestley spent the rest of his life defending the old phlogiston theory.

The years with Shelburne were "the most fruitful period of Priestley's scientific career" -- plus publishing at least 17 first editions on religion, education, and metaphysics. [Schofield 1966, 138] Priestley recalled: "When I went to his lordship, I had materials for one volume of *Experiments and Observations on Different Kinds of Air* [gases], which I soon after published, and inscribed to him; and before I left him, I published three volumes more, and had materials for a fourth, which I published immediately on my settling in Birmingham. He encouraged me in the prosecution of my philosophical inquiries, and allowed me forty pounds per annum for expenses of that kind, and was pleased to see me make experiments to entertain his guests, and especially foreigners." [I-i, 201] Shelburne also provided laboratories at both his Bowood and London homes for Priestley.

An evaluation of Priestley's scientific achievements was given 27 years after his death by William Henry, a physician and fellow of the Royal Society. Of Priestley's primitive laboratory equipment, Henry wrote, "All his contrivances for collecting, transferring, and preserving different kinds of air ... were exceedingly simple, beautiful, and effectual."

Of Priestley's candid accounts of his experiments, Henry wrote: "He unveils with perfect frankness, the whole process of his reasoning, which led to his discoveries; he pretends to no more sagacity than belonged to him, and sometimes disclaims even that to which he is fairly entitled; he freely acknowledges his mistakes, and candidly confesses when his success was the result of accident, rather than judicious anticipation, and by writing historically and analytically, he exhibits the progressive improvement of his views, from their first dawnings, to their final and distinct development." Henry wrote that Priestley was not competitive with other scientists: "Free from all little jealousies of contemporaries or rivals, he earnestly invited other laborers into the field which he was cultivating; gave publicity in his own volumes to their experiments; and, with true candor, was as ready to record the evidence which contradicted, as that which confirmed, his own views and results. Every hint, which he had derived from the writings or conversations of others, were unreservedly acknowledged."

Henry concluded, "...it would be difficult to produce an instance of a writer more eminent for the variety and versatility of his talents, or more meritorious for their zealous, unwearied, and productive employment." [Henry 1831]

While Priestley was earning that accolade in his laboratory, he was also engaged in controversial psychological and cosmological speculation. The controversy about matter and spirit is still tacit in philosophical and theological speculation.

Priestley's conclusion that all organisms, including the brain, were composed of matter was called "materialism," which in this context means, not that physical well-being and material posses-sions are the greatest good in life, but that matter with its energy is the only reality, and that everything in the universe, including mind, thought and feeling, can be explained in terms of physical substan-ces organized according to natural laws ordained by the Creator. There was no evidence, said Priestley, of the existence of a spiritual soul that pre-exists birth, and persists after death.

But he did not share the late 18th century notion that "materialism" meant that human beings were analogous to mechanisms, without freedom of action. Though he did occasionally use the word "machines," according to Priestley human beings were not machines, but self-determining organic structures.

Nor did he reduce thought to a function of particles of matter: it was the "system" that functioned as the mind. He wrote: "A certain quantity of nervous system is necessary to such complex ideas and affections as belong to the human mind; and the idea of self, or the feeling that corresponds to the pronoun 'I' ... is not essentially different from other complex ideas, that of our country, for instance. ... [It is] a part of the world subject to that form of government, by the laws of which we ourselves are bound, as distinguished from other countries, ... the term self denotes that substance which is the seat of that particular set of sensations and ideas...." [III, 284] The self was not a separate entity; it was the complex of body and mind.

In his *Disquisitions on Matter and Spirit* Priestley defined the issue: "It has generally been supposed that there are two distinct kinds of substances in human nature, and they are distinguished by the terms matter and spirit. ... Matter is that kind of substance of which our bodies are composed, whereas the principle of perception and thought belonging to us is said to reside in a spirit, an immaterial principle, intimately united to the body; while the higher orders of intelligent beings, and especially the Divine Being, are said to be purely immaterial." [III, 218]

The basis of the "immaterial" concept was the Newtonian as-sumption that matter was solid, impenetrable, and inert; having no inherent energy, it was inconceivable that matter could be organized to function as the mind. According to Newton, matter consisted of solid atoms, held together or kept apart by attractive and repelling powers transmitted by "aether." The human capacity for thought was then popularly ascribed to a separate entity, the spirit or soul.

Priestley wrote: "Spirit has of late been defined to be a substance entirely destitute of ... relation to space, so as to have no property in common with matter; and therefore to be properly immaterial, but to be possessed of the powers of perception, intelligence, and self-motion." He countered: "It is maintained, in this treatise, that the notion of two substances that have no common property, and yet are capable of intimate connection and mutual action, is both absurd and modern.... [i.e., not Biblical]." [III, 219]

Priestley had precedents for his rejection of the concept of spirit. He recommended the study by his contemporary, the Bishop of Carlisle, of "the use of the Words Soul, or Spirit, in Holy Scriptures." The Bishop had concluded that "neither these words nor any other stand for a purely immaterial principle in man, or a substance wholly separable from, and independent of body," and that immortality came only at the resurrection of the dead. In support of his findings, the Bishop quoted his friend Dr. Taylor: "We can never prove, that the soul of man is of such a nature, that it can .... live, think, act, enjoy, ... separate from, and independent of, the body. All our present experience shows the contrary. The operations of the mind depend, constantly and invariably, upon the state of the body; of the brain in particular." The Bishop also quoted from earlier authorities: Mr. Layton, in "Search for Souls" (1702), had written "that the human soul's separate subsistence is a fiction, such as hath not a real being in the nature of things." And Dr. Coward had written in his "Second Thoughts concerning Human Soul" (1702) that "the notion of a spiritual, immortal substance in man is erroneous; and ... man's immortality begins not until the resurrection." [II, 258 note]

For advancing such heretical ideas, Priestley was caricatured and denounced--while the Bishop was not. But Priestley was the first avowed Christian to claim that matter rather than the soul was the seat of cognition. [Rice 1969, 108] He was not content with denials of the soul; he proposed a theory of how the Creator had endowed the material brain, without a soul, with ability to function as mind.

He had changed his mind. He wrote: "Like the generality of Christians in the present age, I had always taken it for granted, that man had a soul distinct from his body, ... and I believed this soul to be a substance so entirely distinct from matter, as to have no property in common with it." [III. 201]

Before he obviated the soul in favor of a physical mind, in his critique of Scottish idealism he had opposed the assumption that the soul by intuition had direct knowledge of moral and religious eternal truths. Now he denied that the Holy Spirit, since it did not share a common substance with matter, was the Divine agency for creating and sustaining the universe, and that the soul was the animating principle that gave life to the body at birth and departed at death. Such ideas, claimed Priestley, were corruptions of Christianity from Platonism. Instead, he pointed out that in the Genesis account of creation, the animating principle was breath: "And the Lord God formed man of the dust of the ground, and breathed into his nostrils the breath of life, and man became a living soul." [The Revised Standard Version of Genesis 2:7 ends "... became a living being."]

He argued that it was more conceivable a material substance could be organized to think than that a spiritual substance could. He reiterated that the powers of sensation, perception, and thought "have never been found but in conjunction with a certain organized system of matter," nor was there any instance of a person retaining a capacity for thought when the body and brain were dead. He came to the reasonable conclusion that "the seat of the sentient principle in man,was the material substance of the brain." [III, 242]

He commented: "I am rather inclined to think that, though the subject is beyond our comprehension at present, man does not consist of two principles so essentially different from one another as matter and spirit.... I rather think that the whole man is some uniform composition, and that the property of perception, as well as the other powers termed mental, is the result ... of such an organical structure as that of the brain. Consequently, that the whole man becomes extinct at death, and that we have no hope of surviving the grave but what is derived from the scheme of revelation [resurrection of the body]." [III,181]

To account for the capacity of a corporeal substance to be organized for thinking, Priestley "spiritualized" matter. [Schofield 1978, 351] He resolved the problem posed by the assumption that matter was solid and inert, and hence incapable of thought, by claiming that matter was energized so it could be organized to perform the mental functions of the brain.

He wrote of his critics: "... by whatever name they may choose to call the substances, is of no consequence. If they say that, on my hypothesis, there is no such thing as matter, and that every thing is spirit, I have no objection.... The world has been too long amused with mere names." [III, 236] However, in order not to mislead his readers, Priestley frankly chose to say "that man is wholly material, rather than wholly spiritual, though both terms were within my option." [IV, 142]

To defend materialism, as a distinguished scientist and theologian Priestley pursued the dialectics of conflicting opinions to a paradoxical theological position, in the process integrated science and theology, and proposed psychological and cosmological concepts that were progressive for his time.

Priestley derived the physical hypothesis for his transformation of matter from *Theoria Philosophia Naturalis* written in opposition to the solid atom hypothesis by Joseph Roger Boscovich, a Croatian Jesuit mathematician, astronomer, professor, fellow of the Royal Society in London, and director of optics for "the marine in Paris." In a letter to Boscovich, Priestley reminded him that they had "many agreeable conversations ... at Paris, in which I frequently expressed a high approbation of your work." [Schofield 1966, 167]

Boscovich had accepted Newton's theory of gravity and applied it to the substance of matter, which Newton said was composed of solid atoms held together or kept apart by attractive and repelling powers. Boscovich rarefied atoms. In contrast to Newton's solid atoms, Boscovich speculated that matter consisted of geometrical points (not substantial) surrounded by concentric spheres of repulsive and attractive forces, and sensible bodies consisted of complex structures of such points. The apparent solidity of atoms resulted from the negative and positive action of the forces, just as the planets were held in their courses by gravity, or the poles of a magnet attracted or repelled.

Based on his own observations in his scientific experiments, as well as the speculations of others, Priestley elaborated and applied Boscovich's theory. "Boscovich seems to suppose that matter consists of power only, without any substance," Priestley commented, and added, "Mr. Michell supposes that wherever the properties or powers of a substance are, there is the substance itself, something that we call substance being necessary to the support of properties...." [Schofield 1966, 117]

John Michell was an Anglican clergyman, a fellow of the Royal Society, and Priestley's neighbor in Leeds who collaborated with Priestley in his book on vision. Michell had demonstrated that light had mass, which intrigued Priestley, and invented a way to manufacture magnets.

In his *Disquisition*, Priestley had reflected Boscovich's theory by writing, "Matter has in fact no properties but those of attraction and repulsion." His friend and critic Richard Price opened a dialogue by objecting that matter could not be solely energy: "Matter, if it be anything at all, must consist of solid particles or atoms occupying a certain portion of space, ... and it must be the different form of these primary particles and their different combinations and arrangement that constitute the different bodies and kinds of matter in the universe. -- This seems to have been Sir Isaac Newton's idea of matter." [IV, 21] Priestley agreed and revised his definition, writing that "The complete definition is evidently this, viz. that matter is an extended substance [occupying space], possessed of certain powers of attraction and repulsion." [IV, 23]

Priestley speculated that particles of matter were so infinitesimal "that for anything we know to the contrary, all the solid matter in the solar system might be contained within a nutshell, there is such a great proportion of void space within the substance of most solid bodies." [III, 230]

The proof that matter was not solid, said Priestley, was the expansion and contraction of metals with changes of temperature. [III, 27] This fact modified Price's assertion of Newton's theory that atoms are "uncompounded, and incapable of being resolved into smaller particles," and affirmed the compressibility of particles since they were held in solid form by powers of attraction and repulsion in a void.

Nor was matter "inert." It possessed powers of attraction and repulsion, as Boscovich claimed, which meant that matter had inherent energy that acted at a distance. The resistance of matter to compression, which made it appear solid, explained Priestley, resulted from "a power of repulsion." On the other hand, for matter to take form required "mutual attraction" of its elements; "This power of attraction, therefore, must be essential to the actual existence of all matter, since no substance can retain any form without it." [III, 223] Matter is thus inherently and continuously active, a dynamic equilibrium of forces, not Newton's conglomeration of inert atoms, and was not incompatible with being organized for thought and feeling.

Priestley acknowledged that in the state of information at that time--he did not have sufficient facts, he did not know the inner structure of matter. He was speculating, using his imagination and reasoning-by-analogy to arrive at a theory that was at least not inconsistent with the empirically known. [III, 240]

He also modified his theory of the source of energy. In the 1772 publication of his *Institutes*, he accepted the reigning theory that matter was constantly charged with energy by the Divine source, and wrote: "As the matter of which the world consists ... is altogether incapable of moving itself ... so all the powers of nature ... can only be the effect of the Divine energy, perpetually acting upon them, an energy without which the power of gravitation would cease, and the whole frame of the earth be dissolved." [II, 14]

Ten years later, in *Disquisitions*, his concept had changed: "Suppose ... that the Divine Being, when he created matter, only fixed certain centers of various attractions and repulsions, extending in all directions, and consequently carrying their peculiar spheres of attraction and repulsion with them, ... it cannot be denied that these spheres may be diversified infinitely, so as to correspond to all the kinds of bodies that we are acquainted with...." [III, 239] Then he made the bold suggestion of "every thing being the Divine power." [III, 240] Thus, the locus of all energy was in the universe, though originally endowed by the Creator. That's the theory prevailing today - that the universe has inherent energy.

Priestley became odious, not because of his physics, but because he applied his insights from physics to theology, which threatened the faith of many orthodox Anglicans or Dissenters. He integrated science and theology.

For instance, on heresy, his Catholic friend Boscovich who could not read English, was incensed at the implications and applications of his theory in physics that Priestley had made in his *Disquisitions*. Boscovich alleged in a letter to Priestley that a friend "assured me ... that ... you teach in your work pure and unconcealed materialism, ... that you claim to deduce this from my theory of matter, in this way making me a party to a doctrine that I detest and abhor as impiety in religion and senseless in sound philosophy." [Schofield 1966, 169]

Priestley responded, "I have only adopted your theory of the nature of matter, without supposing that you had the most distant idea of the use I have made of it." Then Priestley revealed the theological motivation that impelled his interest in the nature of matter: "As to my doctrine itself, it is the object of my work to prove it to be the only one that is consonant to the genuine system of revelation, and that the vulgar hypothesis [of soul] which I combat, has been the foundation of the grossest corruptions of true Christianity; and especially of the church of Rome, of which you are a member; but which I consider as properly antichristian, and a system of abominations little better than heathenism." [Schofield 1966, 167] Priestley developed this theme a few years later in Birmingham in *An History of the Corruptions of Christianity*, based on the scientific grounds of his materialism.

By eliminating the radical distinction between matter and spirit, Priestley had justified his surmise that "man does not consist of two principles so essentially different from one another as matter and spirit," and that there was no immortal soul as a separate substance. The conclusions Priestley drew were that the hope of a future life could not be based on the "heathen doctrine" of soul, and that the merely human Jesus could not have pre-existed with God as a specially created soul.

He anticipated that his materialism would "rather shock and offend many of my friends," but hoped any controversy would clarify what was true, and would convince his readers that the dualistic hypothesis, "when considered in connection with the facts, is no less revolting" than his monistic hypothesis. [III, 239] It did shock the orthodox who believed in the Trinity, and his Arian Unitarian friends who believed in the pre-existence of Christ as an immortal soul. He was publicly derided as "no soul Priestley," but was delighted with an epitaph by the Welsh poet David Davis:

Here lies at rest,
In oaken chest,
Together packed most neatly,
The bones and brains,
Flesh, blood and veins,
And soul of Dr. Priestley.

Richard Price, an intimate friend of Priestley, on reading his *Disquisitions* had challenged that materialism implied that God was material and led to atheism, which prompted a candid and friendly controversy published in 1778 as *A Free Discussion of the Doctrines of Materialism and Philosophical Necessity Between Dr. Price and Dr. Priestley*. Price had suggested the publication, but when he perused the work before publication he commented, "I am afraid the discussion it contains will be too dry and metaphysical to be generally acceptable."

Price may still be right but, since "spirit" and "spiritual" in our culture have become "buzz words," high-sounding but with little definition, this 18th century discussion is today of more than antiquarian interest. When we speak today of "the life of the spirit," are we referring to experience in another realm of being? Or, when we speak of "spiritual values," are we referring to esoteric values, or to shared values that are not consumed in the enjoyment of them, such as creative works of the mind--art, scientific discoveries, literature, poetry, music, and ethical principles that enrich all life?

Price and Priestley were clarifying their concepts of the nature of reality: Price maintained that there were two substances--matter and spirit--and that human beings were composed of both, while God was wholly spirit (dualism). Priestley maintained that there was only one substance, matter in all its permutations (monism).

Richard Price, ten years Priestley's senior and his colleague in the Unitarian Dissenter ministry, was born in Wales, the son of a Dissenter minister. After the death of both his parents when he was 16, he went to an academy in London under the patronage of his uncle, where he enjoyed studying mathematics, philosophy, and theology. After four years, he became assistant minister of a Dissenter meeting house in London. "His circumstances were considerably improved" by an inheritance on the death of his uncle; he married Sarah Blundell (they had no children), and moved to Newington-Green where he was chosen as minister of a Dissenter congregation. He was so discouraged by his small congregation that he thought he was "totally unfit for the office of a public speaker," but he was called as minister of the much larger Gravel-pit Meeting in Hackney in 1770, where he also taught in the Dissenter New College. His beloved wife died in 1786, and he died in 1791 of a "disorder in his bladder," after two months' illness. [XX, 495] Priestley was a pallbearer at his funeral, delivered the funeral sermon at the Gravel Pit Chapel, and a few months later, after the Birmingham Riot, succeeded Price in that prosperous pulpit.

Price contributed mathematical papers to the Royal Society, was elected a fellow, and later was one of the sponsors for Priestley's election to the Society. He was a member of the Whig Club in London and in 1776 published *Observations on the Nature of Civil Liberty, the Principles of Government, and the Justice and Policy of the War with America*, which rapidly went through many editions, including in the Colonies. He was hailed by the president of the National Assembly of France as "the apostle of liberty." The pamphlet provoked a storm of replies, including one by Edmund Burke, who opposed the war with the American colonies as inexpedient, but never denied the right of Parliament to tax the colonies. [Thomas 1924, 74] (Priestley's *The First Principles of Government* had been published eight years earlier than Price's *Observations on the Nature of Civil Liberty*.)

Price's actuarial tables, based on statistics (some supplied by Priestley) rather than speculation, made significant contributions to computing life insurance risks and premiums, which made the insurance and annuity business much more reliable by giving it a scientific method. The Equitable Society hired Price as consultant for many years; he rode into London almost daily on his white horse, and made the Equitable Society the first sound insurance company in the world. By request of the House of Commons, Price computed tables for a plan enabling the laboring poor to provide support for themselves in sickness and old age by weekly savings from their wages--a precursor of Social Security. The Commons approved the plan in 1789, but it was rejected by the Lords. [Thomas 1924, 59]

Priestley had been introduced to Price about 1761 on an early visit to London, and enjoyed "his particular friendship" on subsequent visits and when living there.

As an Arian, Price believed in the immortal soul and the pre-existence of Christ, and was distressed by Priestley's stance.

Price was "partial to Platonism" and learned Greek so he could study Plato in his own language. He shared all that is original and useful in the Scottish common sense philosophers, said Priestley. [III, 146] Price believed that intuition of self- evident truths of morality and of the existence of God, without reasoning or induction from facts, was all that was required for understanding truths "which are incapable of proof." [III, 149]

In Price's view, the soul was the agent for the intuition of eternal truths and he objected to Priestley's no-soul. Price spoke for many of his contemporaries in England and the later Transcendentalists in America when he wrote: "I must ... confess to Dr. Priestley, that I am in some degree rendered averse to his doctrine by my pride. I have been used to think of my soul as so real and substantial, as to be the very principle that gives reality to the sensible qualities of bodies, and consequently to the whole dress of the external world; as an essence of heavenly origin, incorporeal, uncompounded, self-determining, immortal, indestructible, ... possessed of faculties which (however the exercise of them may be subject to interruptions) make it an image of the Deity, and render it capable of acting by the same rule with him, or participating in his happiness, and of living for ever, and improving under his care. But if Dr. Priestley is right, my soul is literally the off-spring of the earth; a composition of dust; incapable of all agency; a piece of machinery moved by mechanical springs, and chained to the foot of fate; all whose powers of thought, imagination, reflection, volition, and reason, are no more than a result from the arrangement and play of a set of atoms, all unthinking and senseless. -- What can be more humiliating than this account?" [IV, 97] Other critics, particularly the orthodox, denigrated Priestley, but did not write with the candor, or clearly define their personal belief, as did Price.

Priestley redefined the soul as "that system of intelligence which we call the soul of man." [III, 283] The soul therefore was not a uniquely human attribute, since all animals had some intelligence. He wrote: "They differ from us only in kind, having all the same mental, as well as corporeal powers that we have, though not to the same extent...." [III, 252] He noted that the Hebrew word in the Bible translated "living soul" is also used to refer to all living creatures. He supported his argument with verses from Ecclesiastes 3:18: "For that which befalleth the sons of men befalleth all beasts.... As one dieth, so dieth the other. Yea they have all one breath. So that a man hath no pre-eminence over a beast.... All are of the dust, and all turn to dust again." [III, 312]

Human beings may not have "pre-eminence" over other living beings, but they do have an advantage, wrote Priestley: "The great superiority of man over brutes consists in the greater comprehensiveness of his mind, by means of which he is ... capable of reflection .... and, therefore, of enjoying the past and the future, as well as the present. And what is most extraordinary and interesting to us, this power, as far as appears, has no limits." [IV, 317] His belief in the infinite perfectibility of mankind was shared by Price, who wrote that there were not "any limits beyond which knowledge and improvement cannot be carried." [Thomas 1924, 110]

To Priestley, evil spirits were as incredible as good spirits; both were obviated by materialism: "The notion of madness being occasioned by evil spirits disordering the minds of men, though it was the belief of heathens, of the Jews in our Savior's time, and of the apostles themselves, is highly improbable; since all the facts may be accounted for in a much more natural way...." [VII, 309] He claimed Jesus was mistaken when he attributed the cure of madness to driving out evil spirits.

If there was no "spirit," how could God be a spirit? Earlier, he had believed that God was a spirit: "Since God is omnipresent without being the object of any of our senses, he comes under the description of what we call a spirit, or something that is immaterial." The power of God was manifest in the Holy Spirit.[VII, 332] And he believed that "God anointed Jesus of Nazareth with the Holy Spirit and with power." [XVI, 126]

Priestley was placed in a dilemma when he developed the theory that all being was composed of one substance, matter; was God also corporeal? His dilemma was compounded by his conviction that creation required a "first cause" possessed of an intelligence capable of design, a self-existent Creator. He changed his mind again. The inner logic of his physics led him to the verge of acknowledging that the Creator was of one substance with creation, or at least that God was "not immaterial."

Priestley believed that a spiritual God could not have created a material world; it was impossible "to conceive even the possibility of mutual action without some common property, by means of which the things that act and re-act upon each other may have some common connection." [III, 263]

Price challenged: "It seems evident that Dr. Priestley's principles go to prove, that the Deity is material, as well as all inferior beings. He would otherwise have no common property with matter, by which it would be possible for him to act upon it." [IV, 42]

Priestley responded that the material he meant, of which the creation and creator were made, had quite different properties from Newton's definition of matter--being dynamic rather than an inert solid--and ought to have a different name. [IV, 42] Price did not recognize that Priestley had "spiritualized" matter with inherent energy, and continued to insist "that the laws which govern matter, or its attractions and repulsions, are not the actions or properties of matter itself, but effects of the constant operation of a higher cause."

Price pushed Priestley's hypothesis that mind is a function of organized matter in the brain to the analogy that God is corporeal, an "atheistical conclusion" held by the French philosophers who "make nature the only Deity." Price wrote: "I am fully of opinion, that if that mass of flesh and blood we call the brain....may be that sentient and intelligent being we call the mind; then that mass of corporeal substance which we call the world, may be God; and it must be unphilosophical to search farther than itself for its cause. ... such indeed is the tendency of his principles and manner of reasoning." [IV, 51]

Priestley reaffirmed the necessity of a first cause by the watch-ergo-watchmaker analogy, later popularized by Reverend William Paley. Priestley insisted that "when we see the parts of which the universe consists, to be arranged in such a manner, as, from analogy, we have reason to believe, that no other than an intelligent being could arrange them, we conclude that an intelligent being, visible or invisible, has arranged them." [IV, 52]

He often quoted the English poet, Alexander Pope who in his 1732 poem *An Essay on Man* had written:

All are parts of one stupendous whole
Whose body Nature is, and God the soul....

But emotionally, Priestley could not accept Pope's hypothesis that God was the soul of nature. From his boyhood conditioning as a Calvinist, he was an ardent Christian who believed in a sovereign, intelligent Creator independent of nature--though he never used the word "supernatural." He referred to God as "Father," "Creator," "author," "ultimate authority," "Divine Being," "Supreme Being," but never as a supernatural being. He was a reformer, not a skeptic, and could not accept the idea of a self-created world proposed by unbelievers in special revelation.

He speculated: "Supposing ... that intelligence could result from the present arrangement of such bodies as the sun, the earth, and the other plants, etc. (which, however, is so unlike the uniform composition of a brain, that the argument from analogy entirely falls) so that all that is intellectual in the universe should be the necessary result of what is not intellectual in it, and, consequently, there should be what has sometimes been called a 'soul of the universe', the hypothesis is, in fact, that of a deity, though we ourselves should enter into the composition of it, and there would be a real foundation for religion. But our imagination revolts at the idea, and we are compelled, as the easiest solution of the phenomena, to acquiesce in the belief of an intelligent uncaused Being, entirely distinct from the universe of which he is the author." [IV, 336] Priestley's Christian faith could not accept the ultimate logical implications of his monistic materialism.

With characteristic frankness, he reviewed alternate hypotheses with which he disagreed. He quoted from what he called "the bible of atheism," *The System of Nature* published anonymously in France in 1770: "If we ask whence came matter, we say it existed always. If we be asked whence came motion in matter, we answer that, for the same reason, it must have been in motion from all eternity....These elements ... being continually in action on one another, always acting and reacting, always combining and separating, attracting and repelling, are sufficient to explain the formation of all the beings that we see. ... To go higher, for the principle of action in matter, and the origin of things, is only removing the difficulty, and wholly withdrawing it from the examination of our senses...." Priestley countered that he was "unable to account for what is visible without having recourse to a power that is invisible...." [IV, 383]

David Hume, whose heresy precluded appointment to professorships in Scottish universities, denied the necessity of an intelligent first cause: "How shall we satisfy ourselves concerning the cause of that Being whom you suppose the author of nature. If we stop and go no farther, why go so far? Why not stop at the material world? How can we satisfy ourselves without going on 'in infinitum'? -- By supposing it to contain the principle of its order within itself, we really assert it to be God, and the sooner we arrive at that Divine Being, so much the better." To suppose that motion comes from an external source, he said, "is mere hypothesis, and hypothesis attended with no advantages." Priestley again asserted that motion must have come "from a superior and intelligent being ..." [IV, 369]

Hume proposed an organic analogy for creation by suggesting: "If the universe bears a greater likeness to animal bodies and vegetables, than to the works of human art, it is more probable that its cause resembles the cause of the former than that of the latter: and its origin ought rather to be ascribed to generation or vegetation, than to reason or design." [IV, 372] He argued: "does not a plant or an animal ... bear a stronger resemblance to the world, than does any artificial machine, which arises from reason and design?" [IV, 374] With an implicit anthropomorphism, Priestley protested that living organisms had no design or purpose in their reproduction, while the Creator by analogy with human creators must have a design for his productions.

Another contemporary of Priestley, the declared atheist William Hammon, published a pamphlet opposing Priestley's theology. Hammon wrote: "The perpetual industry, intelligence and provision of nature, must be apparent to all who see, feel or think. I mean to distinguish this active, intelligent and designing principle, inherent as much in matter as the properties of gravity, or any elastic, attractive or repulsive power, from any extraneous force and design, in an invisible agent.... my theory makes a God of this universe, or admits of no other God, or designing principle than matter itself, and its various organizations." [IV, 413] Priestley recoiled from such an atheistic conclusion, which Price had claimed was implied by Priestley's own materialism.

Price did not understand the emerging systems-theory in Priestley's materialism. Price charged that Priestley's claim that he was himself "an organized system of matter" implied, since each atom was a distinct substance, that he was composed of a system of beings, each capable of thought. [IV, 59]

Priestley did not reduce thought to a function of individual atoms; thought was a function of the organization or system of particles. Consciousness and thought, he said, "judging from appearances, which alone ought to determine the judgment of philosophers," was a function of "an organized system, which requires a considerable mass of matter." [III, 285]

From Priestley's work in chemistry, he knew the synergistic effect of organization: "I find no difficulty in conceiving that compound substances may have properties which their component parts cannot have." [IV, 64] He explained: "It is well known that chemical compounds have powers and properties which we could not have deduced from those of their component parts, or their new arrangement; as the power of 'aqua regia' to dissolve gold, when neither the spirit of nitre, nor the spirit of salt, of which it is composed, will do it." [IV, 100] He asked rhetorically, "Has not the whole ... a property, or power, which does not, in the least degree, belong to any of its parts." The emergent power of chemical compounds was analogous to the new capacities for thinking and feeling of the "organized system" of human beings when "the breath of life was imparted." [IV, 101]

To Priestley, the universe was organic: "the connection that all persons, and all things, necessarily have, as parts of an immense, glorious and happy system (and of which we ourselves are a part, however small and inconsiderable), with the great Author of this system, makes us regard every person, and every thing, in a friendly and pleasing light." [III, 508] The unity of the universe as "one connected system," he thought, supported the concept of one God; a Trinity of creators was incongruous. [VI, 46] Though he could not identify the Creator with the Creation, Priestley did deny that the Creator was a spiritual substance: "I think I may conclude ... that our modern metaphysical notions concerning the strict immateriality of the Divine Being were certainly not drawn from the Scriptures." [III, 322] He added: "And though ... we are utterly confounded when we attempt to form a conception of a [creative] being properly pervading and supporting all things, we are still more confounded when we endeavor to conceive of a being with no extension, no common property with matter, and no relation to space." [III, 323] Only a Creator of the same substance could create a material universe.

He never resolved that paradox.

Priestley's materialistic interpretation of human and cosmic nature did not become the trend of the future. Instead, "romantic idealism" prevailed in Unitarianism--in England through the influence of James Martineau, and in America through the influence of Channing and Emerson.

But materialism, in Priestley's sense, continued to be the ground of empirical science. And materialism was affirmed by Thomas Jefferson in an 1820 letter to John Adams: "I can conceive thought to be an action of a particular organization of matter formed for that purpose by the Creator, as well as that attraction is an action of matter, or magnetism of a loadstone." [Boorstin 1963, 115] Jefferson was delighted with Priestley's scientific demolition of "spiritualism." To Jefferson, "the only realm of being was the realm of tangible things ... the nature of the creator could be adequately sensed through the visible universe. Materialism was involved in all his principal beliefs about man." [Boorstin 1963, 118]

Benjamin Rush, a Philadelphia physician who admired Priestley and attended him during his critical illness, and who was a signatory of the Declaration of Independence, also was a materialist. In his *Inquiry Into the Cause of Animal Life*, Rush claimed that what God breathed into Adam at creation was not a soul but air; he had witnessed the process at the birth of many infants, when breath brought them to life.

Price, in his discussion with Priestley, was not only defending a spiritual creator; he cherished the spiritual soul as the autonomous agent of free will, and asserted that Priestley's materialism implied a mechanistic determinism that deprived human beings of initiative and responsibility. Priestley published *The Doctrine of Philosophical Necessity Illustrated*, including Dr. Price's views on the subject of free will. As a youth, Priestley had defended absolute freedom of the will against a "necessitarian"--the will acted by necessity. Priestley revised his opinion on reading Hartley in college and became a necessitarian, believing that each choice was a necessary consequence of dominant motives in the mind from a person's circumstances, experiences, education, and information. But it was the person's own motives and the choice was self- determined, if free from external control. He reasoned that since man was wholly material, he was subject to the same natural laws of cause and effect as the rest of nature--even in the exercise of his will. His conviction was that all events had causes, that motives were causes, and that all decisions and actions had motives. Causes of acts of the will were the strongest motives present in the mind. The motives were determined by association with previous personal experiences of pain or pleasure, or by information about the experience of others, as Locke wrote.

Price believed that "consciousness" assured man of his free will, and wrote: "It is very plain, that motives can have no concern in effecting his determination, or that there is no physical connection between his judgment and his views, and the actions consequent upon them. What could be more absurd than to say, that our inclinations act upon us or compel us...." [III, 481] If our choices were necessary, Price said, we were deprived of moral responsibility.

Priestley's response was that necessitarianism did not preclude free will or self-determination; it meant that decisions were made, not in a void, but by the preferences in the mind. The "liberty" of humans he defined as "the power of doing whatever they will, or please, both with respect to the operations of their minds and the motions of their bodies, uncontrolled by any foreign principle or cause." [III, 459] Hence, "the generality of mankind" believe "their volitions are determined only by their own view of things, and influenced and guided by motives operating within themselves."

[III, 505] This makes them accountable for their choices, Priestley wrote, and responsible for the moral improvement of their behavior if the consequences were undesirable. [III, 502] Men were "voluntary agents" who could "do what they please."

Priestley maintained that choices were made on the basis of motives in accord with "some fixed law of nature respecting the will, as well as the other powers of the mind, and everything else in the constitution of nature ... so that every volition or choice, is constantly regulated and determined by what precedes it." All motives ultimately stem from Divine Providence, he wrote, "and therefore all things, past, present and to come, are precisely what the Author of nature really intended them to be, and has made provisions for." [III, 462] By this he meant his confidence in "divine providence" through the laws of nature that made this the best of all *possible* worlds.

In his speculations about human nature and God, his monism confirmed his belief in the homogeneous nature of human beings that shaped both his education and political theories, and implied a non-spiritual Creator. Though he could not fully accept the theological implication of his materialism, he did deny cosmic dualism and advanced concepts that could account for creation without an intelligent first cause: self-acting energy in particles, the synergistic effect of matter organized in systems, and the unity of all being in an interacting system. His doctrine of human nature alarmed and enraged some religious leaders, but inspired the democratic political theory that burgeoned in the American Colonies, in France, and in Great Britain.

Benjamin Franklin, by J. S. Duplessis—Franklin, while in London, was for many years a close friend of Priestley, concerned with scientific pursuits and political science discussions. (Courtesy of the National Portrait Gallery, London.)

Mary and Joseph Priestley portraits in oil by an unknown artist after their 1762 marriage. Photographs courtesy of Diana Gibson Hallowell and the Pennsylvania Historical and Museum Commission.

Dr. Joseph Priestley
1733-1804

Lord Shelburne, as Priestley referred to him, employed
Dr. Priestley as a librarian and literary companion from
1773 to 1780.

Joseph Priestley's home - designed by his wife Mary who did not live to move into it - Northumberland, Pennsylvania, 1798. Administered by The Pennsylvania Historical and Museum Commission. (Photo by John Ruskin Clark).

Priestley's boyhood home where, after his mother's death, he was raised by his Aunt Sarah Keighly from 1742 until he left for college in 1752. "Old Hall" was built in the 17th Century and is now a pub in Heckmondwike, West Yorkshire, England. (Photo by John Ruskin Clark).

VIII

THE HUNTED DEER OF LIBERTY
The First Principles of Government

J oseph Priestley was not a political activist, but his fearless criticisms of the British government and his advocacy of democratic political science made him an influential participant in the political dialogue that ultimately led to reforms of the British Parliament, to the American Declaration of Independence and Constitution, and to the French Revolution. His theories were radical, but not revolutionary -- he believed that all successful political reforms were obtained gradually through the dissemination of information, though he acknowledged that revolution might be necessary to change a despotic government.

Richard H. Lee charged that Thomas Jefferson copied the Declaration of Independence from John Locke's treatise on government. In 1825, Jefferson responded that he had tried "to place before mankind the common sense of the subject. ... All its authority rests on the harmonizing sentiments of the day." [Becker 1922, 25] Priestley was a voice in and popularizer of the "common sense" of political science in his day through his dialogues with liberal political leaders of England, France, and America, and his seminal historical and political publications. Three of the five members of the committee appointed by the Continental Congress to draft the Declaration of Independence were friends and admirers of Priestley--Franklin, Jefferson, and Adams.

From his studies in the physical sciences and in history, Priestley believed that all constructive changes took time. He had an organic theory of government and believed that most successful political reforms were non-violent. His unified theory of knowledge based his political science on the empirical ground of historical experience, not philosophical speculation. He was a leader in the 18th Century Enlightenment--the use of critical reason to examine previously accepted doctrines and institutions, religious and political.

Many of the English settlers in the American Colonies brought with them British Enlightenment ideals of liberty and political reform. Priestley thought it was providential that religious persecution in England drove Pilgrims and Puritans to these shores, assuring that English religious and political institutions, rather than Spanish, dominated in the colonies. He said that David Hume acknowledged that England was indebted for its civil liberties to the principles and spirit of the Puritans.

An international fraternity of men of the Enlightenment in England, France, and America exchanged letters and publications, and produced a ferment of political-reform ideas that were first distilled into a democratic government by the American Founding Fathers.

"The spirit of the times," Priestley thought, inspired a general interest in political reform in Great Britain, in the American Colonies, and on the continent of Europe. Tensions between Britain and her Colonies prompted a re- examination of King George's power, turned a critical eye on all social institutions, and a movement to reform Parliament was beginning. In 1768 Priestley could optimistically write: "This seems to be the time when the minds of men are opening to large and generous views of things. Politics are more extended in practice, and better understood in theory. Religious knowledge is greatly advanced, and the principle of universal toleration is gaining ground apace." [XXII 142]

Priestley believed in progress: the "golden age" was not in the past, as the Renaissance believed, but in the future. He believed that the world was in a state of improvement based on increased knowledge: commerce more equitably distributed production, and improved agriculture produced more food for "the whole family of mankind." He concluded: "If things proceed as they have done in these respects, the earth will become a paradise, compared to what it was formerly, or with what it is at present." [II 7] Franklin shared his optimism.

From his pioneering lectures on English history and constitutional law at Warrington Academy, Priestley was thoroughly grounded in the science of government, based on "historical facts" and not on speculative hypotheses. "Here observation and experience are the only safe guides," he said. [XXIV 35] His *Lectures on History and General Policy*, edited and published in six English and American editions between 1788 and 1826, was adopted as a college text in both England and America. It was recommended by an Englishman to the president of Rhode Island College, who regarded Priestley as very heretical but considered his Lectures "the best book on that interesting subject that I ever met with." It was assigned reading to Yale students, and John Quincy Adams read "this excellent work" in a Boston law office. It was translated into Dutch and French. [Lesser 1974, 223]

The science of government, Priestley wrote, was in its infancy because a study of its historical origins had not been made: "Like other arts and sciences, this is gradually improving; but it improves very slowly, because opportunities for making experiments are fewer. Indeed, hardly any trials in legislation have ever been made by persons who had knowledge and ability to collect from history, and compare the observations which might be of use for this purpose...." [XXII 119] In reading about current events, people in general "are content with seeing how things are, without looking far into the causes and consequences of things." But a philosopher, said Priestley, wishes to see things "in all their connections and relations ... it is only a knowledge of how things were actually brought to the state in which they now are that can enable us to judge how they can be improved." [XXIV 441] He later applied the same procedure to his heretical study of the origins and corruptions of Christianity, which more than his political science enraged the establishment of church and state. He thought that British history had fashioned a "highly improved state of society," whose advantages could not be reaped unless citizens sedulously endeavored to accommodate themselves to it by "social morality, the violation of which ... has the most fatal consequences.... We find ourselves members of a civil society, in which our situation obliges us to have a constant intercourse with great numbers of our fellow creatures, and the rules of this intercourse were established long before we came into the world. Moreover, the nature of things is such, that there is a necessity of obliging every member of the state to conform to the pre-established rules of it, whether he approve of them or not." [XXIV 446] However, in Priestley's concept, citizens were obliged to conform to established rules only in behavior, not in thought or expression; hence, he openly refused to comply with governmental regulations of religion.

Priestley did not project a blueprint of an ideal society; he proposed only policies and procedures by which governments could be gradually improved through small experiments. He warned: "So much does the stability of government depend upon opinion, and so many are the elements ... that enter the composition of such opinions as these, that no wise man will pretend to foresee the consequences of any great change in a complex form of government.... This makes it prudent, when great changes are made, to retain at least the ancient forms and names of offices. For to these it is, in a great measure, that public opinion is attached." [XXIV] Consequently, he sought only a reform of the British system of king, lords, and commons. No great changes should be attempted in a long established government unless, he said, "the minds of the people be prepared for it" by suffering injustices that made them wish for change; even then, if possible, change "should be made partially, and for a time, before it is finally established." [XXIV 267]

Priestley was led to write a systematic political science essay when some of his friends urged him to elaborate on the subject of civil and religious liberty that he had mentioned in his essay opposing a proposed national code of education. They thought he had "placed the foundation of the most valuable interests of mankind [religious freedom] on a broader and firmer basis than Mr. Locke and others who had formerly written on this subject." [XII 3] As Priestley believed that human beings were the instruments of Divine Providence for improving the human condition, and that social improvements followed changed opinions, he responded to the challenge to make his political views more explicit. In 1768 he published *An Essay on the First Principles of Government and on the Nature of Political, Civil, and Religious Liberty*, which had many editions and translations. It was read far and wide, including a 1771 edition in Jefferson's library.

At the Philadelphia Constitutional Convention, Priestley, as well as Locke and others, was quoted in support of limited powers of the federal government. Rebel freeholders in Virginia quoted from Priestley's "First Principles of Government" in arguing against the British Tory position that whatever Parliament enacted must be obeyed. A Dutchman, to support the attempt of his party to democratize the Netherlands, quoted from a translation of "First Principles".

Priestley began his essay with his assumption about human nature: "Man derives two capital advantages from the superiority of his intellectual powers. The first is, that, as an individual, he possesses a certain comprehension of mind, whereby he contemplates and enjoys the past and the future, as well as the present. This comprehension is enlarged with the experience of every day; and by this means the happiness of man, as he advances in intellect, is continually less dependent on temporary circumstances and sensations." The second advantage is that "the human species itself is capable of similar and unbounded improvement...." [XXII 8] To keep pace with intellectual improvements, governments must be susceptible to reform, without violence.

In college, Priestley had studied and adopted the Scottish philosopher John Locke's "social contract" theory of government. As Priestley expressed it in his "First Principles," individuals are "too weak to procure themselves many of the advantages, which they are sensible might easily be compassed by a united strength. These people, if they would engage the protection of the whole body, and join their force in enterprises and undertakings calculated for their common good, must voluntarily resign some part of their natural liberty, and submit their conduct to the direction of the community; for without these concessions, such an alliance, attended with such advantages, could not be formed." [XXI 10]

Locke, a leader in the Enlightenment a century before Priestley, had written that government should be "directed to no other end but the peace, safety, and public good of the people." As Priestley rephrased it, "all people live in a society for their mutual advantage; so that the good and happiness of the members, that is, the majority of members of any state, is the great standard by which every thing relating to that state must finally be determined." [XXII 13]

That passage inspired Priestley's contemporary utilitarian philosopher, Jeremy Bentham, to propose that the function of government was to ensure "the greatest happiness of the greatest number"--a phrase, he wrote in 1821, "for which, upwards of fifty years ago, I became indebted to a pamphlet of Dr. Priestley." When Jefferson composed the Declaration of Independence, among "inalienable rights" of people was "the pursuit of happiness."

Priestley was utilitarian--useful and practical, rather than "ideal" --in judging what controls and laws were proper for government to enact: "We are so little capable of arguing a priori in matters of government, that it should seem, experiments only can determine how far this power of legislature ought to extend; and ... that, till a sufficient number of experiments have been made, it becomes the wisdom of the civil magistracy to take as little upon its hands as possible, and never to interfere, without the greatest caution, in things that do not immediately affect the lives, liberty, or property of the members of the community." [XXII 33] It was not the good of the individual that was the ultimate test; "the whole system of right to power, property, and everything else in society, must be regulated," he said, by the answer to the question, "What is it that the good of the community requires?" [XXII 13]

Though people relinquished some of their natural freedom in order to establish a government, said Priestley, their posterity was not bound by the act: Liberty "every man retains, and can never be deprived of his natural right ... of relieving himself from all oppression." [XXII 12] Revolt may be necessary if the rulers, forgetting that they are servants of the people, abuse their authority and pursue their own interests. If the risks of attempting a revolution were less than the evils they suffered, Priestley asked, "what principles are those which ought to restrain an injured and insulted people from changing, or even punishing their governors ... who have abused their trust, or from altering the whole form of government, if it appeared to be of a structure so liable to abuse." [XXII 18]

Rulers "who employ their power to oppress the people, are a public nuisance, and their power is abrogated ipso facto," said Priestley. "This, however, can only be the case in extreme oppression; when the blessings of society and civil government, great as they are, are bought too dear...." [XXII 27] Government officials rule the state for the public good, and if they abuse that trust, citizens may demand their resignation; if normal channels of protest do not avail, in the interest of the public good every man who has power may "bravely redress public wrongs." [XXII 26]

That in principle oppressed citizens may resort to revolution was gladly heard in America and France. In the early, non-violent days of the French Revolution, Priestley, along with other liberators such as George Washington, was made an honorary citizen of France.

Change is inevitable, thought Priestley: "In spite of all the fetters we can lay upon the human mind, notwithstanding all possible discouragements in the way of free inquiry, knowledge of all kinds, and religious knowledge among the rest, will increase. The wisdom of one generation will ever be the folly of the next." [XXII 125] Since posterity will have accumulated more wisdom, Priestley advised forming governments "such as will easily admit of extension, and improvements of all kinds, and that the least violence, or difficulty of any kind, may attend the making of them." [XXII 140] Our Founding Fathers took care to do that.

Political liberty Priestley defined as the liberty of people to participate in the political process by running for office and voting for candidates, so that their judgment contributed to government policy-making. Civil liberty he defined as "that power over their own actions, which the members of the state reserve to themselves, and which their officers must not infringe"--freedom of thought, expression, and religion. A people's natural and original state was civil liberty, some of which was sacrificed in organizing a government, but they determined collectively how much political liberty they secured in compensation. [XXII 11]

The best security for civil liberty was access to the ballot box. Priestley at first had reservations about universal suffrage, as the poor might vote at the dictates of those on whom they depended. [XXII 14] Not until he was settled in Pennsylvania did he recognize that to disenfranchise the poor was taxation without representation, since they paid heavy sales taxes. [XXII 385] He did not apply that insight to suffrage for women.

Taxes, Priestley said, may be laid on what is possessed or consumed, but he warned that exorbitant taxes destroyed industry and raised the cost of commodities, which made them less competitive in foreign trade. Sales taxes were most advisable, as people paid tax on no more than they chose to consume, he said; on the other hand, sales taxes were a hidden cost that left people ignorant of the amount they contributed to the cost of government. [XXIV 403] There ought to be a limit to the amount of debt posterity could be burdened with: "If our ancestors make a foolish law, we scruple not to repeal it; but if they make foolish wars, and incur foolish debts, we have, at present, no remedy." [XXII 223]

Priestley shared the slogan of the American Colonies, "No taxation without representation." In his "First Principles of Government," he wrote that people who have no vote for representatives in a government that imposes taxes "have reason to fear, because an unequal part of the burden may be laid upon them." [XXII 18] The British Parliament's first scheme for taxing the Colonists by the Stamp Act, which required the purchase of stamps to be fixed to a variety of legal documents, ignored the principles of good government because the Colonists had no representatives in Parliament. After Colonial protest and passive resistance, Parliament repealed the Act in 1766.

The limitation of Locke's political theory that some of Priestley's friends complained of was in freedom of religion. In his first "Letter Concerning Toleration," Locke had maintained that "no opinions, contrary ... to those moral rules which are necessary to the preservation of civil society, are to be tolerated by the magistrates." [XXII] He meant no toleration for Catholics or atheists, but he did warn that the authority of magistrates to suppress idolatry could be misused, at the behest of ambitious clergy, to ruin other orthodox churches. [XXII 72]

Priestley commented, "We have no occasion to confine ourselves within the bounds of Mr. Locke's principles of toleration. His treatise was certainly admirable for the time in which it was written.... It is certainly not advisable to rest solely upon the authority of any man, as if his sentiments and maxims were the perfect and unalterable standard...." [XXII 478]

To preclude abuses possible with Locke's limited toleration, Priestley advocated unqualified and complete religious freedom and tolerance for all beliefs, or for no beliefs--for Catholics, Anglicans, Dissenters, Moslems, Deists, Unitarians, unbelievers or atheists. They could be opposed only by the force of argument--as he did. His defense of radical and inclusive religious liberty threatened the Established Church and alarmed many Dissenters. Jefferson shared the same defense of total religious freedom and of the separation of Church and State in his "Statute of Virginia for Religious Freedom."

Though Priestley vigorously defended the liberty of Dissenters, he noted that "neither the tenor of my theological writings in general, nor the manner in which I have written in the defense of religious liberty in particular, were calculated to procure me the thanks of the bulk of Dissenters. But I think it not less honorable to be the hunted deer, shunned by his companions, than the leader of the peaceful herd." [XXII 458]

With acute self-awareness, Priestley observed: "The man who takes the lead in any body of men whatever, must be a man who gives no offense, by openly espousing obnoxious sentiments; but, whatever he may think privately, must be so much on his guard, as not to be capable of being directly convicted of heresy; or if he cannot conceal his leaning to any unpopular turn of thinking, he must always speak or write with the greatest moderation, so as to give the least offense that the case will possibly admit of. Now it is very proper that there should be such men in the world. I esteem and value them, thinking them very useful in several situations; but it is evident that I have not been one of them." He wrote, he said, with "offensive freedom; with what regard to truth, and with what success, I leave to others and to time to determine." [XXII 456]

In the quest for truth, his maxim was complete freedom for works of the mind in all fields of interest: "truth can never have a fair chance of being discovered, or propagated, without the most perfect freedom of inquiry and debate." [XXII 89] He said, "But, I hope, with that diffidence which becomes all persons who are sensible that they are liable to err, and who are truly willing to be better informed when they do err. If no doubt be ever proposed, and no freedom of speculation indulged, an entire stop will soon be put to our progress in all useful knowledge." [VII 347]

Priestley argued that especially religion was beyond the province of state control, as it prepared people for a future life. The authority of civil government extended only to providing "for the secure and comfortable enjoyment of this life, by preventing one man from injuring another in his person or property." [XXII 35] Religion was "entirely a personal concern." [XXII 69] To French philosophers he wrote, "If I were to address you as politicians on the subject of religion, it would be in the language of the French merchants to your famous Colbert when he asked them what the government could do to favor trade: 'Laissez nous faire'--Let us alone." [XXI 104]

In religion, enrichment or punishment of people by the state, said Priestley, "cannot make them believers. It can only make them hypocrites." [XXI 105] Submit to state authorities, advised Priestley, "but if they would prescribe to you in matters of faith, say, that you have but one Father, even God, and one Master, even Christ, and stand fast in the liberty with which you are made free. Respect a parliamentary king, and cheerfully pay all parliamentary taxes, but have nothing to do with a parliamentary religion, or a parliamentary God." [II xvii]

"All I wish as a Christian," said Priestley, "from the powers of this world, is, that they would not intermeddle at all in the business of religion, and that they would give no countenance whatever to any mode of it, my own or others, but show so much confidence in the principles of what they themselves deem to be true religion, as to think it able to guard itself." [V 495]

In contrast to the independence of the original churches, said Priestley, the clergy of the Established Church functioned as civil officers, with bishops sitting in the House of Lords, and as teachers of the state religion, paid as servants of the Crown. [XXII 79] "This most unnatural alliance of church and state," he said, violated a fundamental Christian principle--"The great doctrine of the kingdom of Christ not being of this world...." [XV 437]

Reforms of the Church of England that Priestley suggested were that the clergy be confined to their ecclesiastical duties, that toleration be complete so that all persons could enjoy the rights of citizens whether or not they conformed to the established religion. [XXII 95-96] He warned the clergy: "Let them take care, lest, for want of permitting a few repairs in their ruinous house, it should at last fall all together about their ears." [XXII 129]

With his commitment to utilitarianism and gradualism, Priestley believed that ecclesiastical authority might continue to be necessary as long as society is imperfect: "If, therefore, I were asked, whether I should approve of the immediate dissolution of all the ecclesiastical establishments in Europe, I should answer, No.... Let experiments be first made of alterations.... Let them be reformed in many essential articles, and then not thrown aside entirely, till it be found by experience, that no good can be made of them." [XXII 95]

Priestley was involved in liberal political circles in London. While still a tutor at Warrington Academy, on the first of what was to become his annual visits to London, he was introduced to Benjamin Franklin and they became good friends. Franklin was in London representing the interests of Pennsylvania and trying to forestall an open rupture between Great Britain and her Colonies. Between 1765 and 1775, 126 articles by Franklin appeared in British newspapers. Franklin advocated a "Plan of Union" based on his expectation that American manufacture and trade would inevitably increase and that the Colonies could not be restricted to agriculture, as Britain intended. Instead, he urged working together toward a relationship in which the American and British people would have equal rights, and in which the Colonies by trade would enrich Britain and extend its empire over the globe. [Tuchman 1984, 157]

When Franklin was charged with espionage in 1774 and summoned to a hearing in Whitehall, Priestley was escorted through the gathering crowd to good seats by his friend Edmund Burke, and heard Franklin humiliated. Franklin had secured copies of letters by the British-appointed Governor Hutchinson of Massachusetts that contained violent invectives against leading citizens of Massachusetts and advised more emphatic measures to suppress the rebellious Colony. When the letters were published in Boston, Massachusetts petitioned Parliament for dismissal of the governor. At the hearing on the petition, by the king's privy council in the "Cockpit," the solicitor general attacked Franklin with sneers and gross abuse, depicting him as a thief and traitor. [Tuchman 1984, 197] Franklin remained silent and would not reveal the source of the leak. [Marvin 1979, 7] The petition was dismissed, and the next day the Crown removed Franklin from his office as Deputy Postmaster General of the Colonies. Priestley called to condole Franklin the morning after the hearing.

Franklin was the delight of the Whig Club that met at the London Coffee House on alternate Thursdays, wrote Priestley, who was also a member of that liberal political-discussion group. James Boswell, Samuel Johnson's biographer, met Priestley at the club, and wrote: "It consists of clergymen, physicians and some other professions.... we have wine and punch upon the table. Some of us smoke a pipe, conversation goes on pretty formally, sometimes sensibly and sometimes furiously. At nine there is a sideboard with Welsh rabbits [cheese dishes] and apple-puffs, porter and beer. Our reckoning is about 18d [British pennies] a head." [Griffith 1983, 5]

Distinguished members of the Whig Club included Sir John Pringle, president of the Royal Society; Edmund Burke, then a Whig member of Parliament; John Canton, an "electrician" member of the Royal Society; Benjamin Vaughan, a former student of Priestley at Warrington Academy and political aid to Lord Shelburne (who later was briefly Whig prime minister when Franklin, John Adams, and John Jay negotiated the Treaty of Paris that so favorably to the Colonies ended the American Revolution); John Lee, a lawyer and member of Parliament who was Priestley's parishioner in Leeds (in whose London home Priestley enjoyed many Sunday evenings of conversation, which "makes life truly valuable," he wrote); and Reverend Richard Price, Priestley's intimate friend and Dissenter colleague.

Distinct political parties began to emerge in Britain with controversies over John Wilkes' imprisonment for seditious libel in 1763, and then over the rebellious American Colonies. Tories were conservative land-owners who had opposed the English Revolution, supported Church and King, and favored suppressing the American rebels, and later the French Revolution. Whigs, on the whole composed of industrialists, commercial interests, and nonconformists, supported the rebel Colonists, advocated electoral, parliamentary and philanthropic reforms, and opposed war against the French revolutionaries.

The French Revolution crystallized party alignments: after 1784, William Pitt the Younger emerged as the leader of the new Tory party, while Charles James Fox became the leader of the revived Whig party. As the hysteria over the violence of the French Revolution increased and war against France was agitated, chauvinism led a large section of the Whigs, under Burke's leadership, to defect to the Tories. Britain embarked on a series of wars against the French, who were led by Napoleon.

Priestley had attended Whig Club meetings during his annual extended visits to London while living in Leeds--where Franklin visited him. After he became Lord Shelburne's literary companion in 1773, he spent all his winters in London, where he said that seldom did many days pass without his seeing Franklin. They always returned together from meetings of the Whig Club. Their conversations were chiefly about the differences with America that threatened to precipitate war. Franklin concluded in March 1775 that efforts to prevent the quarrel from ending in bloodshed were in vain, and prepared to go home. Priestley spent the last day

Franklin was in London with him in his lodging (the building is now being refurbished as a Franklin memorial) reading American newspaper accounts of Colonial reaction to the closing of the Port of Boston by Britain. As Franklin read them, Priestley noted that "tears trickled down his cheeks." [I-i 212] Franklin directed Priestley about what to extract from American papers to place in English papers. [XXV 393]

In response to Franklin's request, in 1774 Priestley addressed a pamphlet to Dissenters on the approaching rupture with America, which Sir George Saville, a member of Parliament and Priestley benefactor, and other friends circulated in great numbers, "it was thought, with some effect." Priestley wrote to the Dissenters of all denominations, "It is most earnestly to be wished that you would ... strenuously exert yourselves to procure a return of men who are known to be friends to civil and religious liberty." [XXII 487] He advised them to "oppose ... every candidate, who, in the present Parliament, has concurred in the late atrocious attempts to establish arbitrary power over so great a part of the British empire, to the imminent hazard of our most valuable commerce, and of that national strength, security, and felicity, which depend on UNION and on LIBERTY." [XXII 498]

Priestley had dedicated his *Chart of History* to Franklin. Franklin, at the Royal Society's request, had reviewed Priestley's accounts of his experiments in *Observations on Different Kinds of Air* and recommended him for the Society's highest honor, the gold Copley Medal, saying "I find there a great number of them [experiments], most quite new, and some I think very curious and important, well deserving for that reason and for the great pains and expense he has been at in making them, the honor of the Society's Medal." [Schofield 1966, 61]

After Franklin left England, they exchanged letters, hand delivered by friends, even during the Revolution. Priestley wrote a letter to Franklin in 1776 advising: "As ... it is most probable you will be driven to the necessity of governing yourselves, I hope you will have the wisdom to guard against the rock that we have fatally split upon; and make some better provisions for securing your natural rights against the encroachment of power, in whomsoever placed." [Holt 1931, 74] The Congress did so in the first ten amendments to the Constitution, after Jefferson, then in France, had prodded Madison.

It took eight months for Priestley's letter to be delivered to Franklin. He responded in 1777 from Paris, where he represented the 13 united states, about the situation in America: "In all probability we shall be much stronger the next campaign than we were in the last; better armed, better disciplined, and with more ammunition. When I was in camp before Boston, the army had not five rounds of powder a man. This was kept a secret, even from our people. The world wondered that we so seldom fired a cannon. We could not afford it, but we may now make powder in plenty." [I-i 297] Priestley was pleased with such news, as were most Dissenters.

Franklin wrote in 1788 from Philadelphia to Benjamin Vaughan in London: "Remember me affectionately ... to the honest heretic Dr. Priestley. I do not call him honest by way of distinction, for I think all the heretics I have known have been virtuous men. They have the virtue of fortitude, or they would not venture to own their heresy; and they cannot afford to be deficient in any of the other virtues, as that would give advantage to their many enemies. ... Do not however mistake me. It is not to my good friend's heresy that I impute his honesty. On the contrary, 'tis his honesty that has brought upon him the character of heretic." [Smith 1920, 5] Franklin asked Priestley to recommend books on religion; Priestley included his own *Institutes of Natural and Revealed Religion*, but the American war for independence broke out and ended the discussion. Priestley would have been gratified, had he known, by Franklin's later summary of his faith, a faith he shared with Priestley and Jefferson. In 1790, Reverend Ezra Stiles, president of Yale, wrote to Franklin, 84 and ill, for the specifics of his faith. Franklin replied: "I believe in one God, Creator of the universe. That he governs it by His providence. That He ought to be worshiped. That the most acceptable service we render Him is doing good to His other children." On the divinity of Christ, he responded: "I think the system of morals of his religion as he left them to us, the best the world ever saw or is likely to see; but I have, with most of the present Dissenters in England [an exaggeration; mostly Priestley and his former Presbyterian followers], some doubts as to his divinity, and think it needless to busy myself with it now, when I expect soon an opportunity of knowing the truth with less trouble." [Alley 1985, 207] Franklin died a few months later, and was not in Philadelphia to welcome Priestley when he fled England to refuge in Pennsylvania.

In 1769 Priestley published *The Present State of Liberty in Great Britain and Her Colonies* anonymously so his religious heresies would not prejudice readers against his case for the Colonies. Of the British policy in America, he wrote: "How preposterous it is, that those who glory in a free constitution for themselves, should wish for power over their fellow subjects, which would make them the most abject slaves; ... that a commercial nation should take measures to cut off the greatest source of their own wealth; and that a nation which, on many accounts, stands in need of peace, should, in asserting her unjust claims, provoke a contest, which, if the Americans be the genuine offspring of Britons, cannot but be attended with the most pernicious consequences to both! Earnestly, therefore, must every friend to Great Britain and the Colonies (whose interest is the same) pray, that this dreadful and unnatural struggle may be prevented, by the success of their constitutional, loyal, and peaceable efforts for freedom, for securing their natural rights as men, and the civil rights which they have hitherto enjoyed as Englishmen." [XXII, 381]

He repeated Franklin's thesis that commerce with the Colonies would enrich Britain more than taxes: the best policy in relation to the Colonies was "to consult the good of the whole, as of one united empire, each part of which has the same natural right to liberty and happiness with the other, to encourage agriculture among them, and manufactures among ourselves, and by no means interfere in their interior government, so far as to lay any tax upon them.... The benefits arising spontaneously from our extensive and increasing commerce with them, will infinitely overbalance all that we shall ever be able to extort from them by way of tax. Thus shall we be mutually the source of strength and opulence to each other...." [XXII 398]

Priestley also was concerned with the state of liberty in Great Britain. He was led to advocate British Parliamentary reform by the famous case of John Wilkes, who was arrested in 1763 for seditious libel against the king by writing in his newspaper that "the Ministry had put lies in the King's mouth." Wilkes' arrest on a general warrant aroused public concern and support for him. He was released on grounds of his parliamentary privilege and expelled from the House of Commons, then fled to France, and was tried in absentia and found guilty. On his return, he was imprisoned but nonetheless was re-elected three times by his Middlesex constituents to a seat in Parliament, which was denied him by Parliament. On his election in 1768, a crowd of supporters had gathered peaceably at the prison, expecting to see a freed Wilkes walk to the House of Commons. The crowd was exasperated when the justices ordered them to disperse by reading them "The Riot Act," and threw stones at the justices. In the ensuing riot, Scottish troops were ordered to fire on the crowd, killing or wounding over a dozen in the "Massacre of St. George's Field." [XXII 391]

Priestley specifically charged that in the Wilkes case the government with impunity violated civil rights by ignoring the writ of habeas corpus whereby an accused must immediately be brought to court and, if warranted, released on bail until the accused can be tried according to law. Priestley specified that the government arrested Wilkes with a general warrant that named no particular person accused under oath; confined him without admitting his nearest friends to speak to him; seized his private papers without a warrant and used them as evidence; restricted the freedom of the press by construing censors as libels; evaded trial by a jury of one's peers and substituted trial by accusation without permitting the accused to confront the accuser; voided the Bill of Rights by refusing to seat Wilkes in Parliament when he was chosen by an informed electorate; and resorted to military force "in a manner contrary to the genius and spirit of our constitution." [XXII 389]

As small changes in Parliament that would help reform a tendency toward despotism, Priestley proposed that all sons of nobility, court pensioners and "placemen"-- appointed to government offices for personal gain without regard to fitness, be excluded from the House of Commons; that sessions of Parliament be shortened; that "pocket boroughs," whose members of Parliament were appointed by the Lords of the Manor, be abolished and all members be elected as they were in the counties; and that all candidates for Parliament take an oath against bribery and corruption. Priestley claimed that "Were these essential points once gained, all the rest would follow of course." [XXII 392]

Priestley justified his call for political reform: "The liberty I have taken with the measures of government, is no greater than the constitution of this kingdom both admits and requires; any thing farther than this, is no concern of mine. I shall contentedly and cheerfully leave the issue up to Providence which disposes of all things." [XXII 380]

More consistent with Priestley's belief that people were the instruments of Providence in human affairs, others were concerned and actively took Providence in hand by organizing a movement to reform Parliament by education of public opinion and by agitation. Societies were formed, petitions prepared, meetings held, pledges demanded of candidates, and publications issued. A "convention" of delegates, in proportion to the population they represented and with universal suffrage, was held in London in 1780, and other counties followed suit. A reform plan was drawn up providing equal election districts, annual elections, all adult males except aliens and criminals franchised, a role of voters kept, voting by secret ballot, no office-holder or pensioner eligible for election to Parliament, and members of Parliament to be paid. [Holt 1952, 95]

The degeneration of the French Revolution induced a reaction that clouded Priestley's hopeful "spirit of the times". France was not blessed, like England, with a tradition based on an unwritten constitution that allowed citizens relative civil liberty, some religious freedom, and Parliamentary checks on the authority of the king. What began in France as an effort to limit the powers of the king by instituting a constitutional monarchy on the English model, which at first was applauded by many in England, deteriorated into a reign of terror; not only King Louis XVI and his Queen but also some 17,000 counter-revolutionaries were executed by the ruling "Convention."

By analogy, the "conventions" of those seeking parliamentary reform in England became suspect. England engaged in intermittent war with France and the tyrant Napoleon from 1793 to 1815. Horrified at the excesses of the French Revolution and the later threats of Napoleonic conquest, the English establishment instituted measures of oppression against those suspected of sympathy with the revolution in France or reform at home. In this hysteria, any further attempts at political and religious reform were feared and oppressed.

The first of a series of political reform acts was not adopted by Parliament until 1832, but they were finally essentially incorporated into English law as Priestley and the reformers had advocated. As the American Colonies formed their new government, they benefited by the example of the British reformers' policies.

In that revolutionary period of English fear and repression, Dissenters were suspected of disloyalty to the Crown because many had supported the American Revolution and the early hopes of the French Revolution. Moreover, Dissenters were still petitioning for relief from state control of their faith, first moved by Anglican clergy on their own behalf. Hence, much of the animus focused on Dissenters, and particularly on Priestley who took no active part in their petitions.

IX

"ONLY LIBERTY FOR THEMSELVES"
"Gunpowder Priestley"

Though the Dissenters' continuing petitions for relief from civil restrictions made them targets for the mounting hysteria caused by the degenerating French Revolution, the first petitioners for more religious freedom were Anglicans. During the Enlightenment, many Anglicans had become restive under the restrictions the Act of Uniformity placed on their theological development. They had to renew their subscription to the Act whenever they were appointed to a "living," advanced to better parishes, or appointed to administrative positions in the Established Church--which often induced a crisis of conscience between Church authority and their changing convictions. Two of the leaders in the Anglican petition for relief from subscription were intimate friends of Priestley.

Impetus for the Anglican effort to obtain relief came from the 1776 publication of *The Confessional*, which attacked the requirement of subscription, and denounced the hypocrisy of Arians, Arminians (Methodists) and others who complied in order to qualify for "preferment" or advancement, regardless of their theological convictions. The book was written by Archdeacon Francis Blackburne, conscientious vicar of Richmond in Yorkshire, whose son at Warrington Academy had been a pupil of Priestley, with whom Blackburne had kept up a correspondence.

Blackburne invited Priestley, W. Turner, and his son-in-law Theophilus Lindsey to his home in the summer of 1769 for several days of "free and amicable discussion," interspersed with rambles in the countryside. Blackburne later wrote, "The company of such worthies as Mr. Turner and Dr. Priestley is one of my luxuries; and the last small taste I had of it, will make me long till another opportunity affords me a second course." [Belsham 1812, 35] He later could rue the meeting, and judged that Priestley's forte was "not in the theological line." [I-i 365] Blackburne wrote a pamphlet against Unitarianism.

Turner was a Dissenter minister of a Presbyterian chapel in Wakefield near Leeds, and a Biblical scholar who collaborated with Priestley in editing the *Theological Repository*.

On his first meeting with Lindsey, wrote Priestley, "a correspondence and intimacy commenced, which has been the source of more real satisfaction to me than any other in my whole life. He soon discovered to me that he was uneasy in his situation, and had thoughts of quitting it. At first I was not forward to encourage him in it, but rather advised him to make what alteration he thought proper in the offices of the church, and leave it to his superiors to dismiss him if they chose." [I-i 82]

Lindsey's "situation" was that he was Vicar of a large Anglican parish with three churches in Catterick, "where he lived in affluence, idolized by his parish." He was considered by his bishop "an ornament to the established priesthood." [I-i,81]

In contrast to Priestley, Lindsey grew up in an "establishment" environment. Born in 1723 (ten years Priestley's senior), the youngest son of a dealer in silks and salt "in easy circumstances," he spent vacations as a youth at the mansions of his noble patronesses--friends of his mother--and graduated from Cambridge University. After serving as a domestic chaplain in the home of the Duke of Somerset, he was sent to the Continent for two years to accompany and supervise the education of the Duke's nine-year-old grandson, who later became the Duke of Northumberland.

On Lindsey's return, he was presented by the Earl of Northumberland with a valuable living in Yorkshire, where he became a visitor in the family of Archdeacon Blackburne. On being "preferred" for the gift of a living in Dorsetshire where he stayed seven years, he married Blackburne's step-daughter Hannah. His study of the Scriptures while in Dorsetshire led him to discard the doctrine of the Trinity and its correlates. To be near Blackburne, with whom he shared concern for Christian liberty and an aversion to ecclesiastical imposition in matters of conscience (though they did not share anti- trinitarianism), Lindsey secured the neighboring vicarage of Catterick. There, in addition to his clerical duties, he supported charity schools for children, spent considerable money on food and clothing for the poor, medicine for the ill, and educational books. It was a policy of Lindsey and his wife to save nothing from his income, but to observe the greatest economy in order to spend the surplus on charity. [Belsham 1812, 16]

Lindsey's scruples about the Trinity were confirmed by his diligent study. He wrote that in the end, be "became fully persuaded, to use St. Paul's express words, 'That there is but one God, the Father, and he alone to be worshiped.' This appeared to be the uniform and unvaried language and practice of the Bible throughout; and I found the sentiments and practices of Christians, in the first ages, corresponding with it." [Belsham 1812, 13] He resolved to quit ministry in the Established Church: "As one great design of our Savior's mission was to promote the knowledge and worship of the Father, the only true God, as he himself tells us, I could not think it allowable or lawful for me ... to be instrumental in carrying on a worship which I believed directly contrary to the mind of Christ, and condemned by him." [Belsham 1873, 21]

Lindsey's intended resignation from his ministry was postponed by the emergence of an Anglican association formed in 1771 to petition Parliament for relief from subscription, which Blackburne had proposed. Blackburne and Lindsey emerged as leaders when 24 clergy and a few lawyers and doctors met at Feathers' Tavern in London to prepare the petition. Lindsey presided and Blackburne chaired the committee that prepared the petition. Lindsey wrote that, though the assembled men differed widely in their opinions, they were united in holding that subscription "was an unjust imposition upon the consciences of men, and an invasion of Christ's authority, the only Lord of conscience; and head of his church." [I-i 144] Lindsey traveled some 2000 miles to secure clergy signatures on the petition, with disappointing results: the majority saw no reason for change, and the timid were unwilling to commit themselves. [Belsham 1873, 31]

Priestley wrote to Lindsey: "I most sincerely wish you success, and hope what you are doing cannot fail to produce good effects. You must permit us Dissenters, however, who are not used to the idea even of spiritual superiors, to smile at your scheme, as an application to the powers of this world for a reformation in the business of religion. As the disciples of a Master whose kingdom is not of this world, I should be ashamed to ask any thing of temporal powers, except mere peace and quietness, ... but I should be sorry to make any application to them which should imply any acknowledgment of their having any other kind of power." [I-i 160]

The motion to introduce the Anglican petition to Parliament was defeated 217 to 71. Lindsey wrote that "Burke declaimed like a Jesuit...." Edmund Burke argued that the Bible was subject to different interpretations and required an authoritative definition of what the Church meant to teach before a man was "authorized by the State to teach it as a pure doctrine, and receive a tenth of the produce of our lands. ... I will not enter into the question of how much truth is preferable to peace. Perhaps truth may be better. But as we have scarcely ever the same certainty in the one that we have in the other, I would, unless truth be evident indeed, hold fast to peace, which has in her company charity, the highest of all virtues." [Holt 1970, 59]

Within a year of Parliament's rejection of the Anglican petition, Lindsey announced, "I am obliged to give up my benefice, whatever I suffer from it, unless I would lose all inward peace and hope of God's acceptance in the end." [Belsham 1812, 42] It was a great personal sacrifice for Lindsey and his supportive wife (they had no children); they had saved nothing for such an eventuality.

They moved to miserable lodgings in London, wrote Priestley, and after struggling for some time,"opened a place of Unitarian worship in London, making use of the Liturgy of the Church of England, as reformed by Dr. Clarke and himself." [X 491] Samuel Clarke was a leading Arian and father of Priestley's liberal tutor at Daventry. Priestley promoted a subscription among his friends to help defray Lindsey's expenses and to outfit a second-floor book-auction room on Essex Street "chapel-wise." That site is now the headquarters and bookstore of the General Assembly of Unitarian and Free Christian Churches.

At the 1774 opening service of the first Unitarian church in England, the respectable congregation included Priestley and Franklin. Priestley noted that Franklin had invited along a friend who "subscribed handsomely toward indemnifying us for the expenses of the chapel...." [I-i 232] For a while, a government informer regularly attended the services, until it was found that nothing seditious was being advocated. The new sect was allowed quietly to emerge among the Dissenters. No other clergy were following Lindsey's example. His hope that dissident Anglicans would populate his congregation was not justified. But his experiment proved viable. Priestley's chapels in Leeds, Birmingham, and Hackney soon followed suit, and many other Dissenter chapels, especially Presbyterian, became avowedly Unitarian.

When Lindsey opened his chapel, Priestley was spending the winter months in London. Their intimacy increased and Priestley wrote: "To his society I owe much of my zeal for the doctrine of the Divine Unity, for which he made so great sacrifices, and in the defense of which he so much distinguished himself...." [I-i 85] In mutual influence, after careful consideration of Priestley's arguments, Lindsey gave up his belief in the miraculous conception of Jesus, and omitted the Apostles Creed that included it from the next edition of his liturgy. [Belsham 1812, 235] When in London, Priestley attended Lindsey's Sunday services, sometimes preaching, and spent the afternoon with the Lindseys.

Lindsey and his wife became the valued editors of Priestley's theological publications, but not of his scientific ones for Lindsey was not concerned with the scientific matters that sometimes were uppermost in Priestley's mind. Priestley wrote to Lindsey about a manuscript: "You know that I always listen to your admonitions ... your cooler and better knowledge of the world, would be of greatest use to me. ... I shall not print any part of it until you have seen it ...." He did listen to their admonitions, though he sometimes ignored their advice.

Blackburne stayed in his parish the rest of his life, altering the unscriptural phraseology of the liturgy, and refusing to renew his subscription, which would have advanced him to a better parish. He had "lost his right arm" he said of the defection of Lindsey to Unitarianism, "though, on the principles of the liberty of private judgment, it might not be opposed." His other clerical son-in-law Dr. Disney, who had married his eldest daughter, also left the Anglican ministry and joined the Unitarians in Essex Street--in 1793, he became Lindsey's colleague in the pulpit of the Unitarian Chapel.

At the time the Anglican petition was rejected, a member of Parliament hinted that if the Dissenters petitioned for relief from the legal restrictions to which they were subject, they might be favorably heard. The Dissenter ministers' organization in London, including Presbyterians, Baptists, Unitarians and Independents, applied to Parliament for relief from the Corporation and Test Acts, which precluded them from appointment to public offices, if not election to Parliament. In 1772 and again in 1773, the petition was accepted in the House of Commons and defeated in the House of Lords. Edmund Burke, then a member of Commons, supported the bill the second time, describing the custom of "liberty by connivance" as nothing "but a temporary relaxation of slavery." [XXII 442]

Priestley summarized the liberty that the Dissenters claimed was: eligibility for all civil offices appointed by the Crown, full liberty to profess and teach all their religious principles without fear of such laws as that of King William--which penalized "blasphemy" of the Trinity-- and the right to celebrate marriage among themselves as the Quakers were allowed to do. "And till these three articles be granted, our toleration is manifestly incomplete, because we remain exposed to civil penalties on account of religious principles, which is the precise definition of persecution." [XIX 180]

In his "First Principles of Government," he had written: "Hitherto, indeed, few of the friends of free inquiry among Christians have been more than partial advocates of it. If they find themselves under any difficulty with respect to their own sentiments, they complain, and plead strongly for the rights of conscience, of private judgment, and of free inquiry; but when they have gotten room enough for themselves, they are quite easy, and in no pain for others. ... The wider we make the common circle of liberty, the more of its friends will it receive, and the stronger will be the common interest. Whatever be the particular views of the numerous tribes of searchers after truth, whether we be called ... Christians, Papists, Protestants, Dissenters, or even Deists, (for all are equal here, all are actuated by the same spirit, and all are engaged in the same cause,) we stand in need of the same liberty of thinking, debating, and publishing. Let us, then, as far as our interest is the same, with one heart and voice, stand up for it." [XXII 137]

As an advocate of radical religious freedom, Priestley knew that he had alienated Dissenters, even those of the "rational kind," and wishing well to the bill, did not participate in the petitions; "I was not particularly concerned in the conduct of it." [XXII 457]

He was not "particularly concerned" with the Dissenters' petitions because he sought complete liberty of belief for all religions, or for no religion, not just for Dissenters or Unitarians. He thought the laws favoring established Christianity were the reason there were so many Deists.

He explained his position in a 1773 *Letter of Advice to those Dissenters who conduct the Application to Parliament for relief from certain Penal Laws*. He wrote that the Puritans were liberal for their time and had won such liberty as the English enjoyed. "But still it was only liberty for themselves, and their own party, that they aimed at." [XXII 262] Priestley thought the Dissenters were doing the same, and should petition for more inclusive religious liberty. The Dissenters had proposed, instead of subscription to the Thirty Nine Articles of the Church of England, substituting a declaration of belief "that the Holy Scriptures of the Old and New Testament contain a Revelation of the mind and will of God." Realizing that many skeptics and unbelievers could not sign such a declaration, Priestley urged: "You have hitherto preferred your prayer as Christians, stand forth now in the character of men, and ask at once for the repeal of all the penal laws which respect matters of opinion." [XXII 442] He challenged: "Let us then act upon this generous principle, and at the same time assert the honor of our country and the dignity of human nature, by petitioning for a bill by which Unbelievers shall be as much at liberty to attack, as ourselves to defend, either Christianity in general, or our particular opinions concerning it. ... Ask for the common rights of humanity."(XXII 443] He based his plea on his concept of human freedom as a natural right. As a Christian, he explained, "I have no occasion to ask for the toleration of any sentiments but my own.... But when the Christian is satisfied, I cannot forget that I am likewise a *man;* and the generosity of the man and of the Christian happily concur, in wishing for the toleration of all the modes of thinking in the world." [XXII 450]

"It is time," said Priestley, "that we no longer halt between two opinions, so very important and opposite to each other, as, whether religion should be left to every man's free choice, like philosophy or medicine, or it should be imposed upon men, whether they choose it or not...." [XXII 234]

His passion for complete toleration was not entirely disinterested. The bill the Dissenters applied for, he said, "would have afforded me no manner of relief. ... You made no complaint at all of a law by which I should still have been liable to the confiscation of all my goods, and even to imprisonment for life." [XXII 444] He meant the Act of Blasphemy promulgated in 1698 to penalize those who "deny any one of the persons in the holy Trinity to be God," which was aimed at Unitarians, though it was no longer enforced. Unitarians were not relieved of this stricture until 1813. Priestley protested that he was doing only what "the law of God required of me.... Christianity expressly requires a public profession of important truths, and even an earnest contention for them." [XXII 447]

Several bishops imagined that Priestley and one or two other violent Dissenters were the sole contrivers of the Dissenters' first petition. At the hearing in the House of Lords, a bishop read extracts from Priestley's writings which "he imagined his audience would call heresy," said Priestley, "to render myself and the Dissenters in general obnoxious to the governing powers." [XXII 456]

In 1778, by unanimous vote of both house of Parliament, Roman Catholics were relieved of old grievous penalties: death for priests

Though the Act granted only partial liberty to Catholics, many Dissenters disapproved and the more extreme Dissenters rioted in the streets against it. Priestley, a trenchant critic of Catholic idolatry, published a pamphlet in support of liberty for Catholics that admonished the rioters that Protestantism needed no defense against Catholicism by civil power. He said, "Christianity addresses itself only to the understandings and hearts of men; and if persuasion fail, it leaves every man to the judgment ... of God." [XXII 500] He wished Catholics to have full liberty to display their religion, and concluded: "Let us strictly adhere to the golden rule of the gospel, a rule of universal application, viz. to do to all others as we would that they should do to us. Let us consider how we would wish to be treated in the Popish countries, and make that the rule of our conduct to Papists in this." [XXII 514] The extreme Protestant Association in London opposed the toleration of Catholics in the Gordon Riots of 1778, which alarmed the public and was a setback to the reform movement; Burke's Bill for Economic Reform was rejected, and many reformers lost their seats in Parliament in the next election.

Nonetheless, encouraged by the relief granted Catholics, the Dissenters petitioned again in 1779 and in 1781 but were defeated. Their next attempt in 1787 was the occasion of another dishonest attack on Priestley.

"Gunpowder Priestley" was the inflammatory libel widely circulated in caricature and verse after an excerpt from his religious writing was read out of context during a debate in Parliament on the Dissenters' 1787 petition. Priestley had arrived from Birmingham for his annual visit in London the day before the debate. John Towill Rutt, who became Priestley's close friend and editor of the 26 volumes of his *Works*, noted: "I was present, March 28, 1787, when Dr. Priestley ... heard 'Sir William Doblen read this paragraph in the House of Commons, with great solemnity'.... The worthy Baronet, I well recollect, dispensed the gunpowder with a deliberation, awfully impressive, grain by grain." [XVIII 544] The excerpt was lifted from a paragraph in *Reflections on the Present State of Free Inquiry in This Country*, which Priestley had published two years earlier. The whole paragraph, with the excerpt in italics, reads:

"Let us not be discouraged, though for the present we should see no great number of churches professedly Unitarian. ... We are now sowing the seeds which the cold of winter may prevent from sprouting, but which a genial spring will make to shoot and grow up; so that the field which today appears perfectly naked and barren, may tomorrow be all green, and promise an abundant harvest. The present silent propagation of truth may even be compared to those causes in nature which lie dormant for a time, but which in proper circumstances, act with great violence. *We are, as it were, laying gunpowder, grain by grain, under the old building of error and superstition, which a single spark may hereafter inflame, so as to produce an instantaneous explosion; in consequence of which, that edifice, the erection of which has been the work of ages, may be overturned in a moment, and so effectually that the same foundation can never be built upon again.* [XVIII 544]

Clearly, the whole paragraph was an analogy of the effectiveness of planting small truths to produce, in time, great changes. But when he ignored Lindsey's advice to delete the grains-of-gunpowder analogy, the phrase was inflammatory, for it was associated with the annual English celebration of Guy Fawkes Day on the anniversary of the discovery of the 1605 plot to blow up Parliament, the king and the queen. "The Gunpowder Plot," led by Guy Fawkes, was a conspiracy of Roman Catholics who were angered by King James the First's failure to honor his promise to grant more toleration to Catholics.

The same day the gunpowder reference was read, Priestley also heard Prime Minister William Pitt argue in the House that the Dissenters' petition was too hazardous to the Church of England, and therefore to the peace and happiness of the civil establishment, to be granted, Priestley, then 54, promptly published a letter to the young Pitt, then 28, defending the Dissenters and admonishing him for abandoning the cause of liberty. Priestley pointed out that the election of Dissenters to the House of Commons, or the king's appointment of Dissenters as peers, or the Dissenters who did not scruple to meet the religious requirement for public office, or the Scotchmen who were promoted in public office without satisfying such a requirement, did not threaten the security of the realm. To quiet the apprehensions of the bishops, Priestley wrote to Pitt, "I shall inform them that the means we propose to employ are not force but persuasion. The gunpowder we are so assiduously laying grain by grain under the old building of error and superstition, in the highest regions of which they inhabit, is not composed of saltpeter, charcoal and sulphur, but consists of arguments; and if we lay mines with such materials as these, let them countermine in the same way...." [XIX 121]

Priestley acknowledged that his letter to Pitt "gave great offense." Yet, six years later, after the Birmingham Riot, when Pitt and Priestley happened to meet at the summer home of William Russell, Pitt gave Priestley a "general invitation to dine with him." [I-i 203]

But the damage of his careless analogy had been done; Pitt won an overwhelming vote against the Dissenters' petition and the slander of "Gunpowder Priestley" continued. A stanza in a popular parody, sung to the tune of "God Save the King," went:

Sedition is their creed;
Feigned sheep, but wolves indeed,
How can we trust?
Gunpowder Priestley would
Deluge the throne with blood,
And lay the great and good
Low in the dust. [XIX 356]

After another try was defeated by only 20 votes, the London Dissenters resolved to procure petitions for the redress of their grievance from all parts of the kingdom and from Dissenters of all denominations. Priestley, in a sermon that all seven congregations in the three denominations of Birmingham Dissenters urged him to print, said: "All that can be advised in this case, (but what, with patience and perseverance, must be effectual,) is a fair and candid representation of our case to the nation at large, and especially to those who have power to give us relief. The voice of reason, of truth, and of right, is sure to be heard, and to prevail in the end; and though prejudice, with which we have to contend, may overbear it, it can only be for a time." [XV 398]

This last effort was ill-timed. British people were increasingly alarmed that the French Revolution might spread to their land. The Dissenters were holding meetings widely to gain support for their 1790 petition and, as Priestley explained, "whether it was on account of these meetings ... or the dread of innovation in general, from the recent example of France [where the Catholic Church had been disestablished], the clergy formed similar meetings, and by their preaching, writings, and other means, excited a more violent opposition than had ever been known before...." The motion was overwhelmingly defeated and "put an end to all the hopes the Dissenters had too fondly entertained of any extension of their toleration in the present reign." [X 94] The Test and Corporation Acts were not repealed until 1828.

Before the Birmingham Riot, Priestley expressed his opinion on the French Revolution in private letters and publicly. In a letter to Lindsey, he wrote that he was happy the French king had not escaped abroad and expressed his hope that the new French Constitution "is now effectually established...." He regretted that the majority of Englishmen hoped that the French Revolution would become a civil war; he said that "the love of liberty is on the decline." [I-i 114} In his 1790 "Letters to the People of Birmingham," he referred to "the late glorious Revolution in France," which corrected nepotism in the established Catholic Church by requiring that clergy and bishops be chosen by the people. [XIX 273] Many people shared Priestley's early high hopes that the revolution would end despotism in France: the Whigs generally; poets such as Wordsworth, Coleridge, Southey and Sheridan; members of Parliament such as Lord Shelburne, Charles James Fox and William Pitt; and most of the Dissenters. [Thomas 1924,122]

Priestley's political writings were primarily defenses of freedom of belief and expression, which were not quoted against him, but he did publish *A Political Dialogue* about his opinions of the French Revolution, which came out too late to have caused the riot. He wrote to Lindsey June 29, 1791, "I enclose a copy of my Political Tract, which will not be printed till I hear from you." [I-i 114] Given the postal delivery-time then between Birmingham and London, and the time for Lindsey to read and return it, and the time to publish it, it could not have been available before the Riot 15 days later. Moreover, as Priestley wrote, it was "the calmest discussion of important subjects," and presented his balanced judgment.

In the *Dialogue* he wrote: "In reality, it is *opinion* that governs the world, and till the general opinion in any country concerning the foundation, the nature, and the uses of government, be changed, all useful revolutions will be impossible, or not permanent." ... "If the minds of the great body of the French nation did not appear to be thoroughly enlightened on the subject of government; had not their former enthusiastic attachment to their monarchs, and the rights of monarchy, received a fatal blow by the late writings in favor of liberty, by the shocking abuses of their government, ... and by the example of America, there could be no dependence at all on their late revolution. The king might sleep, or do what he pleases.... But while the people in general approve of the present [revolutionary] government, all attempts to overturn it will be in vain." [XXV 104]

When asked by his alter ego in the *Dialogue* whether his opinion about the English Constitution had changed, Priestley responded that it had: "There is no good reason why any man should be blind to the defects of his parent state.... Nothing human ... is absolutely perfect; but what is imperfect may be borne with; which I think to be the case with the Constitution of England. I have not, I own, that high veneration which I once had for it, since I have seen others which appear to me to be better. But I think that all the solid advantages of society may be had in ours, with such reforms as it is very capable of. And it will certainly be wisdom in our governors to listen to proposals for reform, rather than run the risk of such convulsions as may be the consequence of an obstinate refusal to reform anything." He suggested reforms: "The power and emoluments of the King may be greatly reduced; nor is it necessary that either his office, or that of the Lords, should be hereditary, or even for life, and neither the Lords nor the King should have an absolute negative on the resolutions of the House of Commons." [XXV 106]

Of a "republic" without a monarch, he said he was far "from wishing that any attempts should be made to reduce the government of England into such a form as this, which I might recommend to a country that had no government at all. Things once established should be respected by speculative politicians, because they will be respected by the people at large; but everything should be put in the way of as much reformation as it is capable of." [XXV 107] In his *First Principles of Government*, he had written of the British Constitution, "If the proposed alterations were violent ones .... I would endeavor to stop the ablest hand that should attempt to reform in this manner; because it is hardly possible but that a remedy so effected must be worse than the disease." [XXII 119]

A year before he died in Pennsylvania, Priestley noted that his non-violent, gradual and empirical theories of social change had been "abundantly verified in the history of the late revolutions in France. Though planned by men of the greatest abilities, and the most extensive reading and experience, they have had consequences that were little foreseen; and the system established at present (A.D. 1803) is the very reverse of every thing that was intended at the commencement of the revolution." [XXIV 35] Napoleon, then reigning in France, had restricted British trade on the Continent and was preparing to invade England.

Priestley's reform proposals were shaped by his unified theory of knowledge. Principles he learned in any field of inquiry he applied to others; his political science was influenced by what he had learned not only in his study of civil history but also of the history of science and religion.

In the preface to his "History of Electricity," he wrote that in "the history of electricity ... we see a gradual rise and progress in things." [XXV 341] "To whatever height we have arrived in natural science our beginnings were very low, and our advances have been exceedingly gradual: and, considering that we ourselves are by no means at the top of human science, ... a view of the manner in which the ascent has been made cannot but animate us in our attempts to advance still higher....." [XXV 343]

In religion, too, constructive and durable changes took time, he thought. In his *History of the Corruptions of Christianity,*he wrote of the Atonement: "We are not ... to expect a sudden and effectual reformation in this or in any other capital article of the corruption of Christianity. To establish this article was a work ... of long time, and therefore we must be content if the overthrow of it be gradual also." [V 153]

In politics also things take time. In an address to the students at Hackney College (where he taught after the Birmingham Riot and the death of Price, and which Burke had denounced, while Price was teaching there, as a "hot bed of sedition"), Priestley said: "Let us consider that all great improvements in the state of society ever had been, and must ever be the growth of time, the result of the most peaceable, but assiduous endeavors in pursuing the slowest of all processes--that of enlightening the minds of men; and that, after all, this noble end has seldom been attained, without great sacrifices from generous individuals...." [XV 438]

Twenty years earlier, Priestley had written: "It would be an infinite advantage to all states if the following maxims were adopted by all their members, viz. to think with freedom, to speak and write with boldness, to suffer in a good cause with patience, to begin to act with caution, but to proceed with vigor. ... By freedom of debate, and writing, the minds of the bulk of any people would in time be enlightened, and their general voice alone would, in a well-regulated state, both command any useful regulation, and enforce the observance of it when it is made. If the constitution was not a good one, this perfect freedom of debate would be the best method of making it be so. In this manner all improvements would be gradual and easy." [XXII 455]

Priestley's onus was bad enough before the riot, but it grew worse when Burke, a friend with whom Priestley shared so much in political theory, published his *Reflections on the French Revolution* in 1790, which Priestley criticized in published letters in 1791 after the riot. Burke then pilloried him from the privileged floor of the House of Commons.

Sketch of Northumberland, Pennsylvania, on the Susquehanna River, with Priestley's home on the far right, by Count Edouard Charles Colbert de Maulevrier in 1798 (the year Priestley moved into his new home). (Courtesy of the Pennsylvania Historical

X

REFLECTIONS ON THE
FRENCH REVOLUTION
"Extirpate the fungus."

The persecution of Priestley was not only local from the Birmingham ruckus with the clergy over his *An History of the Corruptions of Christianity*. He was also pilloried nationally for his political theory in an uneven exchange with Edmund Burke, a member of Parliament, about the French Revolution.

Priestley and Edmund Burke shared the same organic theory of the historical development of governments, though Priestley believed in gradual reforms while Burke, when there was "a wild spirit of innovation abroad," defended the status quo. In less tumultuous times, they might have remained friends and collaborators. Both were not of the establishment, but Priestley identified with the rising middle and industrial class, while Burke was ambitious and enamored of nobility and the Establishment, and switched political-party sides--for which he was rewarded.

Priestley's residence in England after the riot was made intolerable by Burke's continued attacks upon him from the floor of the House of Commons during the mounting "reign of terror," which increased the prejudice against Priestley.

It was not Priestley but gentle and beloved Richard Price who first raised Burke's animosity, though Priestley came to Price's defense after his death. Price was a Dissenter Unitarian minister in London, an intimate friend of Priestley with whom he shared support for the American and French revolutions, and defense of liberty and free inquiry.

Price was the main speaker at the July 14th,1789, dinner in London of the Society for Commemorating the English Revolution of 1688 (which Burke disparaged as "the Society for Revolutions") celebrating the first anniversary of the French Revolution. He prefaced his proposal for a toast to an alliance with France with a sermon that claimed England was so heavily in debt from previous wars that one more war would ruin it. He said, "After sharing the benefits of one Revolution [the English], I have been spared to be a witness of two other Revolutions, both glorious. And now, methinks, I see the ardor for liberty catching and spreading; a general amendment beginning in human affairs; the dominion of kings changed for the dominion of laws, and the dominion of priests giving way to; the dominion of reason and conscience." [Thomas 1924, 128]

He also contended that changed circumstances encouraged a noble purpose--a peace-keeping united nations. France had been regarded as a natural enemy, he said, when it consisted of a "monarch and his slaves," but now with its new "spirit that makes tyrants tremble," the French had "made themselves as free as ourselves. ... We have been an example to them; they are now an example to us." This last phrase most alarmed Burke, who thought the British constitution should be an example to France. Price had a different example in mind: soon France would call on England, he said, "to settle the terms of a confederation for extending the blessings of peace and liberty through the world. Thus united, the two kingdoms will be omnipotent: they will soon draw into their confederation Holland, and other countries on this side of the globe, and the United States of America on the other; and when alarms of war come, they will be able to say to the contending nations, Peace, and there will be peace." [I-ii, 80] He was prophetic, though the United Nations still cannot declare peace.

Price's sermon drew insults from Burke who, reports Rutt, "appears to have been maddened into a fury.... I heard Burke in 1790, assail Dr. Price, in the House of Commons, with those eloquent invectives," which he also later showered on Priestley. [XV, 440] Priestley, who came to the ailing Price's defense, wrote to Price in January 1791: "I am very happy to find that I have given you satisfaction with respect to Mr. Burke's gross abuse of you. These things do not, ... I hope, give you any material disturbance. ... I have sinned beyond forgiveness in many respects, but happily I am not apt to be disturbed at censure from any quarter, when I know it to be ill-founded. With respect to the Church, with which you have meddled but little, I have long ago drawn the sword, and thrown

away the scabbard, and I am very easy about the consequences."
[I-ii, 99] Priestley misjudged the consequences, as he learned in the
riot six months later.

Price died April 19, 1791; otherwise, he might have suffered a riot
in Hackney. Priestley happened to be in London at the time and was
a pallbearer at Price's funeral, and later delivered a commemorative
sermon in Price's chapel.

Edmund Burke, though not himself born into the Establishment,
became its leading spokesman as an orator, writer, and statesman.
He was born in Dublin, four years earlier than Priestley, and
graduated from Trinity College. His father was a lawyer and young
Burke went to London to study law, but soon lost interest. He began
writing and in 1750 published a pamphlet which gained him attention: *A Vindication of Natural Society*. In it, he protested the tendency
to apply purely theoretical critical principles to political and social
institutions that had emerged in historical experience and
demonstrated their practical wisdom by ages of excellent results.
Such was still his premise when he attacked attempts of the French
Revolution to correct political disabilities in the name of a vague
theory of the "rights of man." [Burke 9-11, VII]

Burke was made editor of an annual survey of world affairs and
in 1765 was appointed secretary to Lord Rockingham. Rockingham
was briefly prime minister, but was unpopular because he was
conciliatory toward the American Colonies, repealed the Stamp Act,
and led the Whig opposition to the war in America. Burke was
elected to the House of Commons and, failing re- election, was
appointed to a secure seat in the Commons from Rockingham's
"pocket borough."

At first, Burke was active in constitutional and economic reforms;
he sought to limit the powers of the King, and to give the electorate
more influence and control. He defended the Colonies, arguing that
the revolt of a whole people indicated a serious misgovernment. (He
did not apply the same principle to revolutionary France, arguing
that the Americans were only trying to gain their rights as British
citizens, not to overthrow the British government.) He risked his
popularity by doing all he could to relieve his native Ireland from
English oppression. He criticized the corrupt government of the
British East India Company, and recommended that India should
be governed by a board of independent commissioners in London.

Burke was introduced to Priestley by their mutual friend John Lee
during the time Priestley was living in Leeds. They became good
friends: Priestley was a dinner guest at Burke's, Burke and his son
called on Priestley in Leeds, and in London they had "frequent

interviews." Until the French Revolution, they were congenial on most public issues, including Burke's support of two of the Dissenters' petitions. But their friendship was severed by Burke's alarm at the French Revolution, aggravated by Price's sermon, which prompted Burke to write his *Reflections on the French Revolution*, 1790.

Among the many responses to Burke's *Reflections* was Thomas Paine's *The Rights of Man*, which Priestley considered "the boldest publication he had ever seen on the subject," and which he loaned to his friends. Paine's *Common Sense* of 1776 already had fired support among Americans for their revolution. In *The Rights of Man*, Paine exposed Burke's romantic admiration of the French royalty, particularly the queen whom Burke had once seen, and the clergy of "noble birth," while ignoring the exploited citizens. Paine coined the phrase that Burke "pities the plumage but forgets the dying bird." [Holt 1970, 147] Burke defended the royal family and the many vested interests, but of the oppression and suffering of the French people in general he said nothing. The prime minister, fearing that wide circulation of the *Rights of Man* would incite a bloody revolution in England, had Paine indicted for treason, but Paine escaped to France before his arrest.

Priestley regretted that, after a long friendship, he found himself opposed to Burke on so important a question, that "an avowed friend of the American Revolution should be an enemy to that of the French," and that a friend of civil and religious liberty should favor ecclesiastical establishments. Burke had contemptuously referred to "the gentlemen of the Society for Revolutions," saying that they took from the 1688 English Revolution only the principle of "deviation from the constitution." [XXII, 175]

Priestley's series of *Letters to the Right Honorable Edmund Burke*, some 200 pages published six months before the Birmingham Riot, protested that the same principles were at work in the British as in the French revolutions--the people deposed a king and formed a new government with constitutional restraints on the king. [XXII, 175] Burke's "particular animosity toward Priestley was excited by Priestley's published criticisms of Burke's book. It made Priestley more controversial, but their exchanges were not a "controversy" as Burke never responded to Priestley's factual criticisms; instead, he denigrated Priestley repeatedly on the floor of the Commons, aspersions that were circulated widely in the press.

The basic implication, said Priestley, of Burke's book was: "If the principles that Mr. Burke now advances (though it is by no means with perfect consistency) be admitted, mankind are always to be governed as they have been governed, without any inquiry into the nature, or origin, of their governments. The choice of the people is not to be considered, and though their happiness is awkwardly enough made by him the end of government; yet, having no choice, they are not to be the judges of what is for their good. On these principles, the church, or the state, once established, must for ever remain the same." Such were the principles, said Priestley, "of passive obedience and non- resistance peculiar to the Tories and the friends of arbitrary power" delivered from the pulpits of the high-church party in earlier reigns but intolerable to contemporary believers in liberty.

Burke had written: "The effect of liberty to individuals is that they may do as they please: we ought to see what it will please them to do, before we risk congratulations, which may be turned into complaints. ... Better to be despised for too anxious apprehensions than ruined by too confident a security." [Burke 9- 11, p.l0] He applied his "do as they please" characterization of liberty only to the masses, not to the ruling classes in France.

After revealing Burke's misuse of sources and his misunderstanding of the legitimacy of the first French National Assembly's attempts at constitutional reforms, Priestley wrote, "As you took so much time in preparing your publication for the press, you would have done well to have employed part of it in procuring better information." [XXII, 161]

A week before he died, Priestley published in Northumberland a brief account of his relationship with Burke in which he wrote:

"Though, in my answer to Mr. Burke, I did not spare his principles, I preserved all the respect that was due to an old friend, as the letters which I addressed to him will show." [XXV 397] If he had re-read his Letters to Burke (he seldom re-read anything he had published), he would have noticed that he did not "preserve all respect." In his controversies, Priestley often was ironic but he rarely wrote with such acrimony as he did to Burke: "You appear to me not to be sufficiently cool to enter into this serious discussion. Your imagination is evidently heated, and your ideas confused. ... you lose sight of the great and leading principles on which all governments are founded, principles which I imagined had been long settled, and universally assented to, at least by all who are denominated Whigs, the friends of our own revolution, and of that which has lately taken place in America. To this class of politicians you, Sir, have hitherto professed to belong, and traces of these principles may be perceived in this work of yours." [XXII, 152]

Priestley particularly replied to Burke's defense of the Established Church, since other respondents repudiated Burke's animadversions on the civil constitution of France. Burke held that the majority of English people considered the Church of England essential as the "foundation of their whole constitution"; there was an "indissoluble union" between Church and State. [Burke 9-11, 123]

Priestley charged that Burke confused religion with the Established Church and therefore held that church revenue was sacred and unalienable, and that its wealth and magnificence were necessary to its esteem and influence. If respect for the church was based on its wealth, Priestley asked, what caused the poor Dissenters to grow, and the amazing increase of Methodism? [XXII, 197] Burke decried the French revolutionary government's seizure of monastic lands, except those used for educational or charitable purposes, to pay public debts. Priestley held that the "state has a right to dispose of all property within itself." [XXII, 185]

Burke defended church establishment to serve the faith of the majority of its citizens. Then, reasoned Priestley, the established church in Scotland should be Presbyterian, and in Ireland Catholic, and not the Church of England. [XXII, 188] Priestley compared an established church to "a fungus, or parasitical plant" on the "noble plant of Christianity, draining its best juices....if I wish to preserve the tree, must I not extirpate the fungus....?" [XXII, 203] Religion should be no more established than medicine, which would prescribe certain medicines for all diseases. [XIX, 183] The establishment of Christianity, said Priestley, was contrary to the New Testament maxim "that human authority ought not to be interposed in matters of religion, and, indeed, to our Savior's own declaration that his Kingdom is not of this world." [XIX, 183]

In his *Reflections* Burke "with sufficient asperity" misrepresented the friends of the French Revolution and misquoted Priestley: "Some of them are so heated with particular religious theories, that they give more than hints that the fall of the civil powers, with all the dreadful consequences of that fall, provided they might be of service to their theories, would not be unacceptable to them.... A man amongst them of great authority, and certainly of great talents [his only reference in the book to Priestley], speaking of a supposed alliance between Church and State, says...." [XXV, 397] Then he quoted an excerpt, out of context, from the concluding paragraph of Priestley's *The History of the Corruptions of Christianity*. The whole paragraph, with Burke's excerpt in italics, reads: "It is nothing but the alliance of the kingdom of Christ with the kingdoms of this world (an alliance which our Lord himself expressly disclaimed) that supports the grossest corruptions of Christianity; and *perhaps we must wait for the fall of the civil powers before this most unnatural alliance is broken. But what convulsion in the political world ought to be a subject of lamentation, if it be attended with so desirable an event?* [Burke changed the last word to "effect."] May the Kingdom of God, and of Christ (that which I conceive to be intended in the Lord's prayer,) truly and fully come, though all the kingdoms of the world be removed, in order to make way for it!" [V, 504] In this instance, Burke was a demagogue. It was quotations out of context from Priestley's theological, not his political, publications that Burke used out of context against Priestley's patriotism.

In the whole paragraph, as the last sentence made clear, Priestley was obviously not referring to a political revolution, but to the then widely shared Christian expectation of Divine intervention at the Second Coming of Christ to establish the Kingdom of God on earth. Burke's excerpt, wrote Priestley, was "quoted by many others, in order to render me obnoxious to the English government." [XXV, 397]

The July following Burke's publication and Priestley's *Letters* in response, the Birmingham Riot erupted. It was no local event; it was a consequence of the national hysteria fomented by Burke and other defenders of the establishment. A man who lived in the same house as Burke informed Priestley that when news of the riot reached Burke, "he could not contain his joy on the occasion...." [XXV, 398] When King George III authorized sending troops to quell the riot, he commented, "I cannot but feel better pleased that Priestley is the sufferer for the doctrines he and his party have installed, ... yet I cannot approve of their having employed such atrocious means of showing their discontent." [Holt 1970, 173] The king offered a 100-pound reward for the conviction of any persons concerned with the riot, which dismayed some of the rioters who thought they had the king's backing and complained, "Is he then turned Presbyterian, and are we to be hanged for this?" [XIX, 397]

Burke's reflections on the French Revolution helped to produce the wave of hysteria that later developed into Prime Minister William Pitt's "reign of terror." The Tory policy of trying to suppress the French Revolution by force broke out into a war between France and England in 1793. The British government already had taken fright and had begun persecution at home. A proclamation against seditious publications was issued, the right of habeas corpus was suspended, and the Treasonable and Seditious Meetings acts of 1795 quashed any further efforts for reform.

In England, Horne Tooke, Hardy, Holcroft and others were tried for treason and acquitted. In Scotland, Fyshe Palmer and Muir were condemned and banished. [Holt 1970, 177] Priestley's old friend Thomas Walker in Manchester was "the subject of vicious prosecution by Church and King." [I-ii, 125] He had to defend his home in a riot he helped to quell, and in 1794 a newspaper reported that he and nine others were tried "for seditious practices, in arming men, and providing ammunition, in order to assist the enemies of Great Britain. After a trial of six hours, they were most honorably acquitted. The principal witness was committed by the court, for perjury, he not only prevaricating in the course of his examination, but it being proved that he ... had been hired and bribed to give evidence against Mr. Walker." [I-ii, 210] Walker fled to America, with many others, following Priestley's two older sons who could not find employment in England. [I-ii, 205]

Priestley relayed to Lindsey "an account of the trial of Mr. Winterbottom [a Baptist minister] for seditious expressions in two sermons. He was found guilty ... on the evidence of two very illiterate persons, against the testimony of a great number of his respectable hearers, that he had not used any such language as was ascribed to him. ... Mr. Cook of Cambridge, has also been convicted, on the evidence of the most infamous persons, of seditious words spoken three years ago." Cook emigrated to America where he became a chaplain in the Navy. [I-ii, 206] No formal charges were made against Priestley during the English reign of terror, but continued harassment led him to agree with his wife Mary's desire to emigrate and they too became refugees in the United States.

Unitarians were singled out for attack, especially those who, after studying at Cambridge University, had left the Church to become Unitarian ministers: The Reverend W.Frend of Jesus College, the Reverend T. Fyshe Palmer of Queens' College, and the Reverend J. Jebb of St. John's College

T. Fyshe Palmer had become a Unitarian minister in Dundee and contributed to Priestley's *Theological Repository*. Palmer's offense was that he had corrected the proof of a handbill written by a member of the Society of Friends of Liberty at Dundee which demanded reform of Parliament to save the nation's liberty. Palmer was tried, convicted, and shipped as a convict to Australia. While he was a prisoner awaiting transportation, Lindsey visited him. On his return trip in 1801, his ship was wrecked on the Mariana Islands in the South Pacific, he was imprisoned by the Spaniards and died of a fever. [Holt 1952, 116]

Burke did not remain a Whig. He advocated war with the revolutionary government of France and broke with his friend Charles James Fox over the issue in 1791. He lead a majority of the Whig party in the House of Commons to support William Pitt's Tory government, which did favor war with France. The remaining Whigs unsuccessfully opposed the counter-revolutionary war with France. In 1792, the same year the Convention in France took over and proclaimed the abolition of the monarchy and the establishment of the Republic, sedition trials began in England.

The following spring, Priestley was obliged to defend himself from further slanders by Burke in the House of Commons, which were widely quoted. Since Priestley had no recourse in the Commons, he wrote a letter to the editor of the Morning Chronicle, in which he begged leave to ask Burke "through the channel of your paper, ... what authority he had for asserting, as he did, that 'I gave my name to sentiments in the Correspondence of the Revolution Society in England with Jacobin Societies in France; sentiments adverse to our Constitution? ... I am not, nor ever was, a member of any political party whatever; nor did I ever sign any paper originating with any of them. ... I also wish to ask Mr. Burke what authority he has for asserting, that 'I was made a citizen of France, because I had declared hostility to the Constitution of England?' This assertion, like the preceding, is nothing else than a malignant calumny; being an untruth, which, in the present state of things, is calculated to do me the gravest injury." [XV, 499]

Priestley had been made an honorary French citizen a year after the Birmingham Riot, partly because of his martyrdom. The French Legislative Assembly designated men who "by their writings, and by their valor, have served the cause of liberty, and prepared the emancipation of nations," and declared that "the title of French citizen is conferred on Doctor Joseph Priestley, on Thomas Paine, on Jeremy Bentham [the utilitarian philosopher whose opinions continued to be respected in England and America], on William Wilberforce [who led in the English abolition of the slave trade in which Priestley participated, and was a friend of the Tory Prime Minister William Pitt], ... on George Washington ... and others." [Gibbs 1967, 216] Priestley reminded Burke that at the time Priestley was made a French citizen, "there was no suspicion of a war between England and France. The French king was then living, [and] the constitution of France was then reduced to a limited monarchy, resembling that of England." [XXV, 118] Thomas Jefferson was later made a citizen of France.

To Burke's charge that Priestley had "declared hostility to the Constitution of England," Priestley responded: "Though few of my publications related to politics, I have more than once expressed myself in favor of our Constitution, and I call upon Mr. Burke to show that I have ever written any thing that can, by any fair construction, be said to be against it." [XV, 499] Burke never responded or retracted his charges against Priestley.

Priestley and Burke shared the same basic assumption about the nature of government: it was organic, a slow historical accumulation of wisdom and procedures to facilitate orderly coexistence that could not be changed successfully by sudden and violent reforms in the name of abstract principles. Neither was an idealist, believing that principles of social organization could be derived by speculation based on intuited absolutes. Both believed that stable governments grew from historical experience. Priestley shared Burke's observation that "In history a great volume is unrolled for our instruction, drawing the materials of future wisdom from the past errors and infirmities of mankind." [Burke 9-11, 176] But Burke did not apply that observation to the "errors and infirmities" of the French ancient regime.

Priestley believed that history showed a gradual change and improvement in political systems, while Burke opposed any further changes in established institutions. Priestley was no utopian idealist trying to transform society by violence, as Burke feared, but was an empirical realist who believed in human responsibility for slowly reforming any political system by free inquiry, discussion and experiments. Burke's political organism was dead, not responding to new situations and wisdom, while Priestley's political organism was living, responsive to intentional, though gradual, change by enlightenment: "Were the best formed state in the world to be fixed in its present condition, I make no doubt that, in the course of time, it would be the worst. History demonstrates this truth with respect to all the celebrated states of antiquity; and as all things (and particularly whatever depends upon science) have of late years been in a quicker progress towards perfection than ever; we may safely conclude the same with respect to any political state now in being." [XXII, 119]

At the time, Burke may have been right that during revolutionary furor was no time to initiate reforms, but that was not what he claimed; he defended established institutions against all changes, in spite of their oppressions. When he came to oppose the Dissenter's petitions, he said, "There was a wild spirit of innovation abroad, which required not indulgence but restraint." [Burke 9-11, XVIII]

The execution of the French king and queen, and thousands of other counter-revolutionaries in the French Reign of Terror, brought the majority of English people to Burke's side. Burke prevailed at the time, but if a person's principles are justified by their durability, Burke's policy was expedient and ephemeral. In 1795 he was granted a government pension.

Priestley was vindicated in the long run--British government was gradually reformed, after the defeat of the French at Waterloo, along the lines that Priestley had advocated: all the colonies have become sovereign members of the British Commonwealth of Nations; the monarch's authority is more restricted; members of the House of Commons are salaried; "pocket boroughs" have been abolished; the right to vote is universal; there is de facto freedom of discussion and the press, subject only to the judgment of juries in libel cases; there are no restrictions on freedom of religious belief or worship; the Church of England is still established and its doctrine nominally defined by the state, but it is no longer supported by public taxes; the established church in Scotland is Presbyterian; and in Ireland and Wales there is no established church. France is now a republic.

From the French Revolution, Priestley anticipated only the emergence of a constitutional monarchy, which might have come to pass had not England and other monarchies been frightened and encouraged King Louis XVI to betray the first attempt: he had negotiated with the "estates general" to form a national constitutional assembly to write a constitution. His betrayal of the agreement provoked the seizure of the Bastille, symbol of royal tyranny.

Priestley's political science theory was based not only on his extensive study of and writing on the history of governments for his Warrington classes, but also on the history of the development of science and of religion, all of which he thought were based on the same principles of change and improvement. The transmission and gradual improvement of political science, as of all works of the mind, was to Priestley a function of liberal education.

XI

EDUCATION MAKES THE MAN
"Citizens of the World"

Priestley defended liberty in education and practiced it in his own teaching. Both as the teacher in his private elementary school in Nantwich and as a tutor at Warrington Academy, he introduced practical innovations in education. At Nantwich, he gave his students hands-on experience with scientific equipment, assigned English compositions that he corrected, and provided "a little library, consisting chiefly of books of natural and civil history, with books of travel, which I made them read (as a favor) with the maps before them." [I-i, 64] At Warrington, he is credited with introducing modern history, British constitutional law, economics, and political science in English higher education 60 years before there was a chair of economics at Oxford and more than a 100 years before modern history became a separate discipline. [Chapin 1967, 245]

When Dr. John Brown, an Anglican clergyman, proposed a government code of education, Priestley published a defense of liberty in education. His exposition of the necessity of liberty for human progress was so telling that his friends urged him to expand on the theme, which he did three years later in *An Essay on the First Principles of Government* (1768), and which was influential in the 18th century political science dialogue.

Priestley assumed that human nature would be improved by a variety of experiments in education: "Education, taken in its most extensive sense, is properly that which makes the man. One method of education, therefore, would only produce one kind of men; but the great excellence of human nature consists in the variety of which it is capable. Instead, then, of endeavoring, by uniform and fixed systems of education, to keep mankind always the same, let us give free scope to every thing which may bid fair for introducing more variety among us." [XXII, 46]

Neither Brown nor Priestley believed in innate moral ideas inspiring the conscience, and both believed that education informed the conscience. But Brown believed the conscience should be trained in the established religion of the state, prescribed by law to which all the members of the community should submit, which Priestley claimed was inimical "to liberty, and the natural rights of parents." [I-i, 52] Variable educational opportunities were necessary to the development of human nature, which was violated by relinquishing education to the state, said Priestley: "Education is a branch of civil liberty which ought by no means to be surrendered into the hands of the magistrate; and ... the best interests of society required that the right of conducting it should be inviolably preserved to individuals." [XXII, 54]

The object of education for Brown was to ensure the tranquillity of the state; to Priestley, it was "the forming of wise and virtuous men; which is certainly an object of the greatest importance in every state. If the constitution of a state be a good one, such men will be the greatest bulwarks of it; if it be a bad one, they will be the most able and ready to contribute to its reformation; in either of which cases they will render it the greatest service." [XXII, 44]

Priestley did not think that his generation had reached the ultimate in human development, needing only to be perpetuated. His justification for liberty to experiment in education was practical: "Education is as much an art (founded, as all arts are, upon science) as husbandry, as architecture, or as ship-building. ... Now, of all arts, those stand the fairest chance of being brought to perfection, in which there is opportunity of making the most experiments and trials, and in which there are the greatest number and variety of persons employed in making them. History and experience show, that ... those arts have always, in fact, been brought the soonest or the nearest to perfection, which have been placed in those favorable circumstances. The reason is, that the operations of the human mind are slow; a number of false hypotheses and conclusions always precede the right one; and in every art, manual or liberal, a number of awkward attempts are made, before we are able to execute any thing which will bear to be shown as a master-piece in its kind; so that to establish the methods and processes of any art ... is to fix it in its infancy, to perpetuate every thing that is inconvenient and

awkward in it, and to cut off its future growth and improvement."
[XXII, 44]

He wrote that "if we argue from the analogy of education to other
arts which are most similar to it, we can never expect to see human
nature ... brought to perfection, but in consequence of indulging
unbounded liberty, and even caprice, in conducting it. The power
of nature in producing plants cannot be shown to advantage but in
all possible circumstances of culture. The richest colors, the most
fragrant scents, and the most exquisite flavors, which our present
gardens and orchards exhibit, would never have been known, if
florists and gardeners had been confined in the processes of cultivation.... Many of the finest productions of modern gardening have
been the result of casual experiment, perhaps of undesigned deviation from established rules. ... And why should the rational part of
the creation be deprived of that opportunity of diversifying and
improving itself, which the vegetable and animal world enjoy?"
[XXII, 46]

In Priestley's scheme, allowing such liberty in education did not,
however, relieve the state of responsibility for public instruction.
The arts of reading and writing were so essential that every child
should be instructed in them, with government support. The state
could provide class-rooms and subsidize salaries of teachers,
though the major part of their income would come from charging
fees to parents of all children "that offer themselves." [XXIV 223]

No one in Priestley's generation thought of making school attendance compulsory by law. In fact, child labor was so generally
accepted as part of the social structure in Europe that not until 1890
did organized international efforts begin to restrict the exploitation
of children in field, factory and mine.

Without education, no persons could improve themselves, said
Priestley: "But by means of art we are not only enabled to go far
beyond that low mediocrity in every thing, to which nature alone
could train mankind, but the whole human species is put into a
progressive state, one generation advancing upon another, in a
manner that no bounds can be set to the progress. And this progress
is not equable, but accelerated, every new improvement opening
the way to many others; so that as men a few centuries ago could
have no idea of what their posterity are, at this day, we are probably
much less able to form an idea of what our posterity will attain to,
as many centuries hence." [XXV, 11]

Priestley had no concern about information-overload from the
discovery of new facts and theories: "The greater progress we make
in the analysis of nature, the nearer we come to first and simple

principles, and in fewer general propositions may the whole be comprised." [XXV, 11]

"Experience is the school of nature," said Priestley. [III. 77] "There is a sufficient provision in nature for the education of mankind, provided that sufficient time is allowed for the purpose. But life is so short ... that it is advisable not to depend on experience only; because the knowledge we acquire by that means may come too late." [XXV, 10] Still, when the art of education has done its utmost, "it must be left to nature and experience to confirm us in the lesson." [XXV, 11]

Children should not be protected from the risks of small hurts, which teach more caution than adult restraint, but Priestley warns: "It is necessary, however, to have recourse to admonition, or even absolute restraint, where life or limbs are in danger; because, if the mischief should happen, it will be too late for them to profit by it...." [XXV, 12]

Children learn more from success than from failure: "The only way to give a youth courage, is to accustom him betimes to the exercise of his own powers, and in such circumstances as that he shall have no reason to be discouraged at the outset, ... he must be exposed to some trial, which, if he succeed in it, will leave a favorable impression, and if he be unsuccessful, an unfavorable one; but his situation may be chosen, as that the chance of his succeeding shall be greater than his failing." [XXV, 39]

A sufficient motive to virtue requires teaching with emotion, the association of ideas with feelings. Priestley wrote that "the impression which ideas make upon the mind does not depend upon the definitions of them, but upon sensations, and a great variety of ideas, that have been associated with them; and these associations require time to be formed and cemented." Priestley gave an example: "All persons know what is meant by the term father, and if they are asked, would define it in the same manner; but the man who has never known a father of his own, or, which is nearly the same thing, has had little connection with him ... will by no means have the same feelings when the word is pronounced to him, with the man who was brought up in a constant, uninterrupted intercourse with a father." [XXV, 48]

Priestley's progressive contributions to higher education were made during six happy and fruitful years as a tutor at Warrington Academy. His close friend Clark (who, as his tutor at Daventry Academy, knew of his study of the "learned languages") joined Dr. Benson (London Bible scholar and Priestley benefactor) and Dr. John Taylor (first principal of Warrington) in recommending

Priestley to the trustees of Warrington as the tutor of languages--in 1757 when Priestley at age 24 was minister in his first church in Needham Market. The trustees felt that for the position he was too young and inexperienced, with promise but no reputation, and with defective speech. An older and more experienced Dr. John Aiken was chosen.

Four years later, Dr. Taylor died and Dr. Aiken succeeded him as principal and divinity tutor. Priestley, then at his second church at Nantwich where his flourishing school was evidence of his success as a teacher, was asked to be tutor of languages and literature at Warrington.

When confirmation of the appointment was brought to Priestley, he recorded, "I should have preferred the office of teaching the mathematics and natural philosophy, for which I had at that time a great predilection." Since that position was already filled, Priestley accepted, "though my school promised to be more gainful to me. But my employment at Warrington would be more liberal, and less painful." Besides, he wrote, it "was a means of extending my connections." [I-i, 47] Priestley ambitiously cultivated new friends in his various fields of interest, successfully--his introduction to Franklin came through his connections at the Academy. Warrington Academy was founded by the enterprising John Seddon, a popular young minister in Warrington, to provide a Dissenter school of higher education in the north of England, where the academies had been closed by the death of the ministers who had operated them as private institutions. Seddon proposed an academy administered by trustees responsible to the subscribers and sought the support of wealthy merchants and industrialists in nearby Manchester and Liverpool--Warrington was half-way between them. The traditional rivalry of those cities led to jealous competition for influence and to dissatisfaction among the subscribers, diminishing financial support and dissension between the trustees and the first principal. Nonetheless, the Academy was opened to educate ministers, as Seddon said, "free to follow the dictates of their own judgments in their inquiries after truth," and those going into commerce and the learned professions, giving them a "just concern for the true principles of religion and liberty, of which they must be in future life the supporters." [I-i, 46]

Dr. Taylor in the preface to his divinity lectures to students stated the principles of the liberal, rational Dissenters and of the Academy, which were congenial to Priestley, and charged the students: "that you do constantly ... attend to evidence, as it lies in the Holy Scripture, or in the nature of things and the dictates of reason; banish from your breast all prejudice ... and party zeal; and that you steadily assert for yourself, and freely allow to others, the unalienable rights of judgment and conscience." [Holt 1931, 25]

The town of Warrington was a busy center of manufacturing and trade and, being on a main thoroughfare, had many inns for travellers. Priestley often visited friends in Manchester and Liverpool, each about 20 miles from Warrington. In Liverpool, he would spend the night with Bentley (later Wedgwood's partner in Birmingham]. Since Bentley was an "unbeliever," Priestley disregarded his early-to-bed rule to enjoy long discussions of the evidences of revealed religion.

Priestley moved into his rent-free house in Warrington in May of his first year at the academy and in June married Mary Wilkinson in her home town of Wrexham, Wales. Mary was 21 and Priestley twenty-nine years of age. Her youngest brother William had been a student in Priestley's Nantwich school, and Priestley had often travelled the 20 miles to visit the Wilkinson home to court Mary. There he also met her older brother John (five years Priestley's senior) who was very fond of his little sister. Mary, John, and William were children of Isaac Wilkinson, a farmer and "overlooker" of an iron furnace, whose patent on a "box iron" was lucrative, enabling him to build an iron foundry of his own in North Wales where his sons were employed. John took over the foundry and then built a foundry of his own in Shropshire on the Severn River west of Birmingham, where his brother worked for him. John developed a boring machine that more accurately reamed cannon barrels (as well as steam-engine cylinders for Watt) and manufactured munitions, becoming wealthy, influential, and a benefactor of the Priestley family.

John Wilkinson's "domestic arrangements were of a most peculiar character" [Holt 1952, 63] --he kept his mistress in his home. After the death of his married daughter (his only legitimate child), when he died (after Priestley and his wife) his will left everything to his mistress and his children by her.

Relations between the Priestleys and John were strained in 1791 when Joseph, Jr., who worked for his uncle and was planning marriage, was dissatisfied with his prospects and quit his job. [Lesser 1974, 189] A few months later, after the Birmingham Riot had destroyed his home, Priestley's faith was justified that good came out of evil when he received a "kind letter" from John Wilkinson healing the rift, urging him to disregard "any losses that money can repair" and sending 500 pounds. Then, when Priestley and his family sought refuge in America, John transferred 10,000 pounds in

"French Funds" to Priestley with the assurance that, until they became productive, John would send him 200 pounds a year. Despite Priestley's efforts to collect on the French bonds, they yielded no interest and, until shortly before his death, he continued to receive remittances from his brother-in-law. [I-ii, 121]

Mary's younger brother William also provided financial assistance to the Priestleys through the years. [Primarily to help their sister, but they were also proud of their brother-in- law's achievements in science.]

John and William Wilkinson often quarreled and after one quarrel, William went to France where he opened a foundry that cast and bored cannon barrels, and cast iron sewer-pipes and other iron work for the large Paris waterworks. [Holt 1970, 131]

Priestley's income as a Warrington tutor was inadequate to meet his family's household expenses, so they took in students as boarders. Priestley later reflected that this led to "some valuable friendships," especially with the family of Samuel Vaughan, a wealthy London businessman whose two elder sons boarded with the Priestleys. But Mary found taking in boarders stressful on her frail health, even with the help of a maid. She bore her first child Sarah within the first year of their marriage. Later, while minister in Leeds, Priestley declined a request from Vaughan to take two more sons into his home to educate: "My wife's anxiety about them would be so great that I am afraid it would be prejudicial to her health." [I-i 59] By that time, Mary had born their second child, Joseph.

Still, by his account in his memoirs, Priestley's experience at Warrington was satisfying. He had introduced "public exercises" on Saturday mornings where the tutors, all the students and strangers assembled to hear compositions read, or speeches and scenes from plays. [I-i 53] He wrote: "In the whole time of my being at Warrington, I was singularly happy in the society of my fellow-tutors, and of Mr. Seddon, the minister of the place. We drank tea together every Saturday, and our conversation was equally instructive and pleasing. I often thought it not a little extraordinary that four persons ... should have been brought to unite in conducting such a scheme as this, and all be zealous Necessarians [believing in the necessity of acts of the will], as we were. We were likewise all Arians, and the only subject of much consequence on which we differed was respecting the doctrine of Atonement, concerning which Dr. Aikin held some obscure notions. Accordingly, this was frequently the topic of our friendly conversations. The only Socinian [anti-trinitarian] in the neighborhood was Mr. Seddon of Manchester; and we all wondered at him." [I-i, 58]

However, the Saturday afternoon teas were not only male discussions of theology, as Priestley implies. The tutor's congenial families also attended and Laetitia Aikin, daughter of the principal, records that "both *bouts rimes* and *vers de société* were in fashion with the set." It was their custom to slip anonymous poems into Mrs. Priestley's workbag. The author of one eloquent poem could not be identified until it was correctly guessed that it had been written by Priestley. [Holt 1970, 28]

A sample of Priestley's versification is a hymn, "To God Supreme and Ever Kind," probably composed in Birmingham to go with a "charity sermon" and given for use in the Sunday School:

To God supreme, and ever kind,
Immortal praise be given,
For powers of body, and of mind,
For this life, and for heaven.
....
Since by his bounty you enjoy
All that our hands produce
Still your superfluous wealth employ
To make those hands of use.
To you the book of Science fair
Does all its riches spread

Of this we ask the smallest share,
'Tis simply power to read.
....

[Manchester College, Oxford, holograph]

Laetitia Aikin remained a lifelong intimate friend and correspondent of Mary Priestley. Laetitia married Rochemont Barbauld, a Presbyterian minister who for a time kept a school in which she taught, and she became a popular minor poet. Priestley admits that "I was myself far from having any pretension to the character of a poet ..." and adds, "Mrs. Barbauld has told me that it was the perusal of some verses of mine that first induced her to write anything in verse." [I-i,54] After the Birmingham Riot, Mrs. Barbauld addressed a poem to Priestley:

Stirs not thy spirit, Priestley, as the train
With low obedience and with servile phrase
File upon file advance with supple knee,

And lay their necks beneath the foot of power?
Burns not thy cheek indignant when thy name,
On which delighted science loved to dwell,
Becomes the bandied theme of hooting crowds?
With timid caution, or with cool reserve
When e'en each reverend brother keeps aloof,
Eyes the stricken deer, and leaves thy naked side,
A mark for power to shoot at? Let it be,
On evil days though fallen and evil tongues,
To thee the slander of a passing age
Imports not. Scenes like these hold little space
In his large mind, whose ample stretch of thought
Grasps future periods. Well canst thou afford
To give large credit for that debt of fame
Thy country owes thee. Calm thou canst consign it
To the slow payment of that distant day,
If distant, when thy name to Freedom's joined
Shall meet the thanks of a regenerate land.

Perhaps the best known poem Barbauld wrote about Priestley is "The Mouse's Petition," which was prompted by a mouse, destined by Priestley for scientific experiment, seen on a visit to his home. After Mary Priestley's death in Northumberland, when Priestley learned that Mrs. Barbauld was taking temporary care of one of Priestley's grandchildren in England while their mother Sarah was ill and her husband bankrupt, Priestley wrote, "A friend in need is a friend indeed." [Lesser 1974, 52]

When Priestley moved to Warrington, he said that though he had no particular fondness for the studies he was assigned to teach, "I applied to them with great assiduity." He must have. He taught Latin, Greek, French, and Italian and composed lectures on the theory of language and on oratory and criticism, subtracting some courses when he added new ones.

He had composed the first draft of his grammar for use in his school in Nantwich. At Warrington, he published an expanded version, *A Course of Lectures on the Theory of Language, and Universal Grammar*, including examples from books he read "for amusement," for which he is recognized as "one of the great grammarians of his time," still cited by linguists. [Schofield 1983]

Usage, said Priestley, was normative in a language: "The custom of speaking is the original and only standard of any language." [XXIII, 5] "But our grammarians appear to me to have taken ... a wrong method of fixing our language. This will never be effected by the arbitrary rules of any man, or body of men whatever; because these suppose the language actually fixed already, contrary to the real state of it: whereas a language can never be properly fixed, till all the varieties with which it is used have been held forth to public view, and the general preference of certain forms have been declared, by the general practice afterwards."[XXIII, 8]

Noah Webster shared Priestley's standard of usage in composing *An American Dictionary of the English Language* (1828). Webster wrote; "a language must keep pace with improvements in knowledge, and ... no definable limits can be assigned to future discoveries and advances in science. To arrest the progress of a language is therefore impossible: and, if possible, would be a misfortune."

Mastery of the art of language, wrote Priestley, was a "measure of our intellectual powers; which ... constitutes what is the most obvious, and at the same time a real distinction between the rational and merely animal nature; ... and which, in the same country, renders one man superior to another." [XXIII, 125] Animals, he said, cannot acquire "very abstract or complex ideas; owing, probably, to their want of the power of articulation or speech. They can express their sensations, their joys and sorrows, their hopes and fears, in the clearest manner; but they are ... incapable of discoursing by words or signs, and this is the great instrument of improvement in man, as well as more compass of brain." [XVII, 47] Language is first learned "by imitation only," but learning the rules of grammar makes "a person understand the structure ... of languages," facilitating the use of language and a better understanding of other persons who use the same rules of grammar. [XXIII, 122]

The diversity of languages, said Priestley, was generally believed to have been inflicted by God for building the Tower of Babel, "but it is no impiety to suppose, that this (agreeable to most other operations of the Deity) might have been brought about by natural means." [XXIII, 243]

The transition from speaking to writing, said Priestley, was believed by such great men as Dr. Hartley to have occurred by "supernatural interposition"--the first alphabetical writing was by the finger of God inscribing the Ten Commandments on tablets of stone. [XXIII, 132] Instead, Priestley proposed that writing, like speech, was a human invention, "the result of such a concurrence of accident and gradual improvement as all human arts, and what we call inventions, owe their birth to." [XXIII, 135] Human beings were not Divinely endowed with a complete alphabet. Alphabets emerged gradually: "picture-writing, with the contraction of it into hieroglyphics, and the still further refinement of it into a character like Chinese" preceded the development of alphabets. [XXIII, 135]

Teaching oratory seems incongruous for a stutterer, but one of his former students recalled: "Though not proficient in oratory himself, Dr. Priestley contrived to render himself very useful to the promotion of it among his students. His observations on their defects in speaking, and his directions how to remedy them, were very judicious; and he had the advantage of being able to refer them to excellent practical models in Dr. Aikin and Mr. Seddon." [I-i, 54]

Another of his former students recalled his teaching methods: "What Dr. Priestley added in discoursing from his written lectures ... was pointedly and clearly illustrative of the subject before him, and expressed with great simplicity and distinctness of language, though he sometimes manifested that difficulty of utterance which he mentions in the Memoirs of his Life. ....In order to excite the freest discussion, he occasionally invited the students to drink tea with him, in order to canvass the subjects of his lectures. ... His written lectures he used to permit each student to take and read in his own lodgings. Those on Rhetoric he gave them the liberty of copying, those on History of reading only, as he intended them for publication. From minutes in short-hand, he dictated to each student, by turns, one of the lectures on History, who copied after him in long-hand. From this copy the Doctor told me they were printed, with some additions only, relative to subsequent events." [I-i, 50] By enlisting the help of his students, Priestley reinforced his teaching, and increased his productivity as writer. Priestley was informed that his published *Lectures on History* was used in American colleges; later it also was used at Oxford and Cambridge. [XIX, 214]

Priestley and his colleagues were concerned with transmitting not only facts and skills, but also moral character and a sense of ethical responsibility for the happiness of their fellow human beings and of the world. To this end, said one pupil, they sought to instill virtue in the minds of their students, and reverence for the Supreme Being--the message of the Old and New Testaments, which they thought could be "best promoted by the most thorough, liberal, and unbiased inquiry into the evidence of their divine authority, and the true meaning of their contents." [I-i, 51]

However, Priestley was no moral martinet; he thought it better to connive at some of the "extravagances of youth, which are not of an immoral nature," until they correct themselves, than by an "officious and unseasonable interposition" preclude their learning the error of their ways by experience. "Nature has wisely provided that we should not stand in so much need of artificial education, as is sometimes imagined; and true wisdom will not take too much out of the hand of nature." [XXV, 12]

Higher education was to prepare not merely scholars and clergy, but "the intelligent and useful citizen." At Warrington, wrote Priestley, "I introduced lectures on 'History and General Policy,' on the 'Laws and Constitution of England,' and on the 'History of England.' This I did in consequence of observing that, though most of our pupils were young men designed for situations in civil and active life, every article in the plan of their education was adapted to the learned professions." [I-i, 51] The universities, he pointed out, were intended primarily to train the clergy, and were run by the clergy who continued to teach what they had been taught, "nothing but rhetoric, logic, and school-divinity, or civil law." [XXII, 7]

Instead, he urged that "the studies of youth should tend to fit them for the business of manhood ... not too remote from the destined employment of their riper years." An "active life" included "all those stations in which a man's conduct will considerably affect the liberty and property of his countrymen, and the riches, the strength, and the security of his country," including wealthy gentlemen who in public service would be "standing near the helm of affairs, and guiding the secret springs of government," and the professions of law and of the "higher ranks" of the military. [XXIV, 9] Had he written this catalogue of people in "the principal stations of active life" after his association in Birmingham with leaders of the Industrial Revolution, he would have included the captains of industry who were becoming movers and shakers in England.

Another reason for properly educating youth, Priestley told the London supporters of the Dissenter's New College in Hackney, was to prepare them to participate in the government reforms then stirring--"the new light which is now almost every where bursting out in favor of the civil rights of men, and the great objects and uses of civil government. While so favorable a wind is abroad, let every young mind expand itself, catch the rising gale, and partake of the glorious enthusiasm; the great objects of which are the flourishing state of science, arts, manufactures, and commerce; the extinction of wars, with the calamities incident to mankind from them; the abolishing of all useless [class] distinctions, which are the offspring of a barbarous age (producing an absurd haughtiness in some, and a base servility in others); and a general release from all such taxes and burdens of every kind, as the public good does not require. In short, to make government as beneficial, and as little expensive and burdensome, as possible." [XV, 434]

Why spend so much time studying Latin, asked Priestley, when students know that when they have left the university they will have little occasion to use it. He pointed out that in many private schools and academies, and in university classes where the tutors want to "make their lectures of real use to their pupils," the lectures are in English. [XXII, 18]

"Colleges and schools are not the only places of education," Priestley said. "The world itself is the greatest theater of instruction, as well as action; and the actual wants and business of the age in which men live, form them for acting a proper part in it. Truly great minds, without any other hints than those which are suggested by their situation, will hit upon expedients to remedy abuses, and carry on improvements." [XV, 422] But what they slowly learn from experience they may rapidly teach others "by the art of education."

Education should include the study of human nature and the structure of our own minds with its various effects and operations. That study was not yet called psychology; Priestley called it "moral philosophy." [XXV, 19] And it should include, he said, "natural philosophy" or a knowledge of the external world. To "secure ourselves against the many accidents of life, even the destructive power of lightening itself [i.e., Franklin's lightening rods], not to mention what relates to the cure of diseases to which we are subject, are all derived from an acquaintance with the laws of nature.... The great superiority of modern over ancient times, is owing to our greater knowledge of nature; and the certain consequence of the increase of natural knowledge, will be as great a superiority of future times over the present, as that of the present over the past. It is a great advantage of this study that every new discovery serves as a key to many more of a similar nature." [XXV, 16] Moreover, he said, discovering the natural causes of phenomena and reducing the causes to general rules is "a very high satisfaction." [XXV, 18] The most valuable learning is that "necessary for subsistance," he wrote, so the most important instruction of students is "in such arts as will enable them to support themselves to advantage." [XXV, 14]

Priestley believed that the study of history prepares youth for "the business of life": "The ... higher use of history is to improve the understanding and strengthen the judgment, and thereby fit us for entering upon life with advantage." History presents us with the same problems we meet today and "may be called anticipated experience." Learning about past human experience enables us to bring into the business of living "such a cast of thought and temper of mind, as is acquired by passing through it; which will make us appear to more advantage in it, and not such mere novices upon our introduction to it, as we would otherwise be." [XXIV, 29]

Priestley claimed that "the knowledge of history improves the understanding.... [and] tends to free the mind from many foolish prejudices, particularly an unreasonable partiality for our own country, merely as our own country, which makes a people truly ridiculous in the eyes of foreigners. It was a want of acquaintance with history that made the Chinese mandarins express astonishment to find their country make so small a figure in a map of the world which the Jesuits showed them. ... National prejudices likewise produce a most unreasonable aversion to foreign nations and foreign religions, which nothing but an acquaintance with history can cure." [XXIV, 32]

The study of history for Priestley was not the mere collecting of facts but seeking the connections and consequences of events. "If we read history like philosophers, we must principally attend to the connection of causes and effect in all the great changes in human affairs. We ought never to be satisfied with barely knowing an event, but endeavor to trace all the circumstances in the situation of things which contributed either to produce or facilitate, to hasten or retard it, and clearly see the manner of their operation; by which we shall be better able to form a judgment of the state of political affairs in future time, and take our measures with greater wisdom and a more reasonable prospect of success." [XXIV, 203]

Priestley was among those who assumed that history was to supplant speculative philosophy as the source of moral and political principles. History is cumulative experience that furnishes the mind with known facts and experiments from which to draw conclusions and project plans. It enlarges the field of knowing from experience. True history, said Priestley, is "an inexhaustible mine of the most valuable knowledge. ... Real history resembles the experiments made by air pumps, the condensing engine and electrical machine, which exhibit the operations of nature, and the God of nature himself, ... and are the ground-work and materials of the most extensive and useful theories." [XXIV, 28]

Priestley believed that the facts of history were as much the products of experience as the facts of scientific experiments; both were based on observation and inductive reasoning, and were integrated in his empirical epistemology. The Bible also was history and, once reason had sorted fact from fiction, provided empirical evidence of the truth of Christianity.

He also believed that the history of human experiences strengthened the moral sense by revealing the beneficial effects of virtue and the painful results of vice, an empirical method.

But he did not see that experience was also the source of the moral principles in the Old and New Testament, which he continued to claim were special revelations.

In his Warrington Academy lectures on general history, Priestley dealt with old coins, history of commerce, taxes, agriculture, manufacture, arts, science, fisheries, land value, commercial use of colonies, weights and measures, uses of money, interest, paper money, credit, luxury and frugality, the importance of manufacture, labor as the source of wealth, and the advantages of a balance of trade in an open market. He drew on Adam Smith's *Wealth of Nations* and James Stuart's *Principles of Political Economy*. He also urged the study of geography to prepare young men for an "active life," particularly "commercial geography" about trade and local products suitable for commerce. He added, "A knowledge of chemistry is absolutely necessary to the extension of this useful branch of science." [XXIV, 440]

Priestley also included lectures on the laws and constitution of England, in which he concluded that, from an historical perspective, the current state of the world, and particularly Europe, was preferable to that of any past time. In the introductory address to the course on the history of England, though it stresses the importance of security, commerce and power, Priestley warned students "not to forget ... that we are citizens of the world." [Sugiyama 1984, 81]

For the 16 to 20 year old youths Priestley taught at Warrington, he classified the periods in history and showed the relation of events and their significance. He gave nine lectures on the various sources of history, and 13 lectures commenting on the work of historians. As aids to visualizing the relationship of events and people, he prepared a *Chart of Biography* that included historians, lawyers, orators, artists, poets, mathematicians, scientists, clergy, physicians, and metaphysicians as well as statesmen and warriors from 1100 B.C. to 1800 A.D. A few years later, he published *A New Chart of History*, dedicated to Benjamin Franklin, which proved to be his most popular work. He protested that "in almost all histories, we see little more than what has been done by princes and ministers of state; and it is only from incidental circumstances that we are able to collect what has been thought or done by the people, which has been the progress of science, of arts, of manufactures, and commerce, by which the real welfare of nations is promoted." [XV, 435]

Priestley explained that on meeting "three electricity experimentors" in London in the middle of his fourth year at Warrington, "having composed all the lectures I had occasion to deliver, and finding myself at liberty for any undertaking, I mentioned to Dr. Franklin an idea that had occurred to me of writing a history of discoveries in electricity, which had been his favorite study. This I told him might be an useful work, and that I would willingly undertake it, provided I could be furnished with the books necessary for the purpose." [I-i, 55]

Priestley had already begun his research before he met the three "electrical experimentors" in London. Books arrived from Franklin and other friends. Priestley had a machine to produce static electricity that he used to test disputed experiments, and he went on to do original experiments in his "leisure time." Within a year, Priestley sent a printed copy of his history of electricity to Franklin. To defend himself against charges that he wrote too hastily, he pointed out that, "In the same year, five hours of every day were employed in lectures, ... and one two months' vacation I spent chiefly at Bristol, on a visit to my father-in-law"--and yet the hastily written *History and Present State of Electricity, with Original Experiments* was a classic that established his reputation as a scientist. He explained why it was so successful: "During the course of my electrical experiments in this year, I kept up a constant correspondence with Dr. Franklin, and the rest of my philosophical friends in London; and my letters circulated among them all, as also every part of my History as it was transcribed. This correspondence ... took up much time; but it was of great use with respect to the accuracy of my experiments, and the perfection of my work." [I-i, 57]

In most of his publications, he had the advantage of friendly criticism of his work before publication. His object, he wrote, was not to acquire the reputation of a fine writer, but of a useful one. Nor was it to make money; some of his work was published at a loss, which his benefactors reimbursed in order to encourage him to publish.

After six fruitful and happy years at Warrington, Priestley accepted an invitation to serve as minister of Mill Hill chapel at Leeds at a much better salary. Priestley explained: "Though all the tutors in my time lived in most perfect harmony, though we all exerted ourselves to the utmost, and there was no complaint of want of discipline, the academy did not flourish." The original difference between the trustees and the principal split the trustees, and many of them cancelled their subscriptions of support for the academy. (Warrington Academy later moved to Manchester and finally wound up as Manchester College, Oxford, where it is still struggling to exist.) Priestley concluded: "There being no prospect of things being any better, and my wife having very bad health, on her account chiefly I wished for a removal," though his employment was agreeable "and all the laborious part of it was over." [I-i, 61] Priestley was always concerned for the welfare of his family.

His career and reputation were destroyed by the Birmingham establishment's reaction to his theological polemics against the corruptions of Christianity.

XII

AN HISTORY OF THE CORRUPTIONS OF CHRISTIANITY
"The Platonizing Christians"

While Priestley was minister in Birmingham, he wrote his most challenging criticism of orthodox Christianity. When he had earlier visited Paris, his distress at the numerous unbelievers in Christianity among his enlightened associates in science resulted in his *History of the Corruptions of Christianity*. He became involved in an eight-year controversy in which he was denounced, but not contradicted. He thought that the corruptions were obstacles to belief in pure Christianity, not because they were innovations but because they were pollutions of the gospel. He traced the source of the corruptions to the "heathen philosophy" of Platonism, and marshaled evidence from the New Testament and from the writings of Christian apologists of the first three centuries to substantiate his claim that the early Christians believed in the humanity of Jesus and the unity of God, which were not recent heresies but pristine Christian beliefs. He defended historic Christianity as more credible than the speculative Platonic philosophy that encumbered it.

Priestley's Christian polemic was intended to reform historic Christianity, not attack it. He was continuing the Protestant Reformation of the 17th century: "Those reformers are not to be blamed for not doing more, but to be commended for doing as much as they did. But surely those who came after them are to be blamed, those who have shut their eyes, and have endeavored to shut yours too, from that time to the present day; as if Luther and his brethren had been men divinely inspired and exempt from all error, and as if all wisdom was born and died with them; whereas they only set an example, which those who came after them ought to have followed." [XIX, 240] Those who censure innovators, said Priestley, "are censuring the spirit and example of the very persons whose opinions they have adopted....It is the spirit of inquiry, which, if error be established, necessarily leads to innovation...." [XV, 75] As innovators, he listed Socinus, Arius, Arminius, and Calvin. He did not mention Jesus, a reformer who made innovations in Judaism.

In religion as in science, he thought there should be room for improvement: "My ancestors did not teach me what I teach others; and I am far from supposing that all improvements will end with me. In all cases in which men determine, room should be left for the revision and subsequent determination of other men, who may see farther than they do." [XIX, 189]

In a sermon on "The Importance and Extent of Free Inquiry in Matters of Religion," he warned: "Dissenters ... may think the principles of their dissent from the establishment of their country sufficiently vindicated, and that now we have nothing to do but joyfully acquiesce in our great liberty; only being ready to oppose all attempts that may be made to encroach upon it."

"This, however," he continued, "is the language of those who think they have acquired all useful religious knowledge; whereas, it is probable, that this will never be the situation of man, not even in a future world, and much less in this. In nature we see no bounds to our inquiries. One discovery always gives hints of many more, and brings us into a wider field of speculation. Now, why should not this be, in some measure, the case with respect to knowledge of a moral and religious kind. Is the compass of religious knowledge so small, as that any person, however imperfectly educated, may comprehend the whole, and without much trouble?"

In church history, he noted, "As one controversy has been determined, or sufficiently agitated, others have always arisen; and I will venture to say there never was a time in which there were more, or more interesting objects of discussion before us, than there are at present." [XV, 71]

Prejudice, Priestley knew from his own experience, but was not always aware of, blocked recognition of truths, like a person reading a book "with a particular bias upon his mind. He does not see, or at least he does not regard, any thing but what he is purposely looking for, and wishes to find... In this case it is hardly possible for the mind to perceive its own delusion, and there seems to be no remedy for it." [XVII, 33] Prejudice, he wrote, was a cause of infidelity--when skeptics read the Bible, they noticed only its absurdities. Prejudice was also the cause of the corruptions of Christianity-- when the heathens embraced early Christianity, they mixed their presumptions with it. To Priestley, the Bible was history but could be interpreted differently by people with small differences in their states of mind, with different estimates of the probability of the incidents related, and with different judgments of confidence in the competence of the contemporary witnesses. [XVII, 14] Hence, there could be no authoritative interpretation, just enlightened interpretations.

Emotions influenced judgments, wrote Priestley in a tract, "Considerations on the Differences of Opinion among Christians": "We are generally influenced by a variety of motives in whatever we do. ... especially in cases where the passions and affections are strong....I am satisfied, that the pure love of truth is, on both sides, absorbed in passions of a very different nature." [XIX, 16] Thus Priestley, without rancor, accounted for the differences in interpretations of the Bible between himself, the orthodox, and the unbelievers.

Priestley welcomed the criticisms of Christianity precipitated by the Enlightenment: "Whatever will not bear the test of rigorous scrutiny must now be rejected.... This will be the means of purging our religion from every thing that will not bear this rigorous examination; but it will contribute to the firmer establishment of every thing that will bear it." [XV, 196] Priestley's research in the New Testament and early Christian apologists began with the hypothesis that there were corruptions of historic Christianity. As he candidly acknowledged, he was "fully persuaded that Christ was a man like ourselves," and that "In this state of mind ... I naturally expected to find, what I was previously well persuaded was to be found; and in time I collected much more evidence than I at first expected, considering the early rise, and the long and universal spread, of what I deem to be a radical corruption of the genuine Christian doctrine." He invited his reader to "make whatever allowance he may think necessary for my particular situation and prejudices." [XVIII, 41]

A "prejudice" that he was aware of was his "materialism." He had already established that all human beings were mortal, made of one substance, matter, and that even Jesus had no soul or spirit to have pre-existed with God, though Jesus was divinely consecrated as the Messiah.

In his apologetics, Priestley had two purposes: to purge Christianity of the corruptions that made it unacceptable to thoughtful unbelievers, and to provide evidence to support essential doctrines:

"We now see things in a very different light. We refuse to receive the principles of philosophy, and certainly should not receive those of religion, without being satisfied, from proper evidence, with respect to their truth." [XVIII, 347] He acknowledged, "I am not so little acquainted with human nature, as to expect any great success in this attempt to overturn long-established error...." [II, 485] But, in the preface to *Corruptions*, he did think that the "gross darkness of that night which has for many centuries obscured our holy religion ... is past; the morning is opening upon us; and we cannot doubt but that the light will increase...." [V, 4]

In *An History of the Corruptions of Christianity* Priestley claimed that he clearly described the rise of the doctrine of the Trinity and proved "that the great body of primitive Christians were strict Unitarians; but that the philosophizing [Greek] Christians, offended at the humiliating idea of having a crucified man at the head of their religion, after some time adopted the opinion of his being of a nature higher than human; and that this exaltation of him went on, till they made him to be God equal to the Father; but this was a work of time, and not accomplished in less than four hundred years after Christ." [XIX 256] The specific details of his scholarly evidences of the corruptions are contained in the 500-page volume of his *History*.

The deification of Christ by Platonic Christians was the root corruption, followed by the other corruptions that Priestley described in Socinian terms. The subsequent worship of Christ was "idolatry," a charge that most offended the clergy of the Church of England who made no attempt to refute it. [XXII, 458]

Jesus himself, said Priestley, accepted only the role of the expected Messiah, "referring all his extraordinary powers to God, his Father, who, he expressly says, spake and acted by him ... and it is most evident that the apostles, and all those who conversed with our Lord before and after his resurrection, considered him in no other light than simply as 'a man approved of God, by wonders and signs which God did by him.' Acts 2:22" [V, 14]

But the converts with a Greek education, particularly the apologists "addicted to the doctrine of Plato," wrote Priestley, identified the "logos," the divine reason of Greek philosophy, with Christ who pre-existed with God as an immortal soul, and created the universe: "In order to exalt their idea of Jesus Christ, it being then a received opinion among philosophers that all souls had preexisted, they conceived his soul not to have been that of a common man ... but a principal emanation from the divine mind itself, and that an intelligence of so high a rank either animated the body of Jesus from the beginning, or entered into him at baptism. ... a system which was

not founded on any observation, but was the mere creature of fancy."
[V, 26] He added, "The doctrines of the pre-existence and divinity of
Christ were not fully discovered till the publication of the Gospel of
John, which was one of the last of all the books of the New Testament." [VI, 397] The Gospel of John was written about a century
after the death of Jesus. By then it was clear that the future of
Christianity lay not in the Jewish but in the Greco- Roman world
and the Gospel was recast in terms intelligible to Greek thought.
Priestley, in turn recasting orthodox Christianity in terms intelligible to his enlightened contemporaries, referred back to what he
believed to be the biblical empirical-foundations of historic Christianity.

The revision of the Gospel by philosophical speculation, rather
than by a rational inquiry into historical experience, Priestley wrote,
"taken altogether, will show, in a striking light, the very extensive
mischief that has been done to revealed religion by the introduction
of this part of the system of Heathenism, concerning the soul. ... And,
for my own part, I am satisfied that it is only by purging away the
whole of this corrupt leaven, that we can recover the pristine
simplicity and purity of our most excellent and truly rational,
though much abused, religion." [III, 208]

He asked rhetorically: "If you ask who, then, is Jesus Christ, if he
be not God; I answer, in these words of Peter addressed to the Jews,
after his resurrection and ascension, that 'Jesus of Nazareth' was 'a
man approved of God--by miracles and wonders and signs, which
God did by him.' Acts 2:22 If you ask what is meant by 'man,' in this
place;I answer that man.... must mean the same kind of being with
yourselves. I say, moreover, with the author of the epistle to the
Hebrews, that 'it became him for whom are all things, and by whom
are all things-- to make the captain of our salvation' in all respects
'like unto us his brethren,' that he might be made 'perfect through
sufferings' Heb. 2:l0 & 17, and that he might have a 'feeling of all
our infirmities.' 4:15 ... a mere man, as other Jews, and as we
ourselves are." [II, 394]

That was his ground for becoming a Socinian (Unitarian), as he
explained to the Anglicans of Birmingham: "Socinians believe that
Christ is not God equal to the Father, as your church maintains, but
they say that he was a man inspired of God, or a prophet; that he
was sent of God to teach men the true way to eternal life, and
especially to preach the doctrines of an universal resurrection, and
a future judgment; that in order to enable him to preach these great
doctrines with effect, he was empowered by God to work many
miracles; that he was crucified, died, and was buried; but that God

raised him from the dead, and took him into heaven; where he is to continue till, in God's appointed time, he will come again to raise all the dead, to judge the world, and to give unto every man according to his works." [XIX, 245] That sounds almost like the orthodox claims, except that Christ was a man not equal to God.

Priestley's prejudice that Jesus was "inspired by God" obviated his perception of the sources of Jesus' gospel. Jesus, Priestley wrote, was not "conceived by the Holy Ghost," as the Apostle's Creed declared, but was "the legitimate son of Joseph and Mary." [XIX, 299] He was a common carpenter who Priestley knew could read and write and study the scriptures, but who Priestley thought was "without advantage of any learned education." [XV, 68] He was therefore, by his human nature alone, incapable of devising the system of religion which he founded. [XXI, 180] Priestley thought that Jesus did not require learning to accomplish his divine mission: "We see no reason to think that Jesus' appearing as the Messiah at thirty years of age, required any particular previous knowledge ... his supernatural illumination, and his private meditations ... will sufficiently account for the part that he acted...." [VII, 68] Jesus, said Priestley, "differs from us not with respect to his proper nature, but only in the greater perfection of his nature, and in divine communications." [XV, 40] His miracles attested to his divine mission. [IV, 457]

Priestley was mistaken when he said that Jesus needed no education as his gospel was divinely inspired and original. In spite of Priestley's empirical epistemology, paradoxically he did not recognize that Jesus studied and selectively quoted from the wisdom gained by many generations of human experience recorded in the Old Testament, and that he learned from his own experience and observation, which he taught by analogy in his parables. Priestley overlooked how often Jesus quoted the Old Testament, either to express his own conviction or to change the teaching, as can be easily noted in Bibles published with the texts cross- referenced. In Matthew 4:4,7 and 10, Jesus repeated "It is written," and then quoted from Deuteronomy; in Matthew 5:3,4,5,6, and 7 Jesus paraphrased Old Testament quotations.

Priestley said, "Jesus having nothing materially new to teach, the whole of the moral law having been delivered by Moses and the prophets," he only reminded his hearers to obey them. [XVI, 265] But Jesus did often teach something new about the moral laws he had learned. He transformed Old Testament morality. In "The Sermon on the Mount," [Matthew 5:] he began a number of sayings with "Ye have heard that it was said by them of old time...."and added, "But I say unto you...." He changed "Thou shalt not kill" to "whosoever is angry with his brother shall be in danger of the judgment"; "Thou shalt not commit adultery" he changed to "whosoever looketh on a woman to lust after her hath committed adultery with her already in his heart"; "Whosoever shall put away his wife, let him give her a writing of divorcement" he changed to "whosoever shall put away his wife, saving for the cause of fornication, causeth her to commit adultery"; "An eye for an eye and a tooth for a tooth" he changed to "resist not evil"; and "Thou shalt love thy neighbor, and hate thine enemy" he changed to "Love thy enemies." Rather than accepting the legalisms of the Saducees (the priests who dominated religious and political life in Israel, and who opposed any changes) Jesus challenged the people, "Why do you not judge for yourselves what is right." [Luke 12:57] Jesus was a reformer, a prophet.

The moral and religious insights of Jesus did not come entirely from the scriptures and traditions of his Jewish heritage, nor from a transcendent source, but from his personal experiences with nature and human life, which he reflected in his parables. By vivid and personal insights, he saw the divine meaning in common experience; the natural world was a parable of the Creator. [Fenn 1938, 32] The Kingdom of God would come in the same way as the seeds cast by a man on the ground grew, "he knew not how." [Mark 4:26] Meanwhile, sinners should not be persecuted: like the weeds that sprang up in a field of wheat, whose owner said, "Let them grow together until the harvest," lest pulling out the weeds would also uproot the wheat. [Mat. 13:24] Jesus knew that the multitudes who heard his gospel would have different responses, like seeds that fell on different kinds of soil would grow, or not grow, accordingly. [Mat. 13:3] In the parable of the Prodigal Son, the way the father treated his wayward but repentant son illustrated how God treated human beings, and how society should treat its aberrant citizens. [Luke 13:3] In opposition to the tradition of the Scribes and Pharisees, Jesus introduced a new, less legalistic, morality.

The corruptions continued after the deification of Christ: the Holy Spirit was deified and the doctrine of the Trinity, one God in three persons--Father, Son, and Holy Spirit, was advanced. The Arians developed a position that ascribed divinity to Christ, who was to be worshiped as the soul or spirit that pre-existed with God and created the universe, but retained the concept of one supreme God. Arianism was quashed as heresy by a 4th Century church council that established the Trinity as orthodox, but was the theology accepted by Priestley and his fellow tutors at Warrington Academy.

The orthodox Christians claimed that Adam's "original sin" in the Garden of Eden (he ate the forbidden apple of the tree of knowledge of good and evil and might eat the fruit of the tree of life and live forever--"In Adam's fall we sinned all") was an offense against an infinite God that required an infinite satisfaction ("Christ died for our sins"). Priestley, who had originally questioned orthodoxy on this point, countered that there was no biblical authority for the doctrine. A sin by a finite creature did not require infinite satisfaction. Salvation required only repentance and reformation, which were acceptable to the God of grace and mercy, like the father in the parable of the Prodigal Son. The crucifixion of Christ was not a "propitiation," of an offended God, but was to reveal the doctrine of the resurrection of the body and a future immortal life, with the sanction of morality by retribution for the good or evil done in this life.

Priestley denied Calvin's doctrine that only the "elect" were predestined to be saved, which he said was unknown to early Christians, and was contrary to common sense and reason. Priestley said sin was a personal act to be redeemed by a personal act of contrition and turning to a good life.

Another corruption that Priestley rejected was instantaneous conversion by divine influence; he claimed conversion was a gradual, natural process. As a child, Priestley had been despondent and felt abandoned by God because he did not experience a rebirth by divine grace. At age 46, he claimed that such an expectation was "altogether unscriptural and deceitful." Of his own mature position, he said his "doctrine of the exclusion of all immediate agency of the Deity on the minds of men, restraining them from evil, or disposing them to good, and of his doing this by no other means than by the natural influence of proper instructions and motives, certainly goes to the root of the grossest and most dangerous delusions that the Christian world has, in all ages, been subject to. [XV, 83]

Instead of instantaneous conversion by grace, Priestley claimed that conversion required discipline and study--read the Bible, pray, attend church, honor the seventh day for rest and reflection--to become a proper Christian, "not in name and profession only, but in deed and in truth; because a habit of temper is to be formed, which can only be produced by the long continuance of proper actions. ... If repentance consist of a change of disposition and conduct, it is not even possible that a late, or what we call a death-bed repentance, can be an effectual one." [XV, 13]

Conversion and reformation, he wrote, "takes place according to the usual course of nature...." [XV, 85] He explained: "We are instructed to pray that God would give us, day by day, our daily bread, and it is from God that we do receive our daily bread; but it is only in the natural course of things, and by the use of proper means for procuring it for ourselves. ... When ... operations in surgery are to be performed, we look up to God, but at the same time we never fail to have recourse to the hand of a skilful surgeon." [XV, 95] "A real change of character, from vice to virtue, is only effected in a natural, and, consequently, in a gradual manner." [XV, 97]

The Lord's Supper was originally a shared meal commemorating Christ that was corrupted by the Roman Church into the celebration of a mass bestowing grace, the love and protection of God. Whereas the primitive church had been supervised by officials elected by the members and conversion was voluntary, in the Roman church authority was transferred to the Pope elected by the clergy and enforced by the state.

A further corruption was that the Church of England reformation transferred control of church and doctrine to the secular authorities of king and Parliament. Both Catholic and Protestant leaders persecuted heretics with fire and sword, wrote Priestley, "strengthening the unnatural alliance between Christianity and the powers of this world...." [XV, 427] Dissenters dissented from any human authority in religion, he said, and recognized the authority of only God and Christ.

In the process of determining the pure New Testament faith, instead of accepting the Bible's infallibility, Priestley pioneered in the "higher criticism" of the Bible--what did a text mean to those contemporaries for whom it was written in terms of the time, circumstances, and purpose of the author. ("Lower criticism" is concerned with the accuracy of the translation and the authenticity of the texts.) His historical method anticipated some of the radical findings of 19th and 20th century Bible scholars. His scientific explanations of how God worked, and application of higher criticism to the interpretation of the Bible, weakened the foundation of traditional Christianity. He foreshadowed modern liberal theology by combining a high regard for the Bible's authority with a rejection of its infallibility. The result was his curious amalgam of opinions; some were surprisingly liberal and others very orthodox. He abandoned the defense of Christianity by reference to authorities or by philosophical speculations, and launched the rational historical analysis of the truth of the Christian faith. [Chapin 1967, 97]

During his biblical studies in his first parish, Priestley had arrived at one of his more radical principles of interpretation--that the Bible was not written under supernatural influence. He denied the divine inspiration of the Bible because it led to incredulity: "Christian divines having maintained the absolute inspiration of every word of the canonical books of Scripture, has been attended with very bad consequences, by laying the system of revelation open to so many insignificant, but plausible objections; and this kind of inspiration is as needless, as it is impossible to maintain." [II, 210] Moreover, he said, to guarantee the authenticity of inspiration, every transcriber who could err in copying the Bible, and translator who could mistake the meaning of it, also had to be inspired.

The Bible contained authentic historic records of the dispensations of God to mankind, wrote Priestley, but the authors were not infallible: "The writers of the books of Scriptures were men, and, therefore, fallible; but all that we have to do with them is in the character of historians, and witnesses of what they heard and saw. Of course, their credibility is to be estimated like that of other historians, viz. from the circumstances in which they wrote, with respect to their opportunities of knowing the truth of what they relate, and the biases to which they might be subject. Like all other historians, they were liable to mistakes with respect to things of small moment ... and with respect to their reasoning, we are fully at liberty to judge it, as well as that of any other men, by a due consideration of the propositions they advance, and the arguments they allege." [IV, 467]

This approach, he said, placed "the Gospel history on the same unexceptionable footing with other credible histories, resting on independent testimonies, in consequence of their agreement in all things of importance, and appearing to be independent of each other, by their disagreement in things of no importance." [XX, 14] The Gospel writers were witnesses of events they described, or personally knew people who were, he said. They wrote at a time when other witnesses still lived who could vouch for or deny the truth of the reports, yet the books were widely believed by contemporaries. [IV, 495]

However, Priestley accepted the traditional authorship and date of the Gospels, which was untenable to some scholars of his generation, as well as to modern Bible scholars. To justify his hypothesis that the books of the Bible were genuine history and written by authors who were either contemporaries of the events they wrote about, or had access to contemporary accounts which were not challenged, Priestley believed the traditional ascription of the authors of all books of the Bible. [II, 123] Priestley claimed that the first five books of the Old Testament were written by Moses, though the book of Genesis "must have been collected from tradition." But he did not believe that the "great miracle" story of the creation in six days was historically true: creation came about slowly by divinely ordained natural means. [VII, 306]

Nor did he accept the veracity of the orthodox and Arian doctrine that a pre-existent Christ created the world; we were under no obligation "to believe it, merely because it was an opinion held by an Apostle," Priestley wrote, since it was certainly no part of Christ's own Gospel. [Gordon 1970, 117]

Priestley claimed that the fundamental New Testament revelation was the resurrection of Christ. On this depended the faith in an afterlife for all human beings at the Second Coming of Christ on Judgment Day--along with the orthodox, Priestley believed that retribution was essential for morality.

Revelation, the divine suspension of the laws of nature by miracles, wrote Priestley, was the additional, fuller and clearer knowledge of God, moral behavior and a future life contained in the Bible. God demonstrated the supreme value of morality by the miraculous resurrection of the body of Christ that promised future retribution for all in an afterlife for good or evil done in this life.

Revelation to Priestley did not mean relinquishing reason: "On the contrary ... we ought to make the most use of it, to see that we are not imposed upon.... It is only by the help of that faculty which we call reason, that we can distinguish between any two systems of religion that may be proposed to us. It is by reason only that we can judge both of their previous probability, and also of the positive evidence that is produced in favor of them." [II,117] Evidence in religion, to Priestley, was the same as reports of observation and experience in science. Christianity was an historic faith resting on the evidence of testimony by human witnesses that was not con-tradicted by those in a position to know. He commented that we have "no firmer persuasion concerning anything, than we have of the existence of many things which we have never seen ourselves, nor ever expect to see, and of the truth of facts which we know only from the information of others...." [XXI, 118]

David Hume had argued that miracles--departures from the laws of nature-- contradicted our experience of the constant uniformity of the laws of nature. Priestley argued that "there are doctrines which, to man at least, absolutely require the aid of miracles to their proof; as that of a resurrection from the dead at a future period, which it is impossible for us to learn from any appearances in nature...." [XXI, 135] It was such exceptions to natural laws that caught people's attention and made them believers in revealed Christianity. [II, 109] God, he said, "who ordained and established the course of nature, can alter it." [II, 110] That argument would be even less persuasive today than it was to Priestley's philosophical unbelievers; now scientists understand that natural laws are descriptions of observed regular sequences of events, and are not like civil laws that are enacted and can be nullified. [Clark 1984, 131]

In his defense of the New Testament testimony of witnesses to miracles, Priestley reversed a fundamental canon of historical criticism--that one must remain in doubt when the evidence is inconclusive. Instead, he assumed that the absence of contemporary refutations amounted to convincing support. He shifted the burden of proof from those who alleged a truth to those who denied it. [Chapin 1967, 153] He overlooked the fact that the New Testament was written by believers.

With the increase in knowledge, miracles were no longer necessary or expected, said Priestley: "Christianity, I am confident, will be able, without the aid of any more miracles, to free itself from all its impurities, and command the assent of all the world, even the learned and most skeptical not excluded." [IV, 436] To spread the knowledge of pure Christianity was the work of churches.

From the "prejudices" instilled by the circumstances of Priestley's childhood, we can acknowledge the incongruities in his liberal defense of his devout Christian faith without ignoring the many progressive contributions he made to the understanding of historic Christianity. He was the precursor of the study of the Bible as history, basing his theology on what he perceived to be facts. He integrated science and theology through his unified epistemology, and evaluated religious doctrines by their practical consequences in behavior--virtue was the goal. Where the scholarly study of Christianity has progressed beyond Priestley, it is influenced by the principles he was the first to define and apply. [Gordon 1970, 122]

Priestley was among the earliest to understand that the gospels consisted of separate units whose forms were gradually fixed in the process of oral and written transmission. He concluded that the Sermon on the Mount was not delivered in its present form on one occasion, but was a collection of Jesus' moral maxims given at various times and later consolidated for convenience in teaching his gospel. Priestley even asserted that certain sections incorporated by the evangelists in their histories were spurious, notably the accounts of Christ's birth in Matthew and Luke. [Chapin 1967, 105]

Priestley came to doubt the "ill-grounded opinion" of the Gospel writers concerning the "miraculous conception" of Jesus. [VII, 58] Lindsey was apprehensive about Priestley's publication of his doubt and wished he would restrain himself, "lest it might hurt his usefulness in preventing the reading of his many valuable theological writings." [Belsham 1812, 230] Priestley was "well aware that what I have advanced on this subject will give my enemies fresh occasion for raising a clamor against me." [VI, 9] But, in the cause of promoting what he thought was truth, he was prepared to bear the odium. [VII, 58]

"Our Savior himself, being a man, could not, naturally, be either infallible or impeccable...." (incapable of sin), said Priestley. [VII, 347] "We lose the benefit of his example altogether, if we never consider him as thinking, speaking or acting like other men, that is, as other men of good principles and good sense would naturally speak and act...." [VII, 353] When Jesus cured mental illness, he was incorrect when he assumed a then popular theory and ascribed a disordered mind to possession by evil spirits or demons, said Priestley, though "in reality, no such beings existed." [VII 349]

Belief in spirits led to one of the corruptions, Priestley wrote: Christians came to have an idea "of a local heaven, and of God and Christ residing there," where at death good souls would immediately go, while the souls of sinners "went to some place under the ground; ... but this is not the doctrine of the Scriptures, [and] it could not have been the general opinion of Christians at first...." [V, 220]

A year before the Birmingham Riot, Priestley realized that his theological sentiments had been "no where so unpopular as among the Dissenters themselves...." His opinions gave the greatest offense to those known as "rational Dissenters" (especially Arians), "and it is only of late that the case has begun to be a little otherwise. At one time there were not more than two or three pulpits in England that I considered as open to me." [XIX, 213]

He explained: "What has contributed the most to get me the character [reputation] of a controversial writer, is what I have written in defense of myself when attacked from a variety of quarters, on account of my *Disquisitions concerning Matter and Spirit* and my *History of the Corruptions of Christianity*. I should never have written against Bishop Horsley, any more than against Mr. Burn, if he had not first written against me." [XIX, 228-29] But Priestley had challenged doctrines most essential to their faith and favor.

So great was his confidence in the tacit religious freedom of England that he thought the controversy would soon pass: "The odium I have brought upon myself by maintaining the doctrines of Materialism and Necessity, without attempting to cover or soften terms of so frightful a sound, and without palliating any of their consequences, was unspeakably greater than what this business [regarding the Corruptions] can bring upon me. At the beginning of that controversy I had few, very few indeed, of my nearest friends, who were with me in the argument. They, however, who knew me, knew my motives, and excused me; but the Christian world in general regarded me with the greatest abhorrence. I was considered an unprincipled infidel, either an Atheist or in league with Atheists. In this light I was repeatedly exhibited in all the public papers; and the *Monthly Review,* and other *Reviews,* with all the similar publications of the day, joined in the popular cry. But a few years have seen the end of it.... A similar issue I firmly expect from the present controversy...." [XVIII, 43]

A few years did not see the end of it. It is one thing to innovate cosmological speculations, which interest only the philosophers, and another thing to threaten the faith by which people live or make their living. Priestley had precipitated a major theological controversy; other opponents joined the fray-- Roman Catholics, Methodists, an Arian, and numerous Anglicans-- and over 50 publications sought to refute him. By 1789, the *Gentleman's Magazine* hoped for a respite from the vitriolic articles and letters condemning Priestley as a dangerous enemy of Christianity, and the other articles and letters defending him. After the Birmingham Riot, there was another spate of such articles.

Samuel Horsley, D.D., Archdeacon of St. Albans. which is about 19 miles northwest of the heart of London, initiated the eight-year controversy with Priestley by warning the clergy of the "extraordinary attempt which hath lately been made to unsettle the faith, and to break up the constitution, of every ecclesiastical establishment in Christendom. Such is the avowed object of a recent publication, which bears the title of *A History of the Corruptions of Christianity,* among which the Catholic doctrine of the Trinity, in the author's opinion, holds the principal place." [XVIII, 47] Horsley published his opinions in a series of tracts, and Priestley replied in published letters, hoping to air the truth as he saw it.

Dr. Horsley (the son of a Dissenter minister) said that, after the Platonists brought him "to a right mind," he became convinced that "mysteries"--the Trinity, the Atonement, and the pre-existence of Christ--were necessary to Christianity. He was an accomplished mathematician and member of the Royal Society who had edited an edition of Newton's works.

In his first animadversion on Priestley's *Corruptions,* Horsley said that "the most effectual preservative against the intended mischief would be to destroy the writer's credit, and the authority of his name; which the fame of certain lucky experiments had set high in popular esteem, by proof of his incompetency in every branch of literature connected with his present scheme; of which the work itself afforded evident specimens in great abundance." [Holt 1970, 135] Priestley retorted, "Professing to prove my incompetency in the subject, he has given most abundant proofs of his own, and even of his deficiency in the learned languages." [XIX, 3] Horsley countered: "Dr. Priestley forgets that the main argument with him and with me goes to different points. His point is the antiquity and the truth of the Unitarian doctrine. Mine is Dr. Priestley's incompetency in the subject." [Holt 1970, 135]

Consequently, Horsley's contributions to the controversy were unsubstantial; he attacked Priestley's mistranslations and failure to understand Plato, but he never defended the truth of the Trinity by rebutting Priestley's historical evidences for the biblical unity of God and humanity of Jesus. Horsley twitted Priestley with being "a child" in Platonism. Priestley responded, "This does not, I hope, prevent me from being a man in Christianity." [Gordon 1970, 116]

Priestley wrote that Tertullian claimed that the great body of unlearned ("idiotae") Christians in his time were Unitarians. Horsley translated the Latin word as "idiots." Priestley challenged Horsley to produce any dictionary or quotation from an ancient writer where the word meant "mentally deficient," and cited a number of ancient examples where it meant "unlearned." [XVIII, 191] Horsley charged that most of Priestley's arguments were borrowed from Zwicker, which implied that Horsley had read Zwicker. Priestley learned that Horsley probably had never seen the book, and if he had, had not read it, or he would never have made the charge, as the ideas of Zwicker about early Christian opinions were so different from Priestley's own. [XIX, 19]

Horsley, consistent with his rule in controversy "to strike without remorse at whatever in your adversary you find to be vulnerable, in order to destroy his character and credit," [XIX, 18] threatened Priestley with civil penalties authorized by law, but by "connivance" not enforced. He charged that Priestley might not have made the "declaration" of belief in the Bible required of Dissenters by a recent Act of King George III. Priestley responded "that as I never made the subscription required of all Dissenters before the late act, so neither have I made the declaration which the act makes necessary to my legal toleration, nor have I at present any intention to do it." [XVIII, 257] His reason for not complying was that he did not believe the state had the right to require such a religious test as a declaration of belief in the Bible, which he knew unbelievers could not subscribe to, because it was a violation of complete freedom of religion, or of no religion.

Horsley warned: "If Dr. Priestley ever should attempt to execute the smallest part of what he would now be understood to threaten; it may then, indeed, be expedient that the magistrate should show that he beareth not the sword in vain." Priestley replied that he was then "executing all that I would be understood to threaten, or have ever threatened. I am endeavoring by all means in my power, to rouse the attention of thinking men in this country to the corrupt state of the religion that is established in it, and especially to convince them of the mischievous tendency of worshiping Christ as God...." [XVIII, 302]

Regarding Horsley's suggestion that the state might have to use its power to "nip Dr. Priestley's goodly projects in the bud," Priestley misjudged the spirit of the times when he commented: "But happily 'there is that letteth,' and that is the good providence of God in the increasing light of this age, and the more liberal spirit of the times, which is more and more favorable to free inquiry, and more and more averse to every thing approaching persecution." [XXV, 193]

The attacks on Priestley's *Corruptions* by Horsley and others prompted Priestley to search the Christian writers of the first five centuries for their opinions on the nature of Christ, "as one means of collecting what was the doctrine of the apostles, and the true sense of scripture on the subject." [I-i, 341] His *An History of Early Opinions concerning Jesus Christ*, published in 1786, gave additional evidence that the early Christians were Unitarians, and brought him more antagonists. He published an annual pamphlet "in defense of the Unitarian doctrine against all opponents," and became an influential champion of Unitarianism, which gained more adherents.

The object of Priestley's research was to get at the mind of the Christian people in the earliest period and to make their primary understanding of the Scripture the norm for its true interpretation: "It will be an unanswerable argument," said Priestley, "against any particular doctrine contained in the Scriptures, that it was never understood to be so by those persons for whose immediate use the Scriptures were written...." [VI, 7] In his research on the opinions of early Christian apologists, Priestley concluded: "In those early times, the Scriptures were constantly read by persons better qualified to understand the language of them than we at this time can pretend to be, without suggesting any such notions of the divinity or the pre-existence of Christ, as are now supposed to be clearly contained in them." [XVIII, 148]

The substance of Priestley's conclusion about early opinions concerning Christ were summarized by him in the following paragraphs:

"Both the strongest presumptions, and the most direct positive evidence, show that the common people among the Gentile Christians, were Unitarians, at least between two and three hundred years after the promulgation of Christianity." [VI, 473]

"Athanasius himself [died 371 AD] was so far from denying that the primitive Jewish [Christian] church was properly Unitarian, maintaining the simple humanity and not the divinity of Christ, that he endeavors to account for it by saying, that all the Jews were so firmly persuaded that their Messiah was to be nothing more than a man like themselves, that the apostles were obliged to use great caution in divulging the doctrine of the proper divinity of Christ." [V, 19]

"It is well known, and mentioned [but rejected] by Eusebius that the Unitarians in the primitive church, always pretended to be the oldest Christians, that the apostles themselves had taught their doctrine, and that it generally prevailed till the time of Zephyrinus, bishop of Rome, but from that time it was corrupted; and as these Unitarians are called 'Idiotae' (common and ignorant people) by Tertulian, it is more natural to look for ancient opinions among them, than among the learned who are more apt to innovate." [V, 22]

Common usage, said Priestley, indicated the true beliefs of the early Christians: "We find upon all occasions, the early Christian writers speak of the Father as superior to the Son, and in general they give him the title of 'God,' as distinguished from the Son; and sometimes they expressly call him, exclusively of the Son, 'the only true God;' a phraseology which does not at all accord with the idea of the perfect equality of all the persons in the Trinity. But it might be expected, that the advances to the present doctrine of the Trinity should be gradual and slow. It was, indeed, some centuries before it was completely formed." [V, 36]

Priestley provided references for his critics to check: "I shall not be surprised if those who come after me, especially if they walk over the same ground more leisurely than I have done, should find some things to correct in me. To make this as easy as possible, I have printed my authorities at full length." [VI, 6] He listed 34 of his principal sources, and in his text footnoted his references with page numbers. He remarked that from Greek and Latin his "translations of passages in them are about eighteen hundred." [VII, 200]

Horsley did not deign to read *An History of the Early Opinions concerning Jesus Christ*. He said that he "would not, by an unnecessary and unseasonable opposition to neglected arguments, be the instrument of drawing four volumes, fraught, as the very title imports, with pernicious, heretical theology, from the obscurity in which they may innocently rot in the printer's warehouse." [XIX, 12]

Priestley and his friends were disappointed, as he told Horsley, "because we consider your publications in this controversy as contributing in an eminent manner to the propagation of that great truth for which we think it glorious to contend, and which you oppose." [XIX, 9] Horsley's service to the Church by denigrating Priestley was recognized--he was elevated to Bishop of Gloucester.

"Controversy," said Priestley, "means nothing more than public discussion, without which no question of consequence can be thoroughly and generally understood." [XIX, 229] "I profess to be a controversial writer, because I consider fair controversy as a valuable means of discovering and ascertaining truth...." [XVIII, 473] Echoing Milton, Priestley said, "It is nothing but error that can finally suffer from discussion. Truth ever seeks the light, and challenges investigation." [XVIII, 508]

It was not Priestley's principles so much as his method that aggravated his opponents: he wrote "Can any man maintain the truth of his own opinion, without showing the absurdity of that which is directly contrary to it...." [XXII, 268] Almost a century later Charles Darwin advanced a more radical truth than Priestley, without showing the absurdity of those who heatedly and derisively defended the Biblical story of creation--though Darwin's friends did.

Priestley recognized that fruitful discussions required shared ground-rules: "If we argue with men at all, and expect to gain any thing with them, we must argue from some common principles, or come as near to them as we can." [XXI, 190] Few of his adversaries shared his epistemology; they were not playing by the same assumptions, information, and rules.

Priestley did not conceive of himself as the sole prophet "crying in the wilderness." He was aware that few Dissenters saw things in the same light as he did, but he wished more of them would contribute to the discussion: "Every man has something peculiar to himself, in his manner of conceiving things, or of expressing himself, better adapted to impress a number of other persons than that of any others; and the very idea of a number of writers tends to give an idea of the strength of a cause." [I-ii, 361] He wrote: "I am far from thinking that the great Being who superintends all things, guides my pen any more than he does that of my fiercest opponent; but I believe that by means of our joint labors, and those of all who engage in theological controversy, ... he is promoting his own excellent purposes, and providing for the prevalence of truth, in his own due time...." [XVIII, 44]

Not all of Priestley's controversies were acrimonious; many were frank, courteous, and constructive. His lengthy discussion of materialism and necessity with his good Arian friend Price were friendly, though they differed sharply and explicitly in theology. During the controversy with Horsley, Priestley was pleased that Dr. Horne, Dean of Canterbury, also candidly defended the Trinity: "You, Sir, are as sensible as myself of the importance of this discussion, and have the same wish to conduct it in the most proper, that is, in the most amiable manner, as lovers of truth, and not contenders for victory. ... You say ... 'No mischief will arise from discussion. Truth always had been, and always will be, a gainer by it.'" [XVIII, 322]

Of Priestley, Lindsey wrote to a mutual friend, "Whatever others do, our friend does not put his candle under a bushel, but boldly and honestly holds it up, in his own hand, to give light to others as well as himself." [I-i, 165]

Unfortunately, as Priestley was holding up his candle, the Dissenters in London in 1790 again petitioned for relief from the civil restrictions placed on them by the Corporation and Test Acts, which had been repealed the year before in Catholic Ireland without harm to the minority Anglican established church. The alarmed English clergy organized opposition, said Priestley, "and by their preaching, writings, and other means, excited more violent opposition than had ever been known before.... " The petition was rejected in the Commons by more than two to one. "So much was party spirit inflamed ...," wrote Priestley, "that the Dissenters became the object of more hatred by friends of the court, than they had ever been...." [X, 494 note]

The clergy distributed to the members of the House of Commons a printed paper containing extracts from Priestley's letters to Mr. Burn that misrepresented Priestley's real views and was used by Priestley's old friend Burke in the course of the debate to raise indignation against Priestley. Priestley gave a specimen of the extracts, with the omitted part in italics: "Whether I be more pleased, or displeased, with their present violence, let them judge. The greater the violence, the greater our confidence of final success. *Because it will excite more public discussion, which is all that is necessary for our purpose.*" [XIX, 172]

Priestley acknowledged: "The freedom of my own theological writings in particular has, I find, given much offense,and has been mentioned by many persons, and especially several of the bishops, as a reason why no more liberty should be given to the Dissenters, since they abuse what they already have." [XXII, 456] The bishops assumed that Priestley was an instigator of the petition, though he had little to do with it, except advising the Dissenters to exercise patience and peaceable means in their campaign. Priestley said that Price and himself, "were particularly pointed out as seditious and dangerous persons, the very pests of society, and unworthy of the protection of government." [XIX, 369] Priestley wrote to the bishops: "But all that laws and penalties can do is only to impose silence. But they cannot enforce conviction. On the contrary, wherever they are employed, a suspicion necessarily arises that the proper instrument of conviction, viz. rational evidence, was not to be had...." [XIX, 511]

In Birmingham, party spirit was further inflamed by two Anglican clergymen--Mr. Madan and Mr. Burn-- who had been personal friends of Priestley and whose sermons and writings "to all appearances, contributed most to the fatal catastrophe...." [XIX, 366]

Mr. Madan, "the most respectable clergyman in town," was a young man with whom Priestley had served on a committee for abolishing the slave trade (Priestley had been pleased to be cooperating for once with the clergy, and thought he had found a clergyman "entirely to my mind"). Madan in 1790 preached and printed an "inflammatory sermon," said Priestley, on the subject of the Dissenter's petition, "inveighing in the bitterest manner against Dissenters in general, and myself in particular." [I-i, 4] Madan called the Dissenters proceedings "clamorous and violent; and he intimates that our final views are of a seditious tendency." [XIX, 140] Unitarianism, Madan said, was "the contaminating deamon of heresy." [XIX, 247] Its principles "in this place are evidently gaining ground among Presbyterians; and certainly those principles are not more consistent with the doct ne of the Established Church, and no less dangerous to the State, than any of the tenets of Popery." [XIX, 245] He accused the Dissenters of being in the tradition of regicides: "Is there no reason to see with suspicion their declarations of reverence to the government, and of loyalty to the king, however speciously and pompously announced, when the amount of that reverence has been exactly ascertained by a woeful experience of republican tyranny, and the extent of loyalty has been exactly delineated with the blood of a king?" [XIX, 144]

Madan was referring to the execution of Charles I in 1649, at the end of the English civil war of Royalist vs. Parliamentarians under the leadership of Presbyterian Oliver Cromwell. Priestley explained to the people of Birmingham in his published letters that the king was beheaded when the Presbyterians were overpowered by an army headed by Independents, and the beheading was against the wishes of the Presbyterians, as was "now upon record." He added, "It can therefore only answer the purposes of faction and of bigotry, and by no means of truth, to accuse the Dissenters of putting King Charles to death." [XIX, 146] The clergy were infuriated that Priestley bypassed them and appealed in his letters directly to Anglican laymen and the general public of Birmingham.

Madan's attack made Priestley despair: "His family and connections are respectable; he has had the most liberal education that his country can give. He is a man of a natural good temper, of polished and engaging manners, and the door of preferment is so open to him, that he hardly needs to knock in order to enter. For such a man as he, without provocation, to deal out such gross abuse, and with such uncommon solemnity, shows what we have to expect from the times. If such men as Mr. Madan can divest themselves of all liberality of sentiment, and treat as rebels, and hypocrites, men with whom they have frequent intercourse, and whom they ought to know better, and consequently respect, there is no hope left. If not from such men as he, from whom are we to expect decent treatment? It is a proof that the standard is raised against us, and that all the clergy, and other friends of the court, whether naturally disposed to it or not, must join their ranks in opposing us.." [XIX, 175] In 1792, Madan was appointed Bishop of Bristol, the second clergyman who slandered Priestley to be so elevated.

Mr. Burn, the other Birmingham clergyman who attacked Priestley, was a former Methodist and Dissenter preacher of some ability whom Priestley had first met on the public library committee and, thinking he had "marks of liberality," Priestley had twice invited him to visit. He had a "laudable view to rise in his profession," said Priestley, and to prove his loyalty to the Established Church "might suppose he could not do better than follow the sure foot-steps of those who had succeeded in the same chase before him." [XIX, 174] Of Burns published letters attacking Priestley, Priestley commented: "What he advances in these letters, void of all foundation as it is, is such declamation as I am informed is continually sounded from the pulpits of the churches, and other places of worship, in this town, and, indeed, in many other parts of England, ... representing me as the declared enemy of revelation, and a setter-up of reason in its place." [XIX, 308] Six months before the riot, noted Priestley, in addition to the letters of Burn and Madan, "no less than eight other publications, relating to the controversy, appeared in Birmingham." [XIX, 247]

Burn later regretted his calumny of Priestley: at an 1825 public meeting, he said that "had he to live his life over again, he should have to correct the asperity of feelings and expressions which it was his misfortune to have used in his controversies with a late respectable and highly talented individual." [Ware, Jr., 1834, xxi]

Shortly before the riot and before Priestley's letters to Burke on the French Revolution were published, an attempt was made in Parliament to rescind the act severely penalizing those who voiced anti-trinitarian views. The attempt failed, and it fueled the flames of persecution. Charles James Fox, a Whig member of Parliament who hated anything that savored of oppression and supported the American and French revolutions, as well as earlier Dissenter petitions for relief, in the debate said, "There could be no harm in removing from the Statute Book that which we are afraid, or ashamed, to enforce."

Edmund Burke, in reply, claimed it was "no longer a theological question, but a question of legislative prudence." He argued that it was imprudent to accept the motion because "Unitarians were associated for the express purpose of proselytism," aiming "to collect a multitude sufficient by force and violence to overturn the Church," and this "concurrent with a design to subvert the State." In mock-heroics, he implored Members of Parliament "not to wait till the conspirators met to commemorate the 14th of July, shall seize the Tower of London and the magazines it contains, murder the governor and the Mayor of London, seize the King's person, drive out the House of Lords, occupy your gallery and thence as from a high tribunal, dictate to you." [Holt 1952, 327] Thus, the storm that soon broke over Priestley was agitated in high places, and finally drove him to asylum in America.

XIII

"BEWARE, FOR A PRIESTLEY HAD ENTERED THE LAND"
"A Unitarian by myself"

After the Birmingham Riot, Priestley found shelter in London with a former Warrington pupil and family friend, William Vaughan, who was so fearful for Priestley's life that he provided women's clothing for Priestley to wear should he go out. By October, Priestley decided that his only hope for peace lay in exile and had begun to send funds to John Vaughan, a younger brother of William and also a former Priestley pupil then living in Philadelphia, and asked him to look for a future home for the Priestleys in the New World. [Geffen 1961, 20]

When Priestley arrived in London, a scurrilous handbill was distributed that denounced him as "an enemy both to the religious and political institutions of this country, a fellow of treasonable mind," and he was repeatedly caricatured as seditious. Published letters, articles and pamphlets charged that he raised the mob that turned on him, and urged that the laws be implemented against him "as a blasphemer of God, and a disturber of the peace." He was many times burned in effigy, sometimes along with Tom Paine, and received numerous threatening letters from all parts of the kingdom.

The Royal Society shunned him. When his Unitarian friend and scientist Thomas Cooper, an Oxford graduate, was twice denied membership in the Royal Society, though endorsed by several prominent scientists, Priestley concluded that high churchmen dominated the Society and that more communications from him would not be acceptable. Cooper preceded him to America.

For three years after fleeing Birmingham, Priestley served as successor to his deceased friend Richard Price in the pulpit of the wealthy Unitarian Dissenter Chapel in Hackney near London. He also volunteered without pay to teach science and history in the nearby Dissenter New College, which Burke had denounced while Price was a tutor as a "hotbed of sedition."

Priestley's call to the Hackney pulpit was not unanimous; some older members feared that his notoriety would reflect on the chapel, and withdrew. Neighbors were alarmed at his settlement near them; on the first anniversary of the Riot they feared that his home would again be attacked. Servants feared to live in his home. Priestley withdrew his acceptance of an invitation to preach the annual sermon at a Dissenter charity because the treasurer was so alarmed he could not sleep. But in Hackney Priestley preached to "unusually crowded audiences," and continued his popular religious education of young people. Among his parishioners was John Towill Rutt, later editor of his *Works*.

At the trial of the Birmingham rioters, which Priestley and his son William attended, 20 of the estimated 2000 participants, were apprehended, 13 were tried, five were found guilty, two were pardoned, and three "ruffians" were executed. The jury awarded Priestley damages of 2500 pounds sterling, though his well-supported claim (painstakingly prepared by Mary) was for 4100 pounds. During the trial, the Judge charged the jury that "Dr. Priestley's house was pulled down because he was a Dissenter; you know very well that is no reason at all; Dr. Priestley's life is irreproachable." A proposal was made in Parliament that an inquiry be held into the conduct of the Birmingham magistrates relating to the riot, but was opposed by the government. Priestley's immediate offer to be questioned by the government about the riot was ignored.

In sympathy and support, Priestley received gifts of money from friends and relatives, including a generous gift from his brother-in-law John Wilkinson, and many letters of support from Dissenter ministers (he returned a gift of money from one group of them). Anglican clergy expressed dismay at the "rancorous sentiments" of some of their colleagues, and Anglican laymen were among the first to afford him substantial assistance.

However, with continued abuse and threats, he reluctantly agreed to follow his sons, who had no prospects in England, to America. Mary, who was again spitting up blood, was already determined to go. On April 7, 1794, with a crowd of well-wishers at the Thames dock to see them off, Priestley and his wife sailed to sanctuary in Pennsylvania, sadly parting from their married daughter whose husband refused to emigrate. At that time, many Dissenters less notorious than Priestley were fleeing from England to America due to the increasing bigotry and persecution, which culminated in the Pitt Government's suspension of habeas corpus.

The voyage to America, with adverse winds, took two months, during which Priestley pursued his scholarly studies--though it was difficult for him to find a place to write--and Mary nursed passengers sicker than she. Finally disembarking at New York, they were met by their son Joseph and his wife. The next morning the Priestleys were welcomed by leading citizens, including the governor, the Episcopal Bishop, college administrators, leading merchants, and deputations from the city and from various societies. A newspaper editorial wrote, "England will one day regret its ungrateful treatment to this venerable and illustrious man."

No clergy invited him to preach, and when he attended a Presbyterian church, the minister pointedly refused to give communion to any who disbelieved in the divinity of Christ. An English tourist recorded that the "violence of the clergy" against Priestley's Unitarian doctrine was of great service "for many principal families of New York, chiefly English, have stepped forward and determined to have a Unitarian chapel there." [Belsham 1812, 384] After he was settled in Pennsylvania, Priestley received a written invitation to give a course of lectures and form a Unitarian society in New York. He declined, being "much weakened" and unwilling to move again.

Priestley was already well-known and admired in the United States. In New York, the Medical Society addressed him: "Permit us, Sir, to wait upon you with an offering of our sincere congratulations on your safe arrival, with your lady and family, in this happy country, and to express our real joy in receiving among us a gentleman whose labors have contributed so much to the diffusion and establishment of civil and religious liberty, and whose deep researches into the true principles of natural philosophy have derived so much improvement and real benefit, not only to the sciences of chemistry and medicine, but to various other arts, all of which are necessary to the ornament and utility of human life." [I-ii, 254]

The Associated Teachers of New York greeted him: "As laborers in those fields which you occupied with such distinguished eminence, the arduous and important task of cultivating the human mind, we contemplate, with peculiar satisfaction, the auspicious influence which your personal residence in this country will add to that of your highly valuable scientific and literary productions, by which we have already been materially benefited." [I-ii, 250]

When the Priestleys arrived in Philadelphia in June, he was greeted with honors as a scientist and with dread as a Unitarian theologian. A few months later another English refugee, Bakewell and his family, arrived in Philadelphia. Mr. Bakewell wrote: "I went several times to the Baptist meeting... under the care of Dr. Rogers. This man burst out, and bade the people beware, for 'a Priestley had entered the land'; and then, crouching down in a worshiping attitude, exclaimed, 'Oh, Lamb of God! How could they pluck thee from thy throne!'" [I-ii, 263 note] As frequently happened when people personally came to know Priestley, Dr. Roger's dread was transformed into friendship. Both were members of the American Philosophical Society, and on Priestley's later visits to Philadelphia, he frequently by invitation called on Dr. Rogers, "who was strongly attached to Dr. Priestley, and took pleasure in cultivating his acquaintance." [I-ii, 264]

The American Philosophical Society hailed Priestley on his arrival in Philadelphia as "an illustrious member of this institution" and "as a virtuous man, possessing eminent and useful requirements." [I-ii, 261] This Society, of which Priestley had been a member for nine years, had been instigated by Franklin fifty years earlier and was "associated for the purpose of extending and disseminating those improvements in the sciences and the arts which most conduce to the substantial happiness of man." Benjamin Franklin, having died four years earlier, was not in Philadelphia to welcome his friend of many years.

Priestley also was greeted by old friends from England. A small group of English Unitarians, including a former pupil John Vaughan who then was a prosperous Philadelphia merchant, urged him to stay in Philadelphia and organize a Unitarian church, with the added inducement that there would soon be an opening for him as professor of chemistry at the College of Philadelphia. The position did come open some months later, but Priestley was settled in Northumberland and declined the offer--he explained that he did not know the ordinary routines of chemistry well enough to teach it.

Philadelphia at that time was the capital of the United states, and of Pennsylvania, and the political, economic, commercial, and cultural leadership of the new nation were all concentrated there. It was the wealthiest and largest city, with a population of about 70,000, and was highly industrialized. The College of Philadelphia, later the

University of Pennsylvania, had an enrollment of about 300 students, including students of the medical school. The city had a theater, public library, hospital, paved and lighted streets, and 500 public pumps for water.

Philadelphia, however, did not attract the Priestleys, partly because it was unhealthy--the previous year between 4,000 and 5,000 people had died in a yellow fever epidemic. Priestly wrote that his wife had taken "an unconquerable aversion to Philadelphia, and my evil genius having brought her hither, I must give her the choice of a place of residence." Joseph, Jr., later added that "what had greater weight with him than anything else was that my mother, who had been harassed in her mind ever since the riots in Birmingham, thought that by living in the country, at a distance from the cities, she should be more likely to obtain that quiet of which she stood so much in need." [Priestley 1806, Vol. II, 169] Priestley did not feel himself to be a strong preacher; in addition to his congenital stammer, at age 61 he was losing his front teeth, "which will affect my speech." He did not realize how much the stress of the riot and persecution had debilitated him.

Moreover, the expense of living in a large city would more than offset any income from teaching. He anticipated sufficient income from the "French Funds" his brother-in-law had given him, which never materialized but was replaced by gifts from friends in England, plus the continued annuities from Lord Shelburne. His own motive for preferring to live in Northumberland was the wish to control his time so he could pursue his scholarly and scientific interests, and his calling to counter the tide of unbelief in Christianity by promoting Unitarianism through his publications.

The Priestleys also wished to be near their sons who were engaged, with Thomas Cooper and other Englishmen, in founding an English community of "the friends of liberty" about 50 miles north of Northumberland--a plan that failed. Priestley and his wife moved on with all their possessions in wagons to Northumberland, a small settlement on the Susquehanna River 130 miles northwest of Philadelphia. It was a five day journey, fording rivers and creeks, and the inns were so disreputable that they sometimes slept in their wagons. They bought a small house whose rooms Mary papered herself, as well as 11 acres fronting on the river for the home they planned to build and land that Henry farmed. When William returned from a year's visit in New England, Henry divided the land with his brother. Priestley cherished the hope that he would head, without salary, a college soon to be established in Northumberland. Building was actually begun by local subscriptions, but financing from the State did not come through.

As soon as Priestley was settled in Northumberland, he began holding Sunday worship services in his home, to which he invited the public. Mr. Bakewell, who had heard Priestley denounced from the pulpit in Philadelphia, moved with his family to Northumberland, where he helped Priestley in the garden and his wife helped Mary with housework--the Priestleys were desperate for servants. Bakewell, who regularly attended Priestley's services, wrote in 1795: "His discourses were usually practical, easy to be understood, and reducible to common life. In his prayers he was devout, and free from the error which many fall into, of multiplying words, when addressing the Divine Being, as though he wanted information. ... A man more satisfied with the dispensations of Divine Providence I never saw, nor one that had imbibed more of the spirit of Christianity." [I-ii, 277 note]

Though Priestley had challenged the infidelity of Deism, in Northumberland he was frequently preached against as a Deist and suffered "greater odium than any professed unbeliever." To counter the slander, he published his religious and political opinions in *Letters to the Inhabitants of Northumberland*, which he thought improved his reputation.

In England, he had esteemed and recommended to his friends the first part of Thomas Paine's *The Rights of Man*--the boldest publication he had ever seen on the subject, but when he found Paine's *Age of Reason* popular in America, he was concerned that Paine's attacks on revelation would mislead the unwary into Deism, and published a tract in refutation. Paine and Priestley had met in London at the home of Benjamin Vaughan, who participated with Franklin and Shelburne at the Anglo-American peace negotiations. Paine and Priestley agreed on "natural religion," but out of ignorance of the Bible, said Priestley, Paine was not aware that he was attacking the corruptions of Christianity, not the original revealed religion.

Priestley moved his Sunday services to a schoolroom with an encouraging accession of new people, including a class of 14 promising young men. By 1800, he reported that he had "succeeded in forming a small society for public worship"--the second avowed Unitarian Society in America. In 1822, a Unitarian minister from England was preaching with some success in Northumberland, and a Unitarian Book Society was organized. In 1834, a chapel was built but the church did not succeed in establishing itself in that small town; by 1910, when the congregation had dwindled away, the chapel was deeded to the American Unitarian Association with the understanding that the building would be maintained as the Joseph Priestley Memorial Chapel and preaching station. It recently has been restored by the Priestley Chapel Associates.

In December 1795, a second tragedy (after the Riot) struck the Priestleys:their youngest son Henry died at age 18. Priestley had intended to educate Henry to carry on his work. Henry was a hard working farmer on his land, which made his father proud. Henry stayed up nights tending the kiln to make lime to finish the stone house he was building, got chilled and went to his parents' home very ill, where he died a few days later. Joseph and Mary greatly grieved the loss of such a promising son.

The following February, Priestley returned to Philadelphia with his daughter-in-law in his son Joseph's wagon. They were houseguests of his devoted Birmingham supporter William Russell, who took them along for tea with President George Washington, where, Priestley wrote, they "spent two hours as in any private family. He invited me to come at any time, without ceremony." [I-ii, 332] Washington was interested in Priestley's ideas; he read and marked one of Priestley's books [Geffen 1961, 32], and later invited him to visit at Mt. Vernon.

William Russell's home had also been burned in the Birmingham riot. Continued harassment drove him from England with his son and two daughters. They sailed for America a few months after Priestley, but did not arrive for a year--the American ship they were on was captured by a French frigate, they were taken prisoner and confined on French prison ships four months. When released, they spent six months in Paris, where they were dismayed by the violent turn of the French Revolution. They finally set sail again for America. They visited the Priestleys in Northumberland with the intention of settling there, but life in the wilderness did not suit them and Russell bought a home in Philadelphia where they lived for a time. They finally settled in Connecticut.

In 1796 Priestley was invited to Philadelphia by a small band of English Unitarians, friends and former students, to give a series of Sunday morning sermons in the new Universalist Meeting House. The Unitarians had contributed "some hundreds of dollars" toward its completion, expecting that they also could meet in the two-story, 300 seat brick building. The walls were still unplastered, the seats were plain benches, and the privy was outside. The shabby building that still stands on Lombard Street has been occupied by a Synagogue since 1888.

While the meeting house was being built, the minister Elhanan Winchester traveled to England to spread the Universalist gospel and called on Priestley in Hackney. They were compatible; both were theological radicals who had lost pulpits because of their unconventional beliefs. Winchester was dismissed from his Baptist pulpit in Philadelphia when he began preaching the new doctrine of Universal Restoration, the ultimate and universal salvation of all people, even the redemption of sinners or of believers in other religions, to eternal life. With the support of a few followers, and especially the personal friendship of Dr. Benjamin Rush, Winchester gathered a Universalist church, one of the earliest to be established in the United States. He was an eminent Universalist leader who introduced scripture authority for Universalism, and published 39 books. [McConkey 1977, 3]

Priestley, like Winchester, believed in ultimate salvation for all. Twenty years before his first meeting with Winchester, he had written in opposition to eternal damnation: "Since ... not reasons of justice or equity could lead men to expect more than an adequate punishment, proportioned to their crimes, there was far from being any reason to imagine that future punishments would be eternal.... If God be a just and righteous governor, it must be in proportion to the sins...." [II, 341 & 357]

Dr. Benjamin Rush had a high regard for Winchester and participated in Universalist affairs. Rush wrote to Winchester, "for if Christ died for all as Mr. Wesley taught, it will soon appear a necessary consequence that all shall be saved." Though he was not a delegate, Rush took an active part in the first Philadelphia Universalist Convention, where he helped draft resolutions condemning slavery and war, and revised and arranged for publication of the *Articles of Faith* and other proceedings. [McConkey 1977, 4]

Winchester returned from England in 1794 seriously ill but resumed his Universalist ministry, preaching as much as he was able. Though he was pleased to provide a meeting place for Priestley's sermon series, his congregation was not.

Mrs. Hart, who attended Priestley's sermons on "The Evidences of Revealed Religion," wrote: "The congregations that attended were so numerous that the house could not contain them, so that as many of them were obliged to stand as sit, and even the door-ways were crowded with people. Mr. Vice President Adams was among the regular attendants"--as were many other members of Congress then meeting in Philadelphia. Priestley dedicated the printed series, with profits going to the Unitarian Society, to Adams who had requested that they be published. Adams, with candidacy on the conservative Federalist ticket for the presidency in mind, repented his suggestion; he confided to Mrs. Adams his fear that "it will give me the character of a heretic," but hoped that "dedicating a book to a man will not imply that he approves everything in it." [Geffen 1961, 31]

Adams had been a friend and correspondent of Priestley since 1787 when Adams was United States Ambassador to England, and he frequently attended Dr. Price's services at Hackney. Adams had passed through New York one day before Priestly arrived, and had asked a friend "to inform the doctor that he should be glad to see him in Boston, which he desired me to tell him he thought better calculated for him than any other part of America, and that he would find himself very well received if he should be inclined to settle there." [I-ii, 234] Priestley would not have been "well received" in Boston where his empirical brand of Unitarianism was appreciated by only a few of the emerging liberal Christians.

At the conclusion of his last sermon in the series, Priestley announced that he would give another the following Sunday on "Unitarianism Explained and Defended," a summary of the Corruptions of Christianity. In the preface to the published sermon, he challenged the Unitarians to form a lay-led society for Sunday worship, preaching and performing the sacraments themselves until they could secure a minister.

Twenty-one men organized themselves as the Society of Unitarian Christians, even though "Unitarian" was an odious word even among the liberal Congregationalists of New England. The Society secured a room as a meeting place in the University of Pennsylvania chapel, courtesy of the Baptist minister who had been so alarmed when "a Priestley entered the land." Later the privilege was withdrawn by the University trustees on grounds that the Unitarians were an "outside" group. They could not meet in the Universalist Church as they had hoped because some of its members were so upset by Priestley's sermons that they insisted Winchester preach a sermon in refutation, and they would not grant the Unitarians the hospitality of their meeting house.

After first trying to secure a Unitarian minister-- Reverend Henry Toulmin living in Lexington, Kentucky, who refused to move--the Unitarians, as Priestley had suggested, held services as a church with lay leadership. William Russell from Birmingham, one of the original organizers and treasurer, was most helpful the few months he lived in Philadelphia. John Vaughan, one of the regular preachers, read published sermons, while Ralph Eddowes and James Taylor composed their own sermons. Eddowes, a former Priestley pupil, was a merchant who fled England the same year as the Priestleys to escape the odium of being a Dissenter during the hysteria over the French Revolution. Thus, what became the first permanent Unitarian church in this country was launched as a "fellowship."

The Philadelphia church had an unfortunate experience with its first minister, William Christie, a long-time friend of Priestley and a merchant of means who had become a Unitarian minister in Scotland. In 1795, he emigrated with his family to America and, after teaching and preaching unsuccessfully in Virginia for four years, moved to Northumberland to be near Priestley. There he preached every other Sunday to Priestley's congregation, delivered the oration at Priestley's grave, and contributed a review of Priestley's theological works to Priestley's *Memoirs*.

In 1807, Christie was invited to be the first ordained minister of the Unitarian Society in Philadelphia, a relationship which lasted only seven months; Christie resigned after he rejected the limitations on his authority as a minister in a revised constitution adopted by the Church. He had learned Priestley's theology, but not his churchmanship--the limitations of the minister's authority in a democratic church. The lay members were used to managing their own society. In 1812, they erected the first avowed Unitarian church building in America, and settled their first successful minister in 1825, William Furness of Boston and Harvard, who served for 50 years.

Five months after his return from a two months stay in Philadelphia, Priestley suffered a third tragedy. Mary had been in poor health and had not accompanied him to Philadelphia. She hoped to get a servant before winter, and worked hard on the new home they were building in Northumberland. She did not live to move into it. Priestley was desolated by her death on September 17th, 1796.

On a Sunday morning she had gone to Priestley's service at Joseph's house, but returned home before the service began. She was seized with a "fever" that rendered her unconscious and she remained so until her death two weeks later. Priestley wrote to Theophilus Lindsey in London: "I never stood in more need of friendship than I do now. ... This day I bury my wife. ... She had taken much thought in planning the new house, and now that it is far advanced, and promises to be every thing that she wished, she is removed to another. For activity in contriving and executing every thing usually done by women, and some things done by men, I do not think she ever had a superior, or in generosity and disinterestedness; always caring for others and never for herself. My loss is proportionably great, though I am thankful that she had been preserved so long. We lived together more than thirty-four years. She, as well as myself, was much affected with the death of Harry

Henry]. Though it is now near nine months since he died, he has never been long out of my thoughts; but this will affect me much more; though I have abundant sources of consolation, for which I am truly thankful [rejoining them in the future life]." [I-ii, 354]

Two years later, Priestley's son Joseph and his family moved with him into the new home, where Priestley said he was a "lodger," but had space for his laboratory and library. The large frame house, now restored, is a Pennsylvania State Monument and a National Historical Landmark.

Priestley returned three more times to Philadelphia. The second time, he preached a sermon series to the Unitarians in the University Chapel, one on "The Case of Poor Emigrants" in which he recommended "to your favorable notice and charitable assistance, the various strangers, or emigrants from different parts of Europe, and the West-India islands, who are now crowding to the shores of America." [XVI 500] He reported to Lindsey in London: "The Unitarian Society is in a most promising state, and the members of it attend with a kind of enthusiasm, and show an attachment to each other similar to the primitive Christians. They gain ground continually, and many who do not openly join them respect them. It is better, I am satisfied, than any congregation with a regular minister." [I-ii, 375] He declared, "I do not know that I have more satisfaction from anything I ever did, than from the lay Unitarian congregation I have been the means of establishing in Philadelphia." [Geffen 1961, 45] However, attendance was small. Adams, by then President, attended only once and disappointed Priestley by not subscribing to the church history he was writing. [Geffen 1961, 50]

On the other hand, Vice President Jefferson wrote that when he lived in Philadelphia there was a respectable congregation of Unitarians "with a meeting house and regular services which I attended, and in which Dr. Priestley officiated to numerous audiences." [Foote 1947,70] At the time, Priestley wrote, "I see a good deal of him." They continued to correspond; Priestley responded to Jefferson's request for advice about founding the University of Virginia. Jefferson repeatedly invited Priestley to be his guest in the White House or at Monticello, but Priestley felt unable to accept because he was in poor health. Jefferson was influenced by Priestley's publications and conversations to adopt Priestley's theology.

Years later at Monticello, Jefferson wrote: "Had the doctrines of Jesus been preached always as pure as they came from his lips, the whole civilized world would now have been Christian. I rejoice that in this blessed country of free inquiry and belief, which has surrendered its conscience to neither kings nor priests, the genuine doctrine of only one God is reviving, and I trust that there is not a young man now living in the United States who will not die a Unitarian." Two years later he added: "The population of my neighborhood is too slender, and is too much divided into other sects to maintain one preacher well. I must therefore be contented to be a Unitarian by myself, although there are many around me who would become so, if once they could hear the question fairly stated." [Foote 1947, 75]

In 1800, Priestley wrote to Thomas Belsham, his friend and successor in the pulpit at Hackney, and zealous Unitarian: "The society of our Unitarians at Philadelphia, I understand, does not increase, which gives me great concern. They have some differences among themselves, and they want a sufficient number of good readers. They have lost many valuable men lately to yellow fever." [I-ii, 429]

In the fall of 1797, a yellow fever epidemic had taken the lives of 988 Philadelphians, including six Unitarians. Also, in 1799 the state capital had been moved from Philadelphia to Harrisburg, and in 1800 the federal capital had moved to Washington, draining many people from Philadelphia.

On his third trip to Philadelphia Priestley accompanied his son Joseph, going on business, and his wife. There Priestley succumbed to a serious illness that was treated by Dr. Benjamin Rush. He had welcomed Priestly to Philadelphia and later wrote of him, "I never met so much knowledge accompanied with such simplicity of manners." Rush was a physician trained at Edinburgh University whose treatment for yellow fever was blood-letting and purge, for which he was criticized. His theory that yellow fever was not carried on ships but bred in the surrounding swamps of Philadelphia proved to be correct and ended the quarantine of the port. He also published his observations on diseases of the mind--the first true American psychiatrist. As a member of the Continental Congress he signed the Declaration of Independence and was a long-time correspondent of Jefferson and Adams, whose rift he mended--and thus fostered their long correspondence in retirement. He suggested, titled and secured a publisher for Thomas Paine's *Common Sense*, which was so popular in preparing the minds of the Colonists for the Revolution.

On Priestley's last trip to Philadelphia with Joseph and his wife the American Philosophical Society held a dinner in his honor. He wrote to Lindsey in London that he was becoming quite deaf and "hardly able to speak loud enough for a large audience," but added "Last night I preached to a very crowded room, and the next Lord's-day I am to administer the Lord's Supper in another house, where some Unitarians regularly meet every Sunday morning. They are the remains of the society of lay-unitarians, and I am not without hopes that it may revive. But I see that a professed minister would be more useful, as making the cause more respectable, by giving it a head. I was not so fully sensible of this before." [I-ii, 306]

Persecution followed Priestley to Pennsylvania, not only for his reputation as a heretic, but also for his political sympathies. A letter to Priestley from John Stone in Paris was seized by the English from a neutral vessel. In his letter, Stone hinted of a future revolution in England. William Cobbett, an unnaturalized English editor of a scurrilous newspaper in Philadelphia, published the letter and accused Priestley of being an "apostle of sedition," and an agent for the French Revolution. Cobbet lost some of his popularity with Federalists when he began to censure President Adams for successfully seeking peace with France. When Dr. Benjamin Rush brought a libel suit against Cobbett for slandering Rush's practice of medicine, Rush was awarded $5,000 in damages, and Cobbett fled to honors in England where his diatribes were republished.

At the time, a state of undeclared war existed between the United States and France, then ruled by the dictatorship of the Directory's "reign of terror." The hysterical Federalist majority in Congress sought to crush all opposition in America and in the summer of 1798 passed the Alien and Sedition Acts that authorized the President to deport any alien or seditious person without a hearing.

Out of loyalty to his native England, Priestley had not become a naturalized citizen of the United States and was "under reasonable apprehension that he would be banished as an alien." [XVI, 498 note] Timothy Pickering, President Adam's secretary of state, tried to make an example of Priestley under the Alien Act. Priestley's friend Thomas Cooper, then living with him, had published political essays in his Northumberland newspaper that criticized the Federalist administration. Priestley had not seen the essays, nor was he consulted, until they were in print. Pickering wrote Adams that Priestley had helped Cooper print and distribute his essays and suggested that Priestley be expelled under the Alien Act. Fortunately, Adams did not approve of the Alien Act, never exercised his authority under it, and responded to Pickering: "I do not think it wise to execute the alien law against poor Priestley at present. He is as weak as water, as unstable as Reuben, or the wind. His influence is not an atom in the world." [Geffen 1961, 53]

Cooper was not so fortunate. Though in an earlier visit to France he had been disgusted with the violent development of the revolution, and had become a naturalized citizen of the United States, he was tried under the Sedition Act, convicted of libel, and served six months in prison while his friends paid his fine of $400 (subsequently repaid to his heirs when the Act was ruled unconstitutional). He went to prison cheerfully as a political martyr. With the ascendancy of the Jeffersonian Democratic Republicans, Cooper, a lawyer, served with distinction as a judge in Pennsylvania and was elected to the American Philosophical Society for his publications in chemistry. He became professor of "natural philosophy" at Carlisle College (now Dickinson College), for which he secured Priestley's laboratory equipment after Priestley's death, and wound up as president of the University of South Carolina.

When Cooper was involved with Priestley's sons in the unsuccessful venture to found a colony for Englishmen north of Northumberland, Priestley feared that Cooper's unbelief in Christianity might corrupt his sons. [Cohen 1983, 10) Cooper, who contributed observations on Priestley's ideas to Priestley's *Memoirs*, wrote that "maturest investigation" did not justify all of Priestley's religious convictions, but that "Theology was a subject on which we agreed to differ: a difference, which though a mutual source of regret, was to neither of us a cause of offense." [Priestley 1806, Vol. II, 467]

Priestley's second son William, who had been present at the riot, had obtained work in France, but with the revolution's increasing violence, had left to join his brothers in Northumberland. William married a woman who his father thought unsuitable, he was jealous of Joseph, Jr.'s favored position, and William was suspected of involvement in a suppressed "ugly affair" of food poisoning in the Priestley home. He moved to Louisiana where he became a successful sugar planter.

At about the same time, Priestley agonized in letters over his daughter Sarah Finch's poor health in England--she had born seven children, her husband had gone bankrupt, and she suffered like her mother from tuberculosis. She died in 1803--though with the slow mails Priestley did not learn of it before his own death five months later.

In his old age and isolation from friends in England with whom he could discuss his ideas, Priestley feared his solitary speculations might lead him astray. They did. He wrote to Rush, who shared his apocalyptic expectation, about his conviction that the triumph of Christianity could not be left to the "slow process of argumentation" but required another miracle--the prophesied Second Coming of Christ, which he thought might come within the lifetime of his younger friends. The signs of the times--the Napoleonic wars and the collapse of the Turkish Empire that presaged the return of the Jews to Palestine—indicated that the Millennium was near. When Rush wrote Adams about the eminent establishment of the Kingdom of God on Earth, Adams responded that "rulers of men would presume too much if they neglected history, experience and philosophy and depended upon the theological interpretations of mysterious predictions...." In a letter to Jefferson 26 years after the event, Adams recalled a conversation about biblical prophecies with Priestley, whom he had invited to breakfast in Philadelphia while he was President. Adams asked Priestley what grounds he had for believing that France would ultimately establish a free government. Priestley responded that his opinion was founded on revelation and prophecy; "There is however, a possibility of doubt." [Cappon 1959, 595]

Two years before his death, Priestley wrote to his London colleague Theophilus Lindsey: "The more I think of the wonderful system of which we are a part, the less I think of any difficulties about the reality or the circumstances of a future state. The resurrection is, really, nothing, compared to the wonders of every day in the regular course of nature; and the only reason why we do not wonder is, because the appearances are common. Whether it be, because I converse less with men, in this remote situation, I contemplate the scenes of nature, as the production of its great Author, more, and with more satisfaction, than I ever did before; and the new discoveries that are now making in every branch of science, interest me more than ever in this connection. I see before us a boundless field of the noblest investigation; and all that we yet know appears to me as nothing, compared to what we are wholly ignorant of, and do not, as yet, perceive any means of access to it."

"I now take great pleasure in my garden; and plants, as well as other objects, engage more of my attention than they ever did before; and I see things in a more pleasing light than ever. I wish I knew a little more about botany; but, old as I am, I learn something continually." [I-ii, 486-87] He had concluded that the resurrection was no more a miracle than the miracles he saw all around him in nature, and he ceased trying to rationalize his faith in the future resurrection of the body on Judgment Day.

Priestley twice declined Jefferson's invitation to visit him in the White House, explaining to Lindsey in 1802, "I shall not be able to visit him as he wishes. Indeed, the state of my health is such as warns me that I have no time to lose, and I am desirous of doing all I can in what remains of my life." [I-ii, 490] He finished his interesting and informative *Church History* and his boring *Notes on all the Books of.*

Scripture that were published posthumously by anonymous sub-scription of friends in England.

Joseph, Jr., in a long letter to Theophilus Lindsey, described Priestley's illness and death: "The first part of my father's illness, independent of his general weakness, the result of his illness in Philadelphia, in 1801, was constant indigestion, and a difficulty of swallowing meat, or any kind of solid food, unless previously reduced by mastication to a perfect pulp. This gradually increased upon him till he could swallow liquids but very slowly, and led him to suspect, which he did to the last, that there must be some stoppage in the oesophagus. Lately he lived almost entirely on tea, chocolate, soups, sago (starch), and the like." [I-ii, 526] His medication included laudanum, a tincture of opium.

To go outdoors, he had to be carried in a chair, and for the first time in his life, illness obliged him to give up conducting worship services. However, he got up and shaved himself, as he always did, until two days before his death.

At family prayers the night before he died, he admonished his grandchildren at his bedside "to continue to love each other." On Monday morning, February 6, 1804, at ten a.m. he dictated some additions and alterations to three pamphlets for publication, and when they were read back to him, he said, "That is right; I have now done." He asked to be moved to a couch and died quietly soon thereafter, with his son and daughter-in-law sitting close by. He was buried in the Northumberland Quaker cemetery next to his son Harry and wife Mary.

The memory of Priestley is best celebrated by the reflections on him by his prominent American friends.

XIV

"A COMET IN THE SYSTEM"
"The example of liberality he set"

After Jefferson's inauguration in March 1801 as third President, he wrote to Priestley, rejoicing that Priestley was recovering from his critical illness in Philadelphia, and adding: "What an effort ... of bigotry. in politics and religion, have we gone through! ... They pretended to praise and encourage education, but it was the education of our ancestors. We were to look backwards, not forwards, for improvement; the President himself declaring we were never to expect to go beyond them in real science. This was the real ground of all the attacks on you. Those who live by mystery and charlatanry, fearing you would render them useless by simplifying the Christian philosophy, the most sublime and benevolent, but most perverted systems that ever shone on man, endeavored to crush your well-earned and well-deserved fame. But ... our countrymen have recovered from the alarm into which art and industry have thrown them. Science and honesty are replaced on their high ground; and you, my Dear Sir, as their great apostle, are on the pinnacle. It is with heartfelt satisfaction that, in the first moments of my public action, I can hail you with welcome to our land, tender to you the homage of its respect and esteem, cover you under the protection of those laws which were made for the wise and good, like you ...." [I-ii, 456]

Jefferson, a leader of the progressive Democratic Republican Party, had served as vice president under President John Adams, supported by the conservative Federalist Party.

Priestley sent a copy of Jefferson's letter to his London friend Lindsey, which Thomas Belsham later included in his *Memoirs of Theophilus Lindsey*. When Adams read it, he wrote an indignant letter to Jefferson protesting the opinion attributed to him, which contributed to their estrangement.

Jefferson shared Priestley's grounds for tolerance. Jefferson wrote in a letter to Rush in 1811 expressing eagerness to be reconciled to his old friend John Adams, "Why should we be dissocialized by mere differences of opinion in politics, in religion, in philosophy, or anything else? His opinions are as honestly formed as my own. Our different views of the same subject are the result of a difference in our organization and experience." [Boorstin 1963, 120] Priestley had written in his 1791 *Letters to the Right Honorable Edmund Burke*, a copy of which was in Jefferson's library: "Objects appear in very different lights to different persons, according to their respective situations, and the opportunities they have for observing them." [XII, 163] ... "So different are men's feelings, from the difference, no doubt, of our educations, and the different sentiments we voluntarily cherish through life...." [XXII, 171] Jefferson incorporated ideas from his wide reading into his own concise, beautifully expressed compositions, without the scholar's habit of identifying his sources.

The long and interesting correspondence of Jefferson and Adams in their retirement, after Rush got the old political rivals to correspond, contains many expressions of their high regard for Priestley, though neither adopted his apocalyptic vision. Their correspondence also reveals how much Priestley shared or influenced the religious and political ideas of two of the Founding Fathers.

Adams wrote to Jefferson of Priestley: "This great, excellent, and extraordinary Man, whom I sincerely loved, esteemed and respected, was really a Phenomenon; a Comet in the System...." [Cappon 1959, 36]

John Adams was a member of, and was buried in, the First Parish of Quincy, Massachusetts, a liberal christian church that became Unitarian before his death. Adams had been a "diligent student" of the writings of Priestley, "this learned, indefatigable, and most excellent and extraordinary man." After Priestley's death, Adams wrote, "Glory to his soul! For I believe he had one; and one of the greatest." If Priestley had lived, Adams said he would have corresponded with him to ask a million questions, "And no Man was more capable or better disposed to answer them candidly than Dr. Priestley." [Cappon 1959, 363]

Jefferson wrote Adams: "You are right in supposing ... that I had not read much of Priestley's Predestination, his No-soul system, or his controversy with Horsley. But I have read his Corruption of Christianity, and Early Opinions of Jesus, over and over again; and I rest on them, and Middleton's writings, ... as the basis of my own faith. These writings have never been answered, by quoting histori-cal proofs, as they have done. For these facts therefore I cling to their learning, so much superior to my own." [Cappon 1959, 369]

Reading Priestley's *Corruptions* inspired, or reinforced Jefferson's anti-Platonism: after laboriously reading Plato's Republic in 1814, Jefferson wrote to Adams, "I had occasionally before taken up some of his other works, but scarcely had patience to go through the whole dialogue. While wading thro' the whimsies, the puerilities, and unintelligible jargon of this work, I laid it down often to ask myself how it could have been that the world should have so long consented to give reputation to such nonsense as this?" [Cappon 1959, 432] "With the Moderns, I think it is rather a matter of fashion and authority. Education is chiefly in the hands of persons who, from their profession, have an interest in the reputation and the dreams of Plato. ... The doctrines which flowed from the lips of Jesus himself are within the comprehension of a child; but thousands of volumes have not yet explained the Platonisms engrafted on them and for the obvious reason that nonsense can never be explained." [Cappon 1959, 433]

Priestley's theory of useful knowledge, based on facts from ob-servation or experience, including historical experience, supported Jefferson's innovations in education. In his "An Essay On A Course Of Liberal Education For Civil And Active Life," written a year before he died, Priestley proposed "some new articles of academical instruction": "The subjects I would recommend are CIVIL HISTORY, and more especially the important objects of CIVIL POLICY; such as the theory of laws, government, manufactures, commerce, naval force, etc., with whatever may be demonstrated from history to have contributed to the flourishing state of nations ... together with those articles of previous information without which it is impossible to understand the nature, connections, and mutual influences, of those great objects." [XXIV, 11] Jefferson consulted Priestley about his plans for the University of Virginia. The subjects Jefferson proposed for the curriculum of the University were "Botany, chemistry, zool-ogy, anatomy, surgery, medicine, natural philosophy, agriculture, mathematics, astronomy, geography, politics, commerce, history, ethics, law, arts, fine arts." [Boorstin 1963, 218] Neither Priestley or Jefferson included speculative philosophy in their curriculums.

Jefferson, in a letter to Adams, was dismayed by the popularity in the United States of the neo-platonic theory of knowledge, which Priestley had earlier opposed in Great Britain in his criticism of the philosophical idealism of the Scottish philosophers: "Our post-revolutionary youth are born under happier stars than you and I were. They acquire all learning in their mother's womb, and bring it into the world ready-made. The information of books is no longer necessary; and all knowledge which is not innate, is in contempt, or neglect at least. Every folly must run its round; and so, I suppose, must that of self- learning, and self sufficiency; of rejecting the knowledge acquired in past ages, and starting on the new ground of intuition." [Cappon 1959, 434]

Jefferson and Priestley shared belief in the necessity of a "first cause" of creation as proof from nature of the existence of God as creator and regenerator, though Priestley also believed in biblical revelations. Jefferson wrote to Adams: "I think that every Christian sect gives a great handle to Atheism by their general dogma that, without revelation, there would not be sufficient proof of the being of a god. ... On the contrary I hold (without appeal to revelation) that when we take a view of the Universe, in it's parts general or particular, it is impossible for the human mind not to perceive and feel a conviction of design, consummate skill, and indefinite power in every atom of its composition. The movements of the heavenly bodies, so exactly held in their courses by the balance of centrifugal and centripetal forces, the structure of the earth itself, with its distribution of lands, waters and atmosphere, animal and vegetable bodies, examined in all their minutest particles, insects mere atoms of life, yet as perfectly organized as man or mammoth, the mineral substances, their generation and uses, it is impossible, I say, for the human mind not to believe that there is, in all this, design, cause and effect, up to an ultimate cause, a fabricator of all things from matter and motion, their preserver and regulator while permitted to exist in their present forms, and their regenerator into new and other forms." [Cappon 1959, 592] Jefferson honored Priestley for "the example of liberality he set" in total freedom of religion. [Cappon 1959, 331] Jefferson's "Statute of Virginia for Religious Freedom," composed in 1777 and adopted by the legislature in 1786, concisely reflects Priestley's advocacy of complete religious freedom in his *Essay on the First Principles of Government*, a 1771 edition of which was in Jefferson's library.

Jefferson's idea of Jesus, in a letter to Benjamin Rush, summarized Priestley's : "To the corruptions of Christianity I am, indeed, opposed, but not to the genuine precepts of Jesus himself. I am a Christian in the only sense in which I believe Jesus wished anyone to be, sincerely attached to his doctrines in preference to all others; ascribing to himself every human excellence, and believing that he never claimed any other." [Foote 1907, 4]

Jefferson sent a copy of Priestley's posthumous publication of *The Doctrines of Heathen Philosophy compared with those of Revelation*, to Adams with the comment that it was "executed with learning and candor, as was everything Priestley wrote: but perhaps a little hastily; for he felt himself pressed by the hand of death." [Cappon 1959, 368] Priestley's progressive ideas had preceded him to America through his publications (20 were in Jefferson's library) and through his correspondence, though he did not correspond with Jefferson until after he had settled in Pennsylvania and they became friends. Boorstin writes that Priestley's "extensive knowledge of languages, theology and church history enabled him to supply the artillery to defend the Jeffersonian view of religion and metaphysics. *A History of the Corruptions of Christianity* ... was a work which Jefferson read again and again and never ceased to admire. The friendship between Priestley and Jefferson deepened, and their philosophic harmony became closer with the years; with no other theologian did Jefferson feel equally at home. Priestley's extraordinary union of the theologian and the physicist qualified him to expound the materialism on which Jefferson, Rush and others rested their faith. There was surely no hyperbole when Jefferson described him as unexcelled for service 'in religion, in politics, in physics.'" [Boorstin 1963, 19] Both Jefferson and Rush shared Priestley's conviction that "mind and body were not separate substances ... for thought itself was nothing but the interaction of material forces." [Boorstin 1963, 112] Jefferson wrote, "I can conceive thought to be an action of a particular organization of matter, formed for that purpose by the Creator...." [Boorstin 1963, 115]

Rush and Jefferson shared Priestley's belief in the value of controversy--Priestley wrote, "A truth that has never been opposed cannot acquire that firm and unwavering assent, which is given to that which has stood the test of rigorous examination," and dedicated his defense of the phlogiston theory to several French critics of the doctrine. Jefferson claimed, "Differences of opinion leads to inquiry, and inquiry to truth." [Boorstin 1963, 126 & 127]

In 1785, Priestley had been made a member of the American Philosophical Society, founded in 1743 "for the promotion of useful knowledge" by Franklin, its first president. Priestley was welcomed by the Society on his arrival, and on his last visit to Philadelphia, the Society gave a dinner honoring him. He had contributed papers to the Society about his experiments before he arrived, and continued to send papers about his experiments in Northumberland.

The response to Priestley by early 19th century New England liberal Christians is recorded in the preface to *Views of Christian*

Truth, Piety and Morality Selected from the Writings of Dr. Priestley by Unitarian and Harvard professor Henry Ware, Jr., which he published in Boston, 1834: "In looking at some of the works of this voluminous writer, I perceived that there were many passages, now unknown, which if collected together, would form a valuable volume of religious instruction, acceptable to devout readers and honorable to the memory of the distinguished author.... Meantime some recent abusive notices of Priestley recalled my attention to the subject, and seemed to present a fitting occasion for a work which would ... do something toward vindicating the character of an injured man; a man, who, with all his errors, and they seem to have been many, was yet distinguished for pure and unalienable devotion to the cause of Christianity, a strong piety, an incorruptible love of truth, and an integrity and simplicity truly apostolic." [Ware 1834, III]

"All his errors" were Priestley's "materialism" that rejected separate spiritual souls, his empirical theory of knowledge that voided unverified intuitions, and his insistence that human wills were conditioned by circumstances, William Ellery Channing of Boston, leading spokesman for the emerging Unitarian movement in New England, as a young man wrote:

"I have just been reading Priestley's Lectures, and have derived considerable advantage from them." [Channing, William H. 1848, Vol 1, 100] Twenty years later, he wrote: "Next to Lardner, the most laborious advocate of Christianity against the attack of infidels, in our own day, was Priestley; and whatever we may think of some of his opinions, we believe that none of his opposers ever questioned the importance of his vindication of our common faith." [Channing, Willim E. 1875, 407] But in 1841, he wrote: "With Dr. Priestley, a good and great man, who had most to do in producing the late Unitarian movement, I have less sympathy than with the 'Orthodox'." [Channing, William H. 1848, Vol. II, 380]

However, some of the New England liberal Christian ministers were inspired and informed by Priestley's Unitarianism. William Bentley of Salem preached Priestley's views by 1791 and gave Priestley pamphlets to a sailing-ship captain to read on a voyage, with the comment that Priestley "will recommend the liberty of thinking for yourself." [Clark 1940, 59] James Freeman of King's Chapel in Boston, who had corresponded with Priestley, in 1795-96 reprinted in Boston Priestley's *Discourses on the Evidence of Revealed Religion* and *History of the Corruptions of Christianity* that, with the example of Freeman, "made it easier for a latter generation to outgrow Arianism." [Wright 1955, 215] John Sherwood of

Mansfield, Connecticut, who had adopted the views of Priestley and was almost driven from his church by the Congregational Consociation of churches, in 1805 published *One God in One Person Only*, one of the first such expositions by an American writer.

Hosea Ballou, Universalist theologian, was influenced by Priestley to change his christology from Arianism to Socinianism-- he had removed references to the "logos" in the 1805 reprint of his *A Treatise on Atonement* that also claimed the unity of God, and reprinted in *The Universalist Magazine* of 1819 Priestley's treatise on the Unity of God, that argued against the pre-existence of Christ. [Cassara 1961, 134]

Priestley also made contributions to science in America, notes a University of Pennsylvania professor: "Isn't it fair to declare that the great majority of chemical students think of Priestley as working only in England, his native land, and never give thought to his efforts during the last ten years of his life? It has been said that he probably inspired and incited the young chemists of this country to renewed endeavor in their science upon his advent here. There is no question that he influenced James Woodhouse and his particular confreres most profoundly, as he did a younger generation, represented by Robert Hare. Priestley again set in rapid motion chemical research in the young Republic. He must therefore have done something himself." [Smith 1920, 2]

Within a year before he died, Priestley conducted an experiment to disprove his old friend Erasmus Darwin's theory of the "spontaneous generation" of living forms in sealed containers, about which Priestley had just read. Priestley said "it is observation of facts, and not conjecture, that must determine the question of probability." To test Darwin's theory, Priestley put water in vessels, some were unsealed and others sealed from penetration by air. Since only the unsealed vessels produced "green matter," algae, Priestley concluded that the germs of algae were in the air, not spontaneously generated, and published his finding in the *Medical Repository* of New York. [Priestley 1803, 122]

The legacy of Joseph Priestley is progressive and prophetic. He is a universal man, a paragon of the Enlightenment. His contributions to the philosophy of science are significant. His discoveries in chemistry are celebrated in the scientific community. His experiments in electricity are recognized as original and significant.

But because of the English prejudice against him resulting from embarrassment over the persecution of him in the Birmingham Riot and subsequently, his seminal contributions are ignored in political science, education, psychology, biology, theology, cosmology, epistemology, and biblical criticism. The real reason for his persecution was his heterodox theology, not the false allegation that he was a seditious revolutionary.

In experimental science he is recognized, but not in works of the mind. He obviated the two cultures of the liberal arts and science, the religious and the secular, the natural and the supernatural, and theology and science. In his unified frame of reference, there was no conflict between them. To him, this was a monistic, not a dualistic, two-story universe.

He had an integrated epistemology; insight and imagination suggested hypotheses, but to him the only way to know whether they were true was by observation and experience, plus reliable reports of the experience of others. Except for his eschatology, he applied the same empirical rules of evidence in science and in theology--he thought science was revealing how the Providence of the Creator worked. He came prophetically close to identifying the Creator with the Creation.

In psychology, he made original contributions. He eliminated the body-mind, physical-spiritual dualism by proposing that thought was a function of the organization of matter in the brain, integrating human nature. He eliminated the soul as a separate substance capable of direct perception of religious and moral truths, and as the agency at death of immediate personal immortality--though he clung to the Biblical hope of the resurrection of the body. He emphasized education as the means of transmitting wisdom in religious as in secular life.

He claimed that the will was conditioned by previous experience and education, yet choices were self-determined if the will was not externally controlled.

With his "materialism," he was not a mechanist or reductionist. He spoke of organic systems, from biological bodies and societies to the universe, the dynamic organization of masses of interacting particles of matter, which could change.

Social organization, for Priestley, was a political science based on experience, not speculation, to which he contributed radical democratic principles grounded on his theory of human nature. Governments were organic, the gradual accumulation of policies and laws by experiments, founded on public support, and subject to gradual improvements as circumstances changed. Violent revolution was a last resort against despotism. Civil and religious liberty were natural rights, requiring unlimited freedom of thought, discussion, and publication, and were protected by access to the ballot box. Only actions could be controlled by authorities in order to provide individual and social security for life and property.

It can be said of Priestley, as Jesus said to those who were offended by his teachings, "A prophet is not without honor, but in his own country, and among his own kind, and in his own house." [Mark 6:4] Priestley is widely remembered and honored for his achievements in his avocation as a scientist, but not for his contributions in his vocation as a theologian and philosopher to the history of ideas, which are still relevant and significant in the state of wisdom of this century.

Index

References

ALLEN, Bernard M. 1932-33. "Priestley and the Birmingham Riots." *Transactions of the Unitarian Historical Society* (England), Vol. 5, No. 2.

BEARD, J. R., Ed. 1846. *Unitarianism Exhibited in its Actual Condition.* London: Simpkin, Marshall and Co.

BECKER, Carl Lotus. 1922. *The Declaration of Independence-Study in the History of Political Ideas.* New York: Harcourt Brace and Company.

BELSHAM, Thomas. 1812. *Memoirs of Theophilus Lindsey, M.A..* London: J. Johnson and Co.

BELSHAM, Thomas. 1873. *A Memoir of the Rev. Theophilus Lindsey, M.A..* London: Williams & Norgate.

BOORSTIN, Daniel J. 1963. *The Lost World of Thomas Jefferson.* Boston: Beacon Press.

BOORSTIN, Daniel J. 1983. *The Discoverers.* New York: Random House.

BOYER, John T., Ed. 1964. *The Memoirs of Dr. Joseph Priestley.* Washington, D.C.: Barcroft Press.

BRONOWSKI, Jacob. 1973. *The Ascent of Man.* Boston: Brown and Company.

BURKE, Edmund 9-11 (1790). *Reflections on the Revolution in France.* London: The Walter Scott Publishing Co.

BURKE, James. 1978. *Connections.* Boston: Little Brown and Company.

CAPPON, Lester J., Ed. 1959. *The Adams-Jefferson Letters*, Vol. II. Chapel Hill: The University of North Carolina Press.

CASSARA, Ernest. 1961. *Hosea Ballou.* Boston: Beacon Press.

CHANNING, William E. 1875. *The Works of William E. Channing, D.D..* Boston: The American Unitarian Association.

CHANNING, William H. 1848. *Memoirs of William Ellery Channing*, Vol. I. Boston: Wm. Crosby and H. P. Nichols.

CHAPIN, Lloyd W. 1967. "The Theology of Joseph Priestley: A Study in Eighteenth Century Apologetics." (Unpublished Ph.D. thesis, Union Theological Seminary in the City of New York) Ann Arbor: University Microfilms, Inc.

CLARK, John R. 1984. *The Great Living System - Religion Emerging from the Sciences.* Boston: Skinner House Books.

CLARK, John R. 1940. "William Bentley and his Place in the Development of Unitarian Theology." (Unpublished B.D. dissertation, The Meadville Theological School, Chicago.)

COHEN, Seymour S. 1983. "Faith and Reason: Joseph Priestley and Thomas Cooper in Pennsylvania." (Unpublished paper presented at the American Chemical Society Symposium on Priestley, Washington, D.C., August 30, 1983.

COMMAGER, Henry Steele. 1947. *Theodore Parker*. Boston: The Beacon Press.

CORY, John. 1804. *The Life of Joseph Priestley*. Birmingham, England: Wilks, Grafton & Co.

DAVENPORT, Derek A. 1983. "*Citoyen* Joseph Priestley," *CHOC News*, Spring, Vol. 1, No. 2.

FENN, William Wallace. 1938. *The Theological Method of Jesus*. Boston: The Beacon Press.

GEFFEN, Elizabeth M. 1961. *Philadelphia Unitarianism 1796-1861*. Philadelphia: University of Pennsylvania Press.

GIBBS, F. W. 1967. *Joseph Priestley, Revolutions of the Eighteenth Century*. New York: Doubleday & Company, Inc.

GORDON, Alexander. 1896. "Joseph Priestley" in *Dictionary of National Biography*, Vol. XLVI. London.

GORDON, Alexander. 1970. *Heads of English Unitarian History*. London: Redwood Press Limited.

HENRY, William D. 1831-32. "An Estimate of the Philosophicall Character of Dr. Priestley." *Report of the British Association for the Advancement of Science*. Vol. 1-2 (no page numbers)

HIEBERT, Erwin N. 1980. *Joseph Priestley - Scientist, Theologian and Metaphysician*. Lewisburg, Pennsylvania: Bucknell University Press.

HOLT, Anne. 1931 & 1970. *A Life of Joseph Priestley*. Westport, Connecticut: Greenwood Press, Publishers.

HOLT, Raymond V. 1952. *The Unitarian Contribution to Social Progress in England*. London: The Lindsey Press.

HUTTON, Catherine. 1875. *A Narrative of the Riots in Birmingham*. (Two letters written in July, 1791, found and printed in 1875: Birmingham Central Library.)

KING-HELE, Desmond. 1977. *Doctor of Revolution - The Life and Genius of Erasmus Darwin*. London: Faber & Faber.

LESSER, Charles Huber. 1974. "Joseph Priestley (1733-1804): The Mind of a Materialist. An Intellectual Biography." (Unpublished Ph.D. thesis, The University of Michigan) Ann Arbor: University Microfilms, Inc.

LINDSEY, Jack. 1970. "Introduction" to *Autobiography of Joseph Priestley*. Cranbury, New Jersey: Associated University Presses.

LOCKE, John. 1977. *An Essay Concerning Human Understanding,* Abridged and edited by John W. Yolton. London: J. M. Dent & Sons, Ltd.

McCONKEY, Thomas W. 1977. "The Church at Four Twelve Lombard Street - A Monument to Liberal Religion." (Philadelphia: Mimeographed MS.)

MERCHANT, Carolyn. 1983. *The Death of Nature.* New York: Harper & Row.

McEVOY, John G. 1975. "Joseph Priestley: Philosopher, Scientist and Divine." (Unpublished Ph.D. thesis, University of Pittsburgh) Ann Arbor: University Microfilms, Inc.

McEVOY, John G. 1975, and J.E. McGuire. "God and Nature: Priestley's Way of Rational Dissent," *Historical Studies in the Physical Sciences,* Vol. 6

McEVOY, John G. 1978. "Joseph Priestley, 'Aerial Philosopher': Metaphysics and Methodology in Priestley's Chemical Thought, from 1762 to 1781." *Ambix,* Vol. 25, Part I, March.

McLACHLAN, Herbert John. 1951. *Socinianism in Seventeenth-Century England.* Oxford: Oxford University Press.

NORTON, David Fate. 1982. *David Hume - Common-Sense Moralist, Sceptical Metaphysician.* Princeton: Princeton University Press.

PRIESTLEY, Joseph. cf. RUTT

PRIESTLEY, Joseph. 1803. "Observations and Experiments relating to equivocal, or spontaneous Generation," *Medical Repository.* New York.

PRIESTLEY, Joseph. "Priestley's Manuscript Letters," Vol. I & II. Dr. Williams Library, London. (Also in RUTT, edited.)

PRIESTLEY, Joseph, Jr. 1806. *Memoirs of Dr. Joseph Priestley, to the Year 1795. Written by himself: With a Continuation to the Time of His Decease, by His Son, Joseph Priestley: And Observations on his Writings, by Thomas Cooper, President Judge of the 4th. District of Pennsylvania: and the Rev. William Christie.* Two Volumes, Northumberland, Pennsylvania.

PRIESTLEY, Timothy. 1804. *A Funeral Sermon, Occasioned by the Death of the late Rev. Joseph Priestley...* (printed 1805).

RICE, Richard Adams. 1969. "Joseph Priestley's Materialist Theory of Cognition: Its Influence and Historical Significance." (Unpublished Ph.D. thesis, Brandeis University) Ann Arbor: University Microfilms, Inc.

RITCHIE-CALDER, Lord. 1982. "The Lunar Society of Birmingham," *Scientific American,* June 1982.

RUSTON, Alan. 1979. "Two Unitarians in France during the Revolution," *Transactions of the Unitarian Historical Society,* Sept. 1979, Vol. XIV, No. 1, London.

RUTT, John Towill, ed. 1972. *The Theological and Miscellaneous Works of Joseph Priestley, LL.D. F.R.S. &c.* Edited, with notes. Containing Memoirs and Correspondence in 26 volumes. (London 1817-32) New York: Kraus Reprint Co.

SCHOFIELD, Robert E. 1966. *A Scientific Autobiography of Joseph Priestley (1733-1804).* Cambridge, Massachusetts: The M.I.T. Press.

SCHOFIELD, Robert E. 1978. "Joseph Priestley on Sensation and Perception," *Studies in Perception: Interrelations in the History of Philosophy and Science,* Peter K. Machamer & Robert G. Turnbull, eds. Columbus: State University Press.

SCHOFIELD, Robert E. 00 "S. T. Coleridge, Joseph Priestley, and Eighteenth-Century British Neo-Platonism." To be published in *FESTSCHRIFT* for J. Bernard Cohen.

SCHOFIELD, Robert E. 1980. Aaron J. Ihde, and Erwin N. Hiebert, *Joseph Priestley - Scientist, Theologian, and Metaphysician.* Lewisburg: Bucknell University Presses.

SMITH, Edgar F. 1920. *Priestley in America.* Philadelphia: P. Blakiston's Sons & Co.

STEPHEN, Leslie. 1949. *History of English Thought,* Vol. I & II. New York: Peter Smith.

SUGIYAMA, Chuhei. 1984. "The Economic Thought of Joseph Priestley, *Enlightenment and Dissent,* No. 3.

THOMAS, Roland. 1924. *Richard Price - Philosopher and Apostle of Liberty.* London: Oxford University Press.

TRANSACTIONS OF THE UNITARIAN HISTORICAL SOCIETY, 1931. Vol. 5, No. 1. (England) "Priestley's Daughter and her Descendents" (no author's name)

TUCHMAN, Barbara W. 1984. *The March of Folly, from Troy to Vietnam.* New York: Alfred A. Knopf.

TURNER, W., Jun. 1840. *Lives of Eminent Unitarians.* London: Published by the Unitarian Association.

WARE, Henry, Jr., ed. 1834. *Views of Christian Truth, Piety and Morality, Selected from the Writings of Dr. Priestley.* Cambridge, Massachusetts: James Munroe and Company.

WILBUR, Earl Morse. 1925. *Our Unitarian Heritage.* Boston: The Beacon Press.

WILBUR, Earl Morse. 1978. *A History of Unitarianism.* Vol. I & II. Boston: Beacon Press.

WILLEY, Basil. 1977. *The Eighteenth Century Background*. New York: Columbia University Press.

WRIGHT, Conrad. 1955. *The Beginnings of Unitarianism in America*. Boston: The Beacon Press.

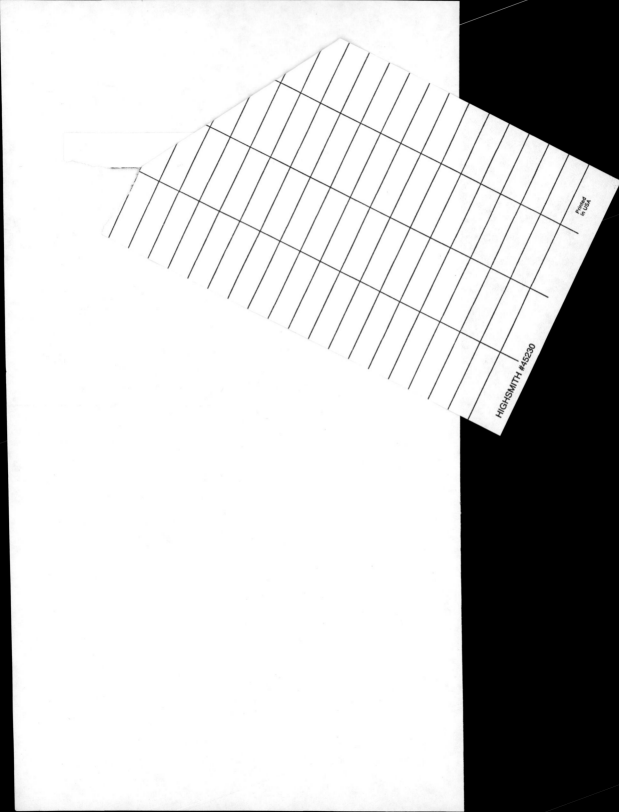

HIGHSMITH #45230

Printed
in USA